DATE		

RESTAURANTS
Chicago-Style

RESTAURANTS
Chicago-Style

Recipes collected by
JAMES WARD

CBI Publishing Company, Inc.
51 Sleeper Street
Boston, Massachusetts 02210

Library of Congress Cataloging in Publication Data

Main entry under title:

Restaurants Chicago–style.

Includes index.
1. Cookery, American—Illinois. 2. Chicago—Social
life and customs. 3. Chicago—Restaurants—Directories.
I. Ward, James, 1932–
TX715.R426   641.5   79–996
ISBN 0–8436–2116–8

Printing (last digit): 9 8 7 6 5 4 3 2 1

Printed in the United States of America

CONTENTS

PREFACE

Restaurants Chicago-Style was written for the restaurant *patron*, in both senses of the word—for the person who offers hospitality and for the person who receives it. After all, the proprietor and the customer have much in common, or the latter wouldn't be breaking the former's bread on a regular basis. This lively rapport, based on shared interests and tastes, is a vital sign of all the Chicago restaurants presented here, from the oldest (Berghoff's) to the newest (Jimmy's Place).

Something else that these Chicago foodservice establishments have in common is a professionalism that guarantees the consistency of their good food . . . whether that food is Mandarin Hot Green Pepper Beef as prepared at Dr. Shen's, Baked Stuffed Pork Chops to delight the patient-patrons at the University of Chicago Hospitals and Clinics, or Chili con Carne as served at the drug store in the Drake Hotel.

The popular "signature recipes" presented here capture not only the tastes but the flavor of the 25 restaurants discussed. Some are mass quantity recipes of special interest to restaurateurs, caterers, or party-givers hosting large groups of people. Other recipes in smaller quantities, are of particular note to home-cooks, as *well* as foodservice professionals. *No* recipe in this book has been cut down for smaller quantity "at home" preparation. Thus the restaurant chef's exact mode of preparation may be followed to the letter (as well as the spirit) of the cookery law, regardless of quantity. The only liberty taken is in format: all recipes are presented in an easy-to-follow, contained listing of ingredients and procedures. Alas, the cost of ingredients (as well as the menu prices mentioned in this book) could not be contained. They reflect the date of publication in this onwards-and-upwards inflationary year.

—*March 1979*

RESTAURANTS
Chicago-Style

INTRODUCTION

Always a brawny, hungry town, Chicago's appetite remains voracious. However, the "Big Potato" no longer symbolizes the city's tastes. Although meat-and-potato restaurants still abound—some of them, the best in the country—Chicago's flirtation with culinary adventure has developed into a long-term romance. In the last five years, the Chicago restaurant market has changed and expanded in menu offerings and geographics, creating new dining-out expectations. The foodservice organizations in and around Chicago covered in this book attest to this new sophistication; indeed, many of them helped to create it. The 200-plus recipes contained here represent contemporary Chicago favorites in all menu categories.

Television chefs and cookbook authors have played an important role in Chicago's growing gastro-worldliness. But, while those experts extolled the joys of doing-it-yourself-at-home, Chicagoans have found that many restaurants do it better.

There was, however, a more important development. As the older middle classes left the city proper, many restaurants followed them to exurbia. They were then replaced by a new group of people—young, affluent, single or recently married—demanding a new kind of restaurant: part foodservice, and sometimes part theatre.

Today, several north-side areas of Chicago are more lively than ever. Many of the region's new foodservice operations are made possible because the audience is on tap. In addition, there is a new breed of "help." There has been a changing of the guard as enthusiastic "part-life" service personnel have replaced an older generation of "full-life" waiters, bartenders, and kitchen folk. These new-life-styled young people don't find serving others degrading, especially when they know they won't have to do it forever. The vitality of at least ten Chicago restaurants covered in this text would be diminished enormously without the roles played by these bright, young performers.

Another gastronomic development in Chicago: the French Revolution! Small but influential groups of French chefs have solidly established themselves and their cuisine as *the* taste-making factor in both city and suburbs. Expensive French bistros have become the place to be, and to be seen in. Perhaps this is no forefront trend, but for Chicago it's an important new element.

Periodic tight money has had little effect on Chicago's high-tab restaurants. The smaller establishments in the middle price range have suffered more, but every professionally run restaurant covered here, regardless of its market, reports that business is up over the preceding year. As the other nemesis, inflation has certainly raised tariffs in the expensive special-preparation restaurants, but fortunately, their upper middle class customers seem immune to inflation as well as to recession. At the moderate and the low ticket end, Chicago still offers some of the most reasonable restaurant prices to be found in any metropolitan area. Chicago's lower overhead, cheaper labor, and in many cases, lower profits, have everything to do with it, despite soaring food costs.

Just as there is a Chicago School of Architecture, so there is a Chicago School of Food Service. Its viability, as in architecture, depends on a balance between two criteria: a respect for the past in what came before; and an alertness to the present in what is new. The 17 foodservice organizations covered in this volume represent 25 restaurants ranging from coffee shops and high-end fast food operations to traditional and innovative white tablecloth establishments, one hotel room service facility, and one high-volume hospital feeding operation. All are owned or managed by knowledgeable and respected professionals. All have the merchandising know-how needed to zero-in on their audience, and to attract and satisfy their guests. But most importantly, all serve outstanding food.

Omissions are legion, as are apologies. The selection is a personal one, but not arbitrary. Although all places presented here are among Chicago's finest, there is no inference intended that they are necessarily *the* "best" or the only top operations in the Chicago area.

However, every restaurant or foodservice unit featured in *Restaurants Chicago-Style* is of particular interest to professionals for reasons that will be recounted in the pages to follow. All of them, by establishing precedents or solving problems, by facing challenges or taking chances, have contributed to the definition of the dynamic Chicago foodservice market.

AVOCADO, SO... ...IAR   2.75
SHRIMP SUPREME ON ICE   3.9... ...HILLED TROUT IN DILL SAUCE   3.50
ALASKAN KING CRAB, LOUIS DRESSING   3.95
BEEFSTEAK TOMATO & ANCHOVIES   2.25
MELON OF THE SEASON   1.50
AVOCADO WITH SHRIMP, 1000 ISLAND DRESSING   3.75

HOT

CREPES FILLED WITH SEAFOOD   3.75   ESCARGOTS IN PASTRY   3.75

SPECIAL APPETIZER OF THE DAY   2.50

SOUPS

ONION SOUP GRATINEE   1.50   SOUP DE JOUR   1.50

SALADS

AVOCADO VINAIGRETTE   1.75
BEEFSTEAK TOMATOES & PURPLE ONIONS   1.75
ARNIE'S TOSSED SALAD   1.75   COLE SLAW   1.50
SPINACH SALAD FOR TWO   3.95
Avocado, Bacon, Mushrooms, Scallions and Eggs, Special Dressing

SPECIALTIES

SLAB OF BABY BACK RIBS   9.50
*Above Served With Au Gratin Potatoes, Cole Slaw and
Sweet & Sour Sauce*

CHICKEN CARUSO   5.95
Whole Chicken Basted in Lemon, Butter, Oregano & A Wisp of Garlic

PEPPER STEAK   8.95
Sliced Tenderloin, Green Peppers, Mushrooms and Tomatoes Served With Rice

FILET OF BEEF WELLINGTON   9.95
Filet Mignon Baked in Pastry

FISH

DOVER SOLE MEUNIERE   10.50   SAUTEED RED SNAPPER   8.95
With Lemon-Butter Sauce

FRESH WHITE GRENOBLOISE   6.95
Sauteed in Butter With Lemon and Capers

Above Served With Parslied Potatoes

VEAL

VEAL PICCATA IN LEMON BUTTER SAUCE   8.95
SICILIAN VEAL   8.95
Lightly Breaded with Garlic, Parsley & Parmesan Cheese

– *ABOVE SERVED WITH LINGUINI* –

VEAL FLORENTINE   8.95
Thinly Sliced Veal Over Spinach, Covered With Mornay Sauce

BEEF

PRIME RIB OF BEEF, WHIPPED HORSERADISH   9.95
SIRLOIN STEAK EL FORNO, SERVED WITH LINGUINI   11.50
Broiled with Parmesan Cheese, Butter, & A Wisp of Garlic
FILET MIGNON, SAUCE BEARNAISE   9.95   NEW YORK SIRLOIN STEAK   11.50
SIRLOIN STEAK ARNIE'S   11.95
Broiled, Topped with Medallions of Lobster, Sauce Bearnaise Glace

Served With Baked, Au Gratin or ARNIE'S Special Baked Potato

VEGETABLES AND POTATOES

ARNIE'S SPECIAL BAKED POTATO   1.00
AU GRATIN POTATOES   .95   BAKED POTATO   .95
CREAMED LEAF SPINACH   .95
FRESH VEGETABLE OF THE SEASON   1.00

DESSERTS

BRANDY ICE   2.50   HOT FUDGE SUNDAE   1.75
CHEESE CAKE   1.50   STRAWBERRIES WITH WHIPPED CREAM   1.85
FRENCH ICE CREAM OR SHERBET   1.50
CHOCOLATE MOUSSE   1.50   MELON OF THE SEASON   1.50
COFFEE   .75   IRISH COFFEE   2.25   TEA   .60

ASK YOUR WAITER ABOUT OUR FLAMBING DESSERTS!

ARNIE'S

A Personal Statement

Arnie's
1030 N. State Street,
Chicago, Illinois.

When the cost of a restaurant was cooly publicized as $1 million, in 1974, "Is it worth it?" was the question everybody asked. In Arnie's case, after five years of operation, the answer is a decisive "Yes!"

The "oohing" and "ahing" still goes on, but the place is so imaginatively planned that the gasps promise to continue. Thus far, Arnie's has realized its business from a variety of audiences. This was owner Arnold Morton's intention, and has been his successful achievement.

Wrapping itself around three sides of a plant-filled, "eternal-summer" atrium, the Morton complex is huge yet cunningly sequestered into four distinct areas. Up front is the seventy-seat "classy saloon" with bar and dance floor for young affluents, single or otherwise. To the north of the bar is the light, bright garden room seating forty, "Spanish surreal" in feeling, with hanging carrousel horses and an abundance of greenery. This room is essentially for "regulars" as is the 130-seat main dining room with its lavender chairs and banquettes, mirrored walls, tables, and magnificent illuminated ceiling of stained glass. More than a nostalgic art deco revival, this room stands on its own design merits. Finally, there is the white wicker room (eighty seats), created especially for women, lunch, and brunch parties.

Service throughout (fifty-five employees) is handled by pleasant young waiters, casually costumed in bow ties and argyle sweaters. "These kids who serve, they're so nice, so uncorrupted in their attitudes, the customers just love it," says Morton in admiration, but not in surprise, because he knew it would be that way.

The food? Very good, indeed. Despite the sophisticated environs, Arnie's chicken/fish/steak menu presents honest,

Arnie's reflects the personality of its owner—a lot of flash, a lot of substance.

straightforward fare at reasonable prices, and the customers know and appreciate it. There are also a number of higher-flying viands: stuffed trout Chablis, Sicilian veal, escargot in pastry, scallops in champagne sauce.

Arnold Morton, with a lifetime in the business—he comes from a Chicago restaurant family and was the prime mover behind Playboy Clubs and Hotels—knows his foodservice. Don't over promise. Keep it good. Deliver.

Spectacular establishments like Arnie's face a special challenge not to be razzled by their own dazzle. Morton certainly is not. In fact, he is quite casual about Arnie's, as well as his private club, Zorine's, (1976) and his suburban spectacular, Arnie's North in Highland Park, (1977). Zorine's, named after Morton's wife, is located in the same highrise building as Arnie's, and is, if possible, even more o'erwhelming— mirrors, chrome, lucite. It could be a Busby Berkeley set, displaying Chicago's most sensational *son et lumiere* show. Arnie's North fills a huge space formerly occupied by a supermarket. It too dazzles with Morton's engaging style of decoration, merchandising, and humor.

Next, Arnold Morton plans a steak house on the level below Zorine's. And then . . . ?

But Arnie's was the first for Morton and remains a successful first for Chicago. "I want Arnie's to be a home for the local crowds," says Morton, "no address on the menus or match boxes. Just Arnie's, the place to be." It promises to be, for a long time to come.

The various areas of Arnie's at first tend to overwhelm with their eclectic color and clutter . . . but not for long, because the restaurant is a very casual, comfortable place to enjoy food, conversation, and the passing scene. At left, the Garden Room, overlooking an atrium, and below, a view of Arnie's main dining room.

ESCARGOTS IN PASTRY

Arnie's

Ingredients: Yield: 16 portions

Escargots	8 dozen
Butter, unsalted	2 pounds
Shallots, minced	8
Garlic, minced	2 tablespoons
Parsley, chopped	$\frac{1}{4}$ cup
Salt	as needed
Pepper	as needed
Thyme	$\frac{1}{2}$ teaspoon
Pernod	8 ounces
Puff Pastry Sheets, frozen	as needed
Water	as needed
Egg Yolks, beaten	as needed

Procedure:

1. Saute shallots, garlic, and parsley in butter to make escargot butter.
2. Saute escargots in butter adding salt, pepper, thyme, and brandy. Allow sauteed escargots to cool.
3. Place 6 escargots in each serving-sized stone crock. Cover with escargot butter.
4. Cut puff pastry sheets to fit crocks and drench each piece with water. Place pastry over top of each crock and brush with beaten egg yolk.
5. Place crocks on a bed of rock salt. Cook in oven at 350°F. for 8 minutes or until pastry is golden brown.

BEEF WELLINGTON

Arnie's

Ingredients:

Yield: 4 portions

Beef Tenderloins, trimmed, 6 ounces each	4
Salt	as needed
Pepper	as needed
Shallots, finely chopped	2
Mushrooms, fresh, finely chopped	8 ounces
Cream, heavy	4 ounces
Commercial Puff Pastry, 8-inch squares	4 pieces
Goose Liver Spread	4 ounces
Egg Yolk, beaten	as needed

Procedure:

1. Season meat with salt and pepper. Sear in hot skillet so that meat is very rare with cold center.
2. Saute shallots and mushrooms until soft. Add cream and reduce to paste.
3. Roll puff pastry out until size is 10 by 10 inches. Place tenderloin filets on pastry squares, cover with mushroom mixture. Place 1 ounce of goose liver spread on top of each.
4. Fold pastry and decorate with cut-outs.
5. Brush with beaten egg yolk. Bake in oven at 350°F. for 15 to 20 minutes.

PEPPER STEAK

Arnie's

Ingredients: Yield: 20 portions

Beef Tenderloin, sliced	7½ pounds
Onions, medium, sliced	5
Green Peppers, large, sliced	5
Mushrooms, sliced	8 ounces
Peppercorns, whole, crushed	¾ teaspoon
Garlic, minced	1 clove
Claret	2½ cups
Mushroom Sauce, canned	2½ cups

Procedure:

1. Saute sliced beef in butter with onions, mushrooms, garlic, and green peppers for about 5 minutes.
2. Add peppercorns and cook another 5 minutes.
3. Add wine and mushroom sauce and simmer 5 minutes more.

STEAK ARNIE'S

Arnie's

Ingredients: Yield: 20 portions

New York Strip Sirloin Steaks, 10 ounces each	20
Lobster Tail Meat, cooked, sliced	2½ pounds
Bearnaise Sauce	as needed

Procedure:

1. Broil steak to taste.
2. Place 2 ounces lobster tail meat on each steak.
3. Cover entire steak and lobster with Bearnaise sauce.
4. Place under broiler, glaze, and serve immediately.

SIRLOIN STEAK AL FORNO WITH LINGUINI

Arnie's

Ingredients:

Yield: 16 portions

New York Strip Sirloin Steaks, 10 ounces each	16
Salt	as needed
Pepper	as needed
Salad Oil	as needed
Garlic Powder	as needed
Parmesan Cheese	1 cup
Drawn Butter	1 cup
Linguini	4 pounds
Ricotta Cheese	8 ounces
Butter	8 ounces
Parmesan Cheese	8 ounces
Salt	as needed
Pepper	as needed
Egg Yolks, beaten	4

Procedure:

1. Rub steaks with salad oil and season with salt and pepper.
2. Broil to taste, then sprinkle each with a touch of garlic powder, a tablespoon of Parmesan cheese, and a tablespoon of drawn butter. Serve with linguini as prepared below.
3. Cook linguini *al dente*. Drain and immediately add the remaining ingredients. Mix well.

SICILIAN VEAL

Arnie's

Ingredients: Yield: 20 portions

Veal Loin	$7\frac{1}{2}$ pounds
Salt	as needed
Pepper	as needed
Flour	as needed
Egg Yolk, beaten	as needed
Bread Crumbs	$2\frac{1}{2}$ pounds
Parmesan Cheese	$2\frac{1}{2}$ pounds
Garlic Powder	$\frac{1}{4}$ teaspoon
Parsley	2 tablespoons
Butter	as needed
Linguini, cooked (see recipe with Sirloin Steak el Forno)	as needed

Procedure:

1. Cut veal into 2-ounce portions and flatten until paper thin.
2. Sprinkle with salt and pepper, dust with flour, and dip into egg yolk.
3. Mix together bread crumbs, Parmesan cheese, garlic powder, and parsley. Dip veal portions into this mixture.
4. Saute in hot butter until golden brown. Serve with linguini.

RACK OF LAMB

Arnie's

Ingredients:

Yield: 4 portions

Saddle of Lamb	6 to 7 pounds
Salt	as needed
Pepper	as needed
Tarragon, fresh	pinch

Procedure:

1. Bone out lamb so that no bones remain and complete eye of saddle and tenderloins are well-trimmed. Season with salt and pepper.
2. Sear and cook to taste, about 30 minutes per pound.
3. Cut into thin slices. Serve with natural juices mixed with fresh tarragon.

STUFFED TROUT CHABLIS

Arnie's

Ingredients: Yield: 30 portions

Trout, boneless, 8 to 10 ounces each	30
Salmon, boneless	5 pounds
Whipping Cream	2½ quarts
Egg Whites	2 dozen
Salt	as needed
Pepper	as needed
Shallots, finely chopped	6
Butter	12 ounces
Chablis	2 cups
Parsley, minced	2 tablespoons

Procedure:

1. Cut salmon into small pieces and put in blender with half the cream, and salt, pepper, and egg whites. Blend until mixture reaches the consistency of a mousse. Stuff trout with the mixture.
2. Place stuffed trout and chopped shallots in baking dishes. Dot with butter and add Chablis. Bake in oven at 350°F. about 15 minutes.
3. Remove trout from oven; place on a hot service platter. Mix pan juices with remaining cream to make a smooth sauce. Add parsley and spoon over trout.

SCALLOPS

Arnie's

Ingredients:

Yield: 20 portions

Bay Scallops, fresh, drained	3 pounds
Shallots, minced	16
Mushrooms, fresh, sliced	1 pound
White Wine	1 pint
Heavy Cream	1 quart
Butter	8 ounces
Flour	8 ounces
Salt	1 teaspoon
Pepper	as needed
Champagne	12 ounces
Heavy Cream, whipped	12 ounces
Egg Yolks, beaten	8
Parmesan Cheese, grated	as needed

Procedure:

1. Combine shallots, mushrooms, and wine and simmer until shallots and mushrooms are half cooked. Drain off liquid and reduce substantially.
2. Mix reduced liquid with 1 quart heavy cream until smooth. Set aside.
3. Blend butter and flour and cook about 2 minutes. Allow to cool completely.
4. Add reduced liquid to the roux; add salt and pepper. Cook, stirring constantly until smooth.
5. Add champagne, scallops, and shallot, mushroom, and wine mixture to roux. Cook slowly for 5 minutes.
6. Fold whipped cream into egg yolks, then fold into scallop mixture.
7. Pour 3-ounce portions into scallop dishes and sprinkle with Parmesan cheese. Place under broiler until lightly browned. Serve immediately.

SHRIMP AND MUSHROOM SALAD

Arnie's

Ingredients: Yield: 32 portions

Salad Shrimp, cooked, peeled, deveined	8 pounds
Mushrooms, fresh, sliced	8 pounds
Salad Oil	1 cup
Olive Oil	1 cup
White Wine Vinegar	$2\frac{1}{2}$ cups
Celery, chopped	3 pounds
Onion, finely chopped	8 ounces
Scallions, finely chopped	1 pound
Oregano, leaf	1 teaspoon
Salt	as needed
Pepper	as needed
Lettuce	as needed
Egg Slices	as needed
Tomato Wedges	as needed
Alfalfa Sprouts	as needed

Procedure:

1. Cut shrimp in half lengthwise and combine with mushrooms.
2. Mix both kinds of oil, vinegar, celery, onion, scallions, and seasoning. Add to shrimp and mushrooms. Cover and marinate 3 hours, mixing frequently.
3. Serve on bed of lettuce and garnish with sliced eggs, tomatoes, and alfalfa sprouts.

SPECIAL BAKED POTATO

Arnie's

Ingredients: Yield: 24 portions

Baking Potatoes, medium	12
Butter, sweet, melted	$\frac{3}{4}$ cup
Half and Half, warm	12 ounces
Sour Cream	4 pounds
Bacon, sliced	8 ounces
Cheddar Cheese, grated	$\frac{1}{2}$ cup
Onion, medium, finely chopped	1
Salt	as needed
Pepper, white	as needed
Butter, melted	as needed
Cheddar Cheese, grated	as needed

Procedure:

1. Scrub potatoes, then rub with a little water and salt. Bake in oven at 400°F. for 1 hour or until done.
2. Fry bacon to medium crispness, remove from pan and mince.
3. Saute onion in bacon drippings, then drain.
4. Scoop out potatoes close to skin. Add butter, half and half, sour cream, bacon, cheddar cheese, onion, salt, and pepper. Beat until smooth.
5. Put mixture into a pastry bag and refill potato skins. Brush tops with melted butter and sprinkle with grated cheese.
6. Bake in oven at 500°F. for 8 or 10 minutes, then put under broiler for 1 or 2 minutes until golden brown.

At The Columbian Exposition of 1893

When cable cars and carriages
clattered past State Street
and Adams, The Berghoff offered
the finest in food and service.
Today that tradition is proudly
maintained by the third generation
in the Berghoff family, offering
its fare in a style that captures
the sturdy spirit of Old Chicago.

17 WEST ADAMS STREET

THE Berghoff RESTAURANT
OPERATED BY THE BERGHOFF FAMILY FOR MORE THAN 75 YEARS

17 WEST ADAMS STREET • CHICAGO, ILLINOIS

SPRING AND MAY WINE TIME AT BERGHOFF RESTAURANT
CHILLED
ROEMER .. 60c
SCHOPPEN 70c
BOTTLE . . $2.75

We have revised and broadened our selection
of desserts to better reflect the traditional
quality and variety that typify the Berghoff
menu. Choose a pastry from our expanded
selection of Continental and American sweets
... the perfect compliment to your meal.

Napoleon   .75
A Light Creamy Treat

Danish Pinwheel   .60
Pastry at its finest

Chocolate Rum Tarte   .75
Rich and Creamy

Black Forest Cake   .90
Something Special

...   .55

... Pie   .55

... Cheese Cake .55

Banquets by Berghoff

THE Berghoff RESTAURANTS
425 N. Wabash • 17 W. Adams • 427-3170

Berghoff
A New Life for an Old Favorite

Berghoff Restaurant
17 W. Adams Street,
Chicago, Illinois.

Berghoff's has been around since the Columbian Exposition. Originally a great German saloon, Berghoff's entered the food business in 1898, offering free sandwiches to accompany their famous Muenchner-style high-malt beer. Eighty years later, Berghoff's is a favorite of 1.25 million customers annually.

In a city that all too often sloughs off the past for the present, Berghoff's demonstrates the success of persistence. As traditions go, it is a lively one.

The people who fill Berghoff's 700 seats and consume approximately 3,300 meals per day (with a check average of $4.60 come from all over. At lunch, sixty-five percent of Berghoff's business, they are conventioneers, downtown business people, and shoppers. Throughout the day, the restaurant has a growing, young clientele from nearby colleges and law schools; in the evening, more conventioneers and "evening-outers" who dine before going to the theatre, opera, or symphony.

Inside Berghoff's organization, there is even more of a generational, as well as national, mix among its 170 employees and management. The Chairman of the Board of the family-held company, the venerable, second generation C.A. Berghoff, is still active day to day. On the other side of the calendar, Berghoff's general managers, Daryl Fenton and Lorrin Barbero, are in their thirties. Both Fenton and Barbero, who handle the front and the back of the house respectively, have come up through the ranks, according to Berghoff custom.

The many-chaptered Berghoff story has a number of fascinating footnotes. Twenty percent of the restaurant's volume is based on liquor sales, befitting a place that still holds

A sampling of Berghoff menus and printed matter demonstrates a knack for blending the old with the new—a key to the Berghoff's multi-generation success story.

Chicago liquor license "Number One," awarded right after the repeal of prohibition. The Berghoff Cafe (formerly "the men's bar" in chauvinist days) still serves Berghoff draft beer and stand-up lunches.

Berghoff's food is purchased fresh, because it does its own butchering and freezing, sometimes investing heavily in futures to maintain a high inventory. As much as 20,000 pounds of shrimp or 50,000 pounds of halibut are purchased when the market is right. For a German restaurant associated with Wiener Schnitzel and Sauerbraten, still big sellers, Berghoff's is one of Chicago's largest seafood houses. Fish accounts for twenty-five percent of total sale.

Also very successful are the recently introduced *haute cuisine* items not usually thought of as Berghoffian: Veal Parisienne, Schweinfilet in Hunter's Sauce, and according to many, "the best Bouillabaisse in Chicago."

With a new kitchen and its word-of-mouth fame rushing on, Berghoff's has a renewed lease on life as it continues to bridge the generations.

Still in its original building on Adams Street (opposite), Berghoff's darkly wooded dining rooms and bars (below) offer hospitality beyond design contrivance.

FLAEDLE SOUP

Berghoff Restaurant

Ingredients: Yield: 50 portions

Flour	1 pound
Milk	½ gallon
Salt	½ ounce
Eggs	8
Chives, chopped	2 ounces
Butter	8 ounces
Consomme	50 portions

Procedure:

1. Mix flour, milk, and salt to a smooth paste.
2. Add eggs and chives. Mix for 1 minute.
3. Put ¼ounce butter in 8-inch frying pan, heat and add 2 ounces of batter. When golden brown, turn and brown other side. Repeat until batter is used.
4. When pancakes are cool, cut into julienne strips.
5. Put strips into soup bowl, add hot consomme, and serve.

GARLIC BUTTER FOR SNAILS

Berghoff Restaurant

Ingredients: Yield: 50 portions

Shallots, minced	6 ounces
Garlic, minced	6 ounces
Parsley, minced	1 pound
Butter	6 pounds
Anchovy Paste	6 ounces
Lemon Juice	2 ounces
Pepper, white, ground	½ ounce
Worcestershire Sauce	1½ ounces
Monosodium Glutamate	3 ounces
Salt	3 ounces

HUHN IM TOPH
"Chicken in the Pot"

Berghoff Restaurant

Ingredients: Yield: 50 portions

Frying Chickens, 2 pounds each	25
Beef Stock	5 gallons
Celery, coarsely diced	2 pounds
Leeks, coarsely diced	2 pounds
Onion, coarsely diced	2 pounds
Carrots, coarsely diced	2 pounds
Noodles	4 pounds
Salt	4 ounces

Procedure:

1. Split chickens in half. Cook in water until tender, about $\frac{1}{2}$ hour. Remove skin.
2. Cook vegetables in beef stock.
3. Cook noodles in salted water, then portion into individual casseroles. Add a half chicken to each, then top with broth and vegetables.

GARLIC BUTTER FOR SNAILS *(cont'd.)*
Procedure:

1. Put all ingredients in mixer and beat until fluffy.

RAGOUT A LA DEUTSCH

Berghoff Restaurant

Ingredients: Yield: 50 6-ounce portions

Lard or Oil	8 ounces
Beef Sirloin	20 pounds
Onion, diced	2 pounds
Brown Gravy, thick	3 quarts
Red Wine	1 quart
Butter	8 ounces
Green Pepper, diced	2 pounds
Mushrooms, fresh, sliced	2 pounds
Worcestershire Sauce	1 ounce
Liquid Hot Pepper Seasoning	$\frac{1}{2}$ ounce
Salt	5 ounces
Pimiento, coarsely diced	3 pounds

Procedure:

1. Cut beef into $\frac{1}{2}$-inch thick strips and saute with onion in lard or oil until golden brown.
2. Add gravy and wine. Simmer 1 hour or until tender.
3. Saute green pepper and mushrooms in butter. Add to meat along with remaining ingredients.
4. Cook 10 to 15 minutes more.

SAUERBRATEN

Berghoff Restaurant

Ingredients: Yield: 50 portions

Beef Round	20 pounds

Marinade

Celery, finely chopped	1 stalk
Carrots, chopped	1 pound
Parsley, chopped	1 pound
Garlic Cloves, cut in half	1 ounce
Onion, diced	1 pound
Peppercorns, whole	1 ounce
Cloves, whole	6
Bay Leaves	8
Juniper Berries	$\frac{1}{2}$ ounce
Salt	6 ounces
Monosodium Glutamate	3 ounces
Water	$\frac{1}{2}$ gallon
Vinegar	$\frac{1}{2}$ gallon
Red Wine	$\frac{1}{2}$ gallon
Lard or Oil	8 ounces
Brown Gravy	10 pounds
Tomato Puree	1 pound
Red Wine	5 ounces
Salt	2 ounces

Procedure:

1. Place beef in a barrel or large jar. Add vegetables, seasonings, water, vinegar, and wine. Marinate in refrigerator 3 to 4 days.
2. Remove meat from marinade and place in roasting pan containing melted lard or oil. Brown in oven at 400°F. for 30 minutes.
3. Reduce heat to 350°F. and add brown gravy, tomato puree, all of marinade, and 2 ounces salt. Cook 1 to $1\frac{1}{2}$ hours or until done.
4. Remove meat and strain sauce for gravy.
5. Add 5 ounces red wine to gravy.

REHPFEFFER
(Venison Ragout)

Berghoff Restaurant

Ingredients:　　　　　　　　　　　　　　　Yield:　50 portions (4 pieces)

Doe Shoulder, Neck, Ribs	25 pounds
Marinade	
Mirepoix	3 pounds
Garlic Clove, cut in half	1
Bay Leaves	6
Cloves, whole	6
Red Wine	$1\frac{1}{2}$ quart
Water	$\frac{1}{2}$ gallon
Fat	8 ounces
Flour	$1\frac{1}{2}$ pounds
Beef Stock	2 gallons
Onions, medium, chopped	4
Bacon, $\frac{1}{2}$-inch dice	1 pound
Tomato Puree	1 pound
Salt	3 ounces
Pepper, black, ground	1 ounce
Sour Cream	$2\frac{1}{2}$ pounds

Procedure:

1. Cut meat into 2-ounce pieces and place in large jar. Add mirepoix, garlic, bay leaves, cloves, wine, and water. Marinate in refrigerator 3 days.
2. Drain meat and reserve marinade. Brown meat in fat in oven at 400°F. about 30 minutes.
3. Sprinkle with flour, add stock and strained marinade. Cook in oven at 350°F. for $1\frac{1}{2}$ hours or until tender.
4. Saute bacon and onions and add to meat. Do not add bacon fat.
5. Add tomato puree, salt, and pepper.
6. Heat through. Remove from oven and slowly stir in sour cream.

HASENPFEFFER

Berghoff Restaurant

Ingredients: Yield: 90 portions (3 pieces each)

Australian Rabbits, 2 pounds each	30
Marinade	
Mirepoix	4 pounds
Red Wine	$\frac{1}{2}$ gallon
Vinegar	$\frac{1}{2}$ gallon
Water	$\frac{1}{2}$ gallon
Garlic Bulb, split in half	1 ounce
Bay Leaves	6
Cloves	12
Flour	2 pounds
Paprika	$1\frac{1}{2}$ tablespoons
Fat	2 pounds
Beef Stock	1 gallon
Bacon, diced	2 pounds
Onion, diced	6 pounds
Tomato Puree	2 pounds
Salt	2 ounces
Pepper, black, ground	$\frac{1}{2}$ ounce

Procedure:

1. Thaw rabbits and cut into pieces by severing legs at joints and cutting backs into 3 sections. Place in crock or jar.
2. Mix mirepoix, wine, vinegar, water, garlic, bay leaves, and cloves. Pour over rabbit and marinate in refrigerator 5 days.
3. Drain and reserve the marinade.
4. Dry rabbit pieces, dredge with flour and paprika, and fry until golden brown.
5. Add reserved marinade and stock and simmer for 2 hours or until tender.
6. Saute bacon and onion for about 15 minutes. Drain. Add bacon, onion, tomato puree, and seasonings to *hasenpfeffer*.
7. Heat through and serve.

SAUSAGE CAKES

Berghoff Restaurant

Ingredients: Yield: 8 to 10 cakes

Pork, ground	2 pounds
Veal, ground	2 pounds
Eggs	2
Salt	as needed
Pepper	as needed
Monosodium Glutamate	as needed
Powdered Sage	as needed
Water	as needed

Procedure:

1. Grind meat and eggs together.
2. Add seasoning to taste. Mix well, using as much water as needed to handle well.
3. Form into patties. Fry until done, turning to brown both sides.

VINEGAR AND OIL DRESSING

Berghoff Restaurant

Ingredients: Yield: $7\frac{1}{2}$ gallons

Vinegar	3 gallons
Water	3 gallons
Oil	$1\frac{1}{2}$ gallons
Salt	6 ounces
Mustard, dry	4 ounces
Celery Salt	4 ounces
Garlic Salt	4 ounces
Bottled Steak Sauce	2 ounces
Worcestershire Sauce	2 ounces
Sugar	8 pounds

Procedure:

1. Blend all ingredients together well.

POTATO PANCAKES

Berghoff Restaurant

Ingredients: Yield: 6 portions

Potatoes, Idaho, AP	4½ pounds
Eggs	3
Flour	1 teaspoon
Salt	as needed
Shortening	as needed

Procedure:

1. Peel and grate potatoes. Drain thoroughly in sieve for about 5 minutes.
2. Mix in eggs, flour, and salt.
3. Drop by spoonfuls into hot shortening in frying pan.
4. Cook to a golden brown on each side.

STRING BEANS, SWISS-STYLE

Berghoff Restaurant

Ingredients: Yield: 50 portions

String Beans, fresh	12 pounds plus 10 ounces
Bacon, cut julienne	2 pounds
Onion, diced	1½ pounds
Butter	10 ounces
Flour	10 ounces
Vinegar	1 to 2 ounces
Chicken Base	3 ounces
Salt	2 ounces

Procedure:

1. Cut beans into 1-inch pieces and cook until tender.
2. Fry bacon, add onion and cook 5 minutes. Drain off fat.
3. Make roux from butter and flour. Stir in stock and cook until thickened. Add bacon and onion and cook 30 minutes.
4. Add vinegar, chicken base, salt, and drained beans.
5. Heat through and serve.

PLUM CAKE

Berghoff Restaurant

Ingredients: Yield: 50 portions

Bread Flour	6 pounds
Cake Flour	3 pounds
Sugar	2 pounds
Salt	2 ounces
Butter, room temperature	2 pounds
Yeast, granular	14 ounces
Milk, whole, lukewarm	$2\frac{1}{2}$ to 3 quarts
Eggs	1 dozen
Plums, fresh, pitted	10 to 12 pounds
Sugar	$1\frac{1}{2}$ pounds
Cinnamon	1 ounce
Apricot Jelly	16 ounces

Procedure:

1. Place first four ingredients in mixing bowl and blend. Mix in butter.
2. Dissolve yeast in $2\frac{1}{2}$ quarts milk and add to bowl; add eggs and more milk, if necessary until dough is smooth.
3. Allow dough to double in size.
4. Divide into two equal portions and pat out on two 18- by 26-inch baking sheets.
5. Arrange plums, pitted side up, on top of dough.
6. Mix sugar and cinnamon and sprinkle over plums.
7. Let rise 1 hour. Bake in oven at 350°F. for 35 minutes.
8. When cool, glaze with apricot jelly.

INTERNATIONAL FLIGHT

Weekly Gastronomic Tour — Served from 5:30 PM

MONDAY
NEW ENGLAND U.S.A.

MAINE LOBSTERS   **Market Price**

Whole live fresh lobsters flown in to us from Portland, Maine weekly

TUESDAY
ALSACE-LORRAINE

CHOUCROUTE GARNI   **$5.25**

Stolen from Germany and embellished by the French — consisting of chopped pickled cabbage (fancy sauerkraut), Alsatian smoked sausage, roast pork, spareribs, apples, clove-studded onions, and even Beer! Served with parsed boiled potato.
Guten Appetit and Bon Appetit!

WEDNESDAY
Moscow, Russia

KULEBIAKA   **$5.95**

From Russia with love! But our Chef Jacques gives you his French version — "COULIBIAC". Fresh salmon in a mousse of perch, fresh mushrooms and rice rolled inside crepes — then encased in a crust and baked to a golden brown.

THURSDAY
Barcelona, Spain

PAELLA   **$5.95**

The Spanish do their thing! — with plump chickens, tiny clams, shrimp, chorizos sausage, green peas and tomatoes, all beautifully mingled with saffron rice and baked to perfection. Buen Provecho!

FRIDAY
MARSEILLES, FRANCE

BOUILLABAISSE   **$6.25**

A hearty Mediterranean fisherman's stew of various seafoods and shellfish including red snapper, bass, halibut, scallops, clams, shrimp, dungenese crabs and all the traditional herbs, with French bread for dunking! *Bon Appetit!*

SATURDAY
LONDON, ENGLAND

BEEF WELLINGTON   **$7.95**

Tenderloin beef filet coated with pate stuffed with mushrooms — then wrapped in a puff pastry and baked as per Lord Wellington's orders. *Jolly Good Eat!*

THE S S T (Sumptious Salad Tray) and

(center black panel)

JOLLY GOOD EATING

HYVA RUOKAHLUA

SMA

VELBEKOMME

BON APPETIT

SMAKELIJK

GERO APETITO

BUONO APPETITO

SMAKLIG MALTID

BETE AVON

GOD APPETIT

KALI ORAXI

SMACZNEGO

THE DINNER FLIGHT

REV UP

TARTAR STEAK ON TOASTED RYE ROUNDS 2.50   SHRIMP COCKTAIL 1.95
COUGERE SWISS (French Fried Swiss Cheese) 1.75
ESCARGOTS BOURGUIGONNE 2.25

TAKE OFF

FRENCH ONION GRATINEE 1.00   THE CHEF'S SPECIAL SOUP .75

AIRBORNE

POACHED FILET OF ENGLISH DOVER SOLE BONNE FEMME	5.95
ROAST YOUNG DUCKLING MANDARIN	6.50
MINIATURE FROGS LEGS PAYSANNE—Garlic Chive Butter (When Available)	6.95
HONEY BARBECUED BACK RIBS	6.45
SLICED TENDERLOIN OF BEEF BURGUNDY	7.75
SOFT SHELLED CRABS MOZAMBIQUE — covered with chopped nuts and sauteed in butter	5.95
BONED BREAST OF CHICKEN CORDON BLEU (with Brocoli, Thinly sliced Ham, Gruyere Cheese covered with Mornay Sauce and Oven Browned)	5.50
NEW YORK CUT SIRLOIN STEAK (a la Roquefort .50 extra)	6.75
VEAL SCALLOPS CUMULUS—Thin Veal slices with Artichokes cooked in Chablis wine, Cream and Lemon	6.95

THE LUXURY LINERS

PRIME FILET MIGNON	8.50
STEAK AU POIVRE — (The French Touch) — Filet Mignon smothered in cracked black pepper and cognac)	7.75
PEPPER STEAK — (The American Way — smothered with fresh tomatoes, mushrooms and green peppers)	7.75

TWELVE O'CLOCK HIGH

Served from 11:00 AM - 2:30 PM

DOWNWIND
Real French Onion Soup (stringy cheese)
The "HANGARBURGER"
Salad   French Fries   2.75

HEADWIND
Sliced Breast of Turkey and fresh cucumbers on French bread oven baked in a cheesy Mornay Sauce topped with bacon bits and crisp noodles
Salad   2.95

TAILSPIN
Oven Faced Toasted Cheddar Cheese, sliced Tomatoes and Bacon   1.95

THE SEAPLANE
Assorted Seafood Platter—Sauce Tartare   3.10

TAILWIND
Grilled Tenderloin Steak Sandwich
Salad   French Fries   Ice Cold Beer   4.75

SUPERSONIC
Sirloin Luncheon Steak   French Fries
Lettuce wedge-Tomato   Toasted Cheese Bread   4.95

THE GYROSCOPE
YOUR CHOICE OF AN OMELETTE WITH
1. Italian Sausage, Potatoes, Scallions and Green Peppers
2. Sliced Fresh Mushrooms   3. American or Parmesan Cheese   2.85

THE AMPHIBIAN
Tiny Pearl Scallops Meuniere, served with
Tartar Sauce   French Fries   2.95

THE FLY-IN
California Crab Salad with Parmesan Bread
(a San Francisco Specialty with Stuffed Celery)   3.75

SKY DIVER PLATTER
Broiled Chopped Sirloin of Beef, Cottage Cheese, Sliced Cucumbers and Tomatoes (practically no calories)   2.75

UP-UP and AWAY (on less calories) Served with Rye Thins
Chilled Shrimp Mimosa—whole shrimp, chopped egg, carrot curls, radishes with cocktail sauce   2.75
Chef's Salad of Crisp Greens, Ham and Turkey slivers and Chopped Egg   1.95

or

"JUST A SANDWICH"
(Served with French Fries)

"HANGARBURGER"
Chopped Steak with sliced Onion and Tomatoes on Sesame Roll   1.85

JETBURGER
Super-large Chopped Steak with Tangy Banana Peppers, or melted Gruyere or Bleu Cheese   2.25

CAPTAIN CHARLIE TUNA
Tuna, Celery, Onions, and Cheese—
all toasted in the oven on French Bread   2.15

AUTOMATIC PILOT
(It's a Mild "Reuben") Sliced Ham, Cheddar Cheese,
Curried Cole Slaw with Chutney grilled on Rye Bread   2.25

PIPER CUB
Cold Sliced Turkey, Lettuce-Tomato, Cranberry Relish   1.75

DAILY SPECIAL SOUP (Cup) .75   FRENCH FRIES .35   PARMESAN BREAD .25
FRENCH ONION SOUP 1.00   ROQUEFORT DRESSING .50
SMALL SALAD .75   DESSERTS .50   COFFEE, TEA or MILK* Hot or Iced .30

15% Service Charge on all Parties of 6 or more

CEILING ZERO

500 ANTHONY TRAIL/NORTHBROOK/ILLINOIS

CEILING ZERO

500 ANTHONY TRAIL/NORTHBROOK/ILLINOIS

CEILING ZERO
Chicago's Best Kept Secret?

Ceiling Zero
500 Anthony Trail,
Northbrook, Illinois.

Business is good: 140 at lunch, perhaps 200 at dinner on weekends, a check average of $12, excluding liquor. With a value beyond its price, imaginative food, and an atmosphere of much charm, how can Ceiling Zero be Chicago's best-kept culinary secret? To a flock of regulars, devoted returnees, Ceiling Zero in Northbrook's Sky Harbor Airport is anything but secret. Yet to many others beyond Northbrook and the immediate environs, the restaurant would seem to hide its lights under a bushel—or in an airport hanger, to be exact.

"Of course, we welcome business, especially new business to fill in certain valleys between peaks. But constant big volume business? We're not set up for it; we couldn't handle it, and provide the kind of food and service we want to offer. Anyway, we are semi-retired . . ." so says Diane Kovler, who, along with her husband Jerry, has operated Ceiling Zero since September 1971. The Kovlers are widely respected professionals with distinguished foodservice backgrounds. For more than fifteen years they had operated, with success and style, Chicago's fashionable Red Carpet restaurant. Famous from East Coast to West, the Red Carpet offered some of the city's finest continental food with Caribbean touches. (The Kovlers were also the former owners and managers of the renowned resort Miranda Hill at Montego Bay, Jamaica.)

Ceiling Zero, if less known, worldwide or even Chicago-wide, is every bit as smartly run an establishment. The restaurant's lunch business comes from the adjacent Sky Harbor Industrial Park area (the actual airport closed in 1973), and from nearby business and professional people. At dinner Ceiling Zero is perhaps *the* place to dine—if you are among the suburban *cognoscenti*.

33

Ceiling Zero offers one of Chicago's high-soaring menus. Of note are the "International Flight" daily specials.

Ceiling Zero is simply designed and thoughtfully executed with a great deal of throw-away chic. Visually the room seems larger than its 40 feet by 80 feet dimensions, but it is quite compact. There are seventy-five to eighty seats at dinner, and 120 at lunch (when the bar area is used for dining). Black, grey, and aircraft aluminum—these are the colors that form a stationary backdrop for the bright reds which appear unexpectedly, and literally move about the room: waitresses appear in brilliant red stewardess costume and bus boys wear red jumpsuits. On tables, there are red placemats and napkins; and over the bar a red nylon parachute is suspended in motion. The Kovlers have done admirable things with lighting. The lively mood at lunch is completely different from the dinner atmosphere when the restaurant has a quiet, flowing, lighter-than-air feeling—durable and "dirigible."

Ceiling Zero is more casual, more "American" perhaps than other Kovler operations. In any case, the restaurant offers a familiar warmth of welcome. Many of Ceiling Zero's twenty-five employees have long been associated with Jerry and Diane. Everything contributes to high hospitality.

But all of this pleasant decor and service aside, it's the distinguished food that makes Ceiling Zero really take off.

Lunch—"12 o'clock high" on the menu—is moderate in price, offering mostly sandwiches, omelettes and special plates, many of them titularly imaginative: "The Gyroscope," "The Amphibian," and "The Hangerburger." Good items, if not unusual.

The "Dinner Flight" menu soars much higher in the realm of fine dining. Dinner begins with various "Rev-Up" hors d'oeuvres. Of particular interest is the french-fried Cougere Swiss cheese appetizer. Superior "standard" entrees include lime-broiled chicken, a splendid Steak au Poivre, and Soft-Shell Crabs Mozambique (available out of season, the crabs are one of the few superb frozen varieties).

The six nightly specials under the designation "International Flight" are the summation of the Kovlers' foodservice expertise. "International" lists six items as good as anything Chicago restaurantdom has to offer, and four of them may be the best dishes in the city. From Alsace Lorraine, Choucrote Garni on Tuesday; from Russia, Coulibiac, fresh Salmon en Croute on Wednesday; from Barcelona, Paella, Thursday; and Bouillabaisse from Marseilles on Friday. Not incidentally, the man who pilots these high flying feats of gastronomy is Chef Jacques Chevalier, a long-time friend and head-of-kitchen from Miranda Hill days.

Jerry and Diane Kovler clearly know what they are about. Although it is a small restaurant, Ceiling Zero is a very big plus on the Chicago dining-out horizon. For Ceiling Zero customers, it's clear flying all the way.

Jacques Chevalier is the imaginative chef behind Ceiling Zero's French, American, and continental dishes.

COUGERE
(a cheese appetizer)

Ceiling Zero

Ingredients: Yield: 15 portions

Bechamel Sauce, thick	1 quart
Parmesan Cheese, grated	$\frac{1}{2}$ pound
Gruyere Cheese, grated	$\frac{1}{2}$ pound
Salt	to taste
Pepper	to taste
Nutmeg	$\frac{1}{4}$ teaspoon
Egg Yolks, beaten	10
Bread Crumbs, fine	as needed

Procedure:

1. Add grated cheese to Bechamel sauce and heat gently until cheese melts. Add seasonings.
2. Stir in egg yolks and stir until thickened. Pour into sheet pan to cool.
3. Cut into small pieces and dust with bread crumbs.
4. Fry in hot oil at 380°F. for 2 minutes.
5. Serve as hors d'oeuvres.

At left, two views of Ceiling Zero's simple but effectively designed main dining room. Located in a former airport hanger, the restaurant's aeronautical theme is a natural.

FRENCH ONION SOUP

Ceiling Zero

Ingredients: Yield: 50 portions

Onion, sliced fine	8 pounds
Butter or Margarine	8 ounces
Beef Stock, strained, warm	1½ gallons
Chicken Stock, strained, warm	1½ gallons
Dry Sherry (optional)	6 ounces
French Bread	50 slices
Gruyere Cheese, grated	2 pounds

Procedure:

1. Saute onion in butter until evenly browned.
2. Add stocks. Bring to boil and reduce heat. Simmer about 45 minutes or until onion flavor is well developed. Skim liquid as required during simmering. Add sherry about 10 minutes before end of cooking period.
3. Sprinkle cheese on bread slices. Place under broiler until cheese melts. Top each serving of soup with a slice.

BOUILLABAISSE

Ceiling Zero

Ingredients: Yield: 20 portions

Olive Oil	1 cup
Leeks, chopped	6
Onion, chopped	1 pound
Carrots, medium, chopped	2
Water	1 gallon
Sea Bass	$2\frac{1}{2}$ pounds
Lake Trout	$2\frac{1}{2}$ pounds
Spanish Mackerel or Halibut	$2\frac{1}{2}$ pounds
Snapper	$2\frac{1}{2}$ pounds
Shrimp, raw, in shells	3 dozen
Dungeness Crab Legs, cooked, in shells	20
Tomatoes, peeled, seeded, chopped	2 pounds
Garlic, chopped	6 cloves
Parsley, chopped	$\frac{1}{4}$ cup
Saffron, crushed	1 teaspoon
Thyme	2 teaspoons
Salt	as needed
Pepper	as needed
Fennel Seed	1 teaspoon
Bay Leaves	2
White Wine	2 cups
Tomatoes, canned	2 #2 cans
Clams, scrubbed, in shells	4 to 5 dozen

Procedure:

1. Saute leeks, onion, and carrots in hot oil until onion is clear.
2. Add water, cut up fish, and all remaining ingredients except canned tomatoes and clams. Simmer $\frac{1}{2}$ hour.
3. Add canned tomatoes and clams. Simmer 5 minutes.

BEEF TENDERLOIN WELLINGTON

Ceiling Zero

Ingredients: Yield: 10 portions

Beef Tenderloin, whole, trimmed	6 pounds
Liver Pate or Foie Gras	1 pound
Veal or Pork Forcemeat	1 pound
Mushroom Buxelle	10 ounces
Pate en Croute	
Flour, bread	12 ounces
Flour, cake	12 ounces
Salt	$2\frac{1}{4}$ teaspoons
Butter	6 ounces
Shortening	6 ounces
Eggs	6 ounces
Water, cold	6 ounces
Egg	1
Madeira Demi-Glace	as needed

Procedure:

1. Roast meat in oven at 400°F. about 45 minutes or until internal temperature registers rare, 140°F. Remove from pan and allow to cool.
2. Combine pate or foie gras, forcemeat, and duxelle and coat tenderloin with the mixture.
3. To make *pate en croute,* mix flours, salt, butter, and shortening together. Combine 6 ounces of eggs with water, add to flour mixture and blend until smooth.
4. Roll out about $\frac{1}{8}$ inch thick, reserving enough dough for decorating. Place tenderloin on dough and wrap, sealing ends on bottom.
5. Cut flowers or designs from reserved dough to decorate top. Brush with beaten egg.
6. Bake in oven at 375°F. about 45 minutes. Cut slices $\frac{3}{4}$ inch thick and serve with Madeira demi-glace.

STEAK AU POIVRE

Ceiling Zero

Ingredients: Yield: 4 portions

Beef Filets, 10 ounces each	4
Pepper, black, cracked	as needed
Butter or Oil	as needed
Brandy	1 ounce
Burgundy Demi-Glace	1 cup.
Cream, heavy	$\frac{1}{2}$ cup

Procedure:

1. Rub filets with pepper and cook to taste in butter or oil.
2. Remove meat, pour off fat.
3. Add brandy to pan and reduce a little. Stir in Burgundy demi-glace and cream. Cook 5 minutes.
4. Pour over meat.

VEAL SCALLOPINE ALLA LUPORI

Ceiling Zero

Ingredients: Yield: 8 portions

Veal Cutlets, boneless, 6 ounces each	8
Oil	as needed
Eggplant, medium	2
Flour	as needed
Tomatoes, fresh, medium, peeled, quartered	4
Salt	as needed
Pepper	as needed
Parsley, chopped	2 tablespoons
Garlic, minced	1 clove
Veal Stock or Gravy	$\frac{1}{4}$ cup
White Wine	$\frac{1}{4}$ cup

Procedure:

1. Pound cutlets until thin and saute quickly in oil. Remove.
2. Peel and slice eggplant; dust with flour and fry in oil. Remove.
3. Add tomatoes to pan, season with salt, pepper, garlic, and parsley.
4. Arrange veal cutlets on platter, top with eggplant. Cover with tomato mixture.
5. Add stock and wine to cooking pan and de-glaze. Pour over portion and serve.

VEAL SCALLOPS CUMULUS

Ceiling Zero

Ingredients:

Yield: 10 portions

Veal Cutlets	10
Flour	as needed
Oil or Fat	as needed
Brandy	2 ounces
Bechamel Sauce, light	3 cups
Cream, heavy	1 cup

Procedure:

1. Coat cutlets with flour and pan fry until lightly browned. Pour off excess fat.
2. Add brandy to frying pan and reduce.
3. Add Bechamel sauce and cream and cook until thickened. Serve over cutlets.

CHOUCROUTE GARNI

Ceiling Zero

Ingredients: Yield: 12 portions

Pork Loin	6 pounds
Salt Pork, sliced	4 ounces
Sauerkraut	8 pounds
Smoked Sausage	3 pounds
Spare Ribs	4 pounds
Onions, large	3
Cloves, whole	as needed
Apples, chopped	3
Garlic, cloves, minced	6
Pepper	4 teaspoons
White Wine	3 cups
Beer	1½ cups
Potatoes, small, boiled	12

Procedure:

1. Line kettle with salt pork. Add apples studded with cloves.
2. Add remaining ingredients except pork loin and potatoes. Simmer about 1 hour.
3. Roast pork loin separately.
4. Serve sliced pork on sauerkraut mixture with hot potatoes.

PAELLA

Ceiling Zero

Ingredients:

Yield: 12 portions

Frying Chickens	3
Olive Oil	as needed
Onion, chopped	1 pound
Green Pepper, chopped	1 pound
Tomatoes, fresh, chopped	1 pound
Garlic, minced	1 bulb
Green Peas, frozen	2 pounds
Rice, raw	3 cups
Clams, scrubbed, in shells	1 dozen
Shrimp, raw, in shells	4 dozen
Chorizo Sausage, thinly sliced	2 pounds
Thyme	$\frac{1}{2}$ teaspoon
Salt	as needed
Pepper	as needed
Saffron	1 teaspoon
Water, boiling	3 cups

Procedure:

1. Cut up chickens and brown in olive oil.
2. Brown onions, green peppers, and tomatoes and add to chicken.
3. Add remaining ingredients, cover and simmer for 20 minutes.

FROG LEGS PROVENCALE

Ceiling Zero

Ingredients: Yield: 10 portions

Fresh Frog Legs, 20 pairs	5 pounds
Milk	as needed
Flour	as needed
Olive Oil	5 cups
Salt	as needed
Pepper	as needed
Butter	10 ounces
Lemon Juice	$\frac{2}{3}$ cup
Parsley, chopped	$\frac{1}{4}$ cup
Garlic, minced	5 teaspoons

Procedure:

1. Dip frog legs in milk; roll in flour. Fry until golden brown in hot olive oil. Place on hot serving dish.
2. Season with salt and pepper.
3. Brown butter in frying pan, add lemon juice, parsley, and garlic. Blend well and pour over frog legs.

DOVER SOLE A LA JACQUES

Ceiling Zero

Ingredients: Yield: 8 portions

Mushrooms, fresh	1 pound
Butter	2 tablespoons
Shallots or Onion, chopped	2 teaspoons
Parsley, chopped	2 teaspoons
Tomato Sauce	1 tablespoon
Salt	as needed
Pepper	as needed
Sole Fillets, whole, 6 ounces each	8
Lemon Juice	as needed
Butter	as needed
Bechamel Sauce	1 cup
Heavy Cream	$\frac{1}{4}$ cup
Butter	1 tablespoon
Lobster Meat, cooked, chopped,	$\frac{1}{2}$ cup
Parmesan Cheese, grated	as needed

Procedure:

1. Wash and trim mushrooms. Save trimmings for later use; chop remainder to yield about 2 cups. Combine chopped mushrooms with 2 tablespoons butter and shallots. Saute until slightly soft, then stir in parsley, tomato sauce, salt, and pepper. Place mixture in oven proof dish.
2. Poach sole with lemon juice, butter, and mushroom trimmings. Arrange cooked sole on top of mushrooms in oven-proof dish. Strain and reserve poaching liquid.
3. Combine Bechamel sauce, cream, and $\frac{1}{2}$ cup reserved poaching liquid. Reduce to desired consistency, then add 1 tablespoon butter and lobster meat. Pour over sole. Sprinkle with cheese. Bake in oven at 400°F. for 10 minutes.

BAY SCALLOPS IN COCONUT CREAM

Ceiling Zero

Ingredients: Yield: 6 portions

Tiny Bay Scallops	2 pounds
Salt	1 teaspoon
Lime or Lemon Juice	1 cup
Onion, chopped	$\frac{1}{2}$ cup
Scallions, including tops	$\frac{1}{2}$ cup
Green Pepper, chopped	$\frac{1}{4}$ cup
Tomatoes, medium, fresh, peeled, chopped	3
Cayenne Pepper or Liquid Hot Pepper Seasoning	dash
Whole Coconuts	2
Water, hot	as needed

Procedure:

1. Combine scallops, salt, juice, and onion. Marinate, with occasional stirring, overnight or at least 6 hours, until scallops have an opaque "cooked" appearance.
2. Drain and squeeze scallops slightly to remove excess marinade. Add scallions, green pepper, tomatoes, and pepper or liquid hot pepper seasoning.
3. To make coconut cream, crack and peel coconuts and cut into small pieces. Put 1 cup pieces with $\frac{1}{2}$ cup hot water into blender and operate at high speed until coconut is reduced to a fibrous liquid.
4. Scrape liquid into a sieve lined with a double thickness of cheese cloth. Wring liquid out thoroughly to extract liquid.
5. Repeat procedure until coconut is used up.
6. Place coconut cream in refrigerator about 1 hour.
7. To serve, place scallops on bed of lettuce and top with coconut cream.

COULIBIAC
(Salmon in Pastry)

Ceiling Zero

Ingredients:

Yield: 12 portions

Yeast, granular	2 packages, $\frac{1}{4}$ ounce each
Water, warm	$\frac{1}{2}$ cup
Milk, lukewarm	$\frac{1}{2}$ cup
Flour	$5\frac{1}{2}$ to 6 cups
Butter	10 ounces
Eggs, beaten	6
Salt	$\frac{1}{2}$ teaspoon
Salmon Fillets	4 pounds
Fish, cooked, chopped	4 pounds
Lemon Juice	2 tablespoons
Parsley, minced	$\frac{1}{4}$ cup
Dill, fresh, minced	$\frac{1}{4}$ cup
Rice, cooked	6 cups
Butter	$\frac{1}{4}$ cup
Salt	2 teaspoons
Mushrooms, sliced	$\frac{1}{2}$ pound
Eggs, hard-cooked, sliced	6
Eggs	2
*French Butter	as needed

Procedure:

1. Dissolve yeast in water, stir in milk and $2\frac{1}{2}$ cups flour. Mix until smooth and allow to rise.
2. Soften 1 cup butter and add to yeast mixture. Blend in 6 beaten eggs, 3 cups flour, and $\frac{1}{2}$ teaspoon salt. Beat well and allow to rise again. Work in additional flour, if needed.
3. Poach salmon and sprinkle with lemon juice. Mix chopped fish, parsley, dill, rice, $\frac{1}{4}$ cup butter, 2 teaspoons salt, and mushrooms.
4. Roll dough into a rectangle and spread with half the chopped mixture. Top with pieces of salmon and egg slices, then with remaining chopped mixture.
5. Roll up, folding and sealing ends. Slash dough and brush with remaining egg.
6. Bake in oven at 375°F. about 1 hour. Slice and serve with French butter.

*Note:

Melt butter and whip smooth.

FILLET OF SOLE BONNE FEMME

Ceiling Zero

Ingredients:

Yield: 25 portions

Sole, Fillets, skinless, 6 ounces each	25
Butter	1 pound
Mushrooms, sliced	$1\frac{1}{2}$ pounds
Shallots, chopped	$\frac{1}{2}$ cup
Parsley, chopped	$\frac{1}{4}$ cup
White Wine	1 cup
Fish Fumet, strained	3 quarts
Butter	$\frac{1}{2}$ pound
Flour	$\frac{1}{2}$ pound
Hollandaise Sauce	1 pint
Whipped Cream, unsweetened	1 pint

Procedure:

1. Roll fish, starting with small end. Divide 1 pound butter between two pans and melt. Place rolled fillets in pans.
2. Sprinkle with mushrooms, shallots, and parsley. Add wine and fish fumet. Bring to a boil on top of range, then place in oven at 400°F. for 10 to 12 minutes or until fish is done.
3. Pour off fumet and strain, reserving vegetables. Boil fumet until reduced to 2 quarts.
4. To make fish veloute, melt $\frac{1}{2}$ pound butter. Add flour and blend. Cook 10 minutes. Stir in fumet and cook until thickened.
5. Return reserved vegetables to veloute. Fold whipped cream into Hollandaise sauce, then stir into veloute.
6. Place fish portion on serving plate and top with sauce. Place under broiler to brown lightly.

CAPTAIN CHARLIE TUNA
(a "12 o'clock high" favorite sandwich)

Ceiling Zero

Ingredients: Yield: 6 portions

Tuna, water pack	13 ounces
Onion, chopped	$\frac{1}{3}$ cup
Celery, chopped	$\frac{1}{3}$ cup
Ripe Olives, chopped	$\frac{1}{3}$ cup
Cheddar Cheese, grated	$\frac{1}{4}$ cup
Mayonnaise	1 cup
Dijon Mustard	1 teaspoon
Swiss or Gruyere Cheese	12 slices
French Bread, long thin loaf	1

Procedure:

1. Drain tuna. Mix with onion, celery, olives, grated cheese, mayonnaise, and mustard.
2. Cut french bread into 6-inch lengths. Split each chunk lengthwise. Spread one side generously with tuna mixture and put 2 slices of cheese on other side.
3. Place open-face on flat pan. Heat in oven at 450°F. about 8 minutes or until cheese melts.

CHICAGO CLAIM COMPANY
Ingenuous and Ingenius

Chicago Claim Company
2314 N. Clark Street,
Chicago, Illinois.

Bright-eyed, bushy-tailed, and ambitious, twenty-nine-year-old Jim Errant, proprietor of the Chicago Claim Company, became a foodservice veteran the hard way, starting at the top while covering all the ladder rungs in his first restaurant venture. Although he is seemingly ingenuous, Errant is genuinely ingenius. And successful. His trendy and classy "limited menu cum brisk-but-gracious service" establishment grosses over $775,000 a year. Errant aims at a wide market (he notes that it covers the twenty-one to fifty-year-old spectrum), emphasizing "volume, quality, and low prices." A dinner check averages $6.00; a lunch check, $4.25.

Volume? Certainly. Chicago Claim's eighty seats turn up to six times during the week; maybe nine times on weekends. Whatever their ages, Claim's dinner customers seem not to mind waiting an hour or more for the main event of their evening—perhaps the house burger, "The Motherlode," a half-pound bargain at $3.45, served with a variety of cheese toppings, fried or sauteed onions, teriyaki sauce, barbecue sauce, or mushrooms. (The Chicago Claim sautees over 300 pounds of fresh mushrooms a week.)

To refer to the Chicago Claim as "chez hamburger" is a misnomer and something of an injustice. Even though it may have the city's most celebrated hamburger, the restaurant offers much more. Among other menu items are a vegetarian omelette, several soups (including red snapper), chicken teriyaki, and french-fried zucchini. The food costs run thirty-six percent and liquor twenty-four percent.

There are forty-two cheerful young people who cook and serve at Chicago Claim. But there's more cheer. The restaurant's stage setting is based on western gold mining days, but presented with restraint: rough hewn wood, pots, and pros-

53

The Chicago Claim Company was the immensely successful prototype for Errant Enterprises' later ventures. A Chicago "first."

pecting pans. In contrast to the usual portrayal of this theme, Chicago Claim has an almost Japanese feeling in its respect for natural materials.

The Claim can change moods. At lunch (60 percent repeat), it is a place to talk business; at dinner, it is a scene to make, the place to be. It provides good transition in a limited space.

Errant may not believe in advertising but he is a publicizer par excellence. When he cuts prices up to fifty percent on New Year's Eve, customers line up for four hours. Rather than buy space, Errant buys the time of a shrewd public relations firm that gets him newspaper items, column attention, and television feature coverage.

For three years the Chicago Claim was a singular experience for Errant. Then, in 1976, he opened Jasands. It is a "novel kind of theme restaurant—'Contemporary' in a landmark building." Errant's new establishment is located in the old McCormick family mansion at Rush and Superior and on Chicago's near north side. It cost approximately $300,000 for renovation and equipment, just about three times the cost of Errant's first gold mine. Scheduled to open in May 1979 is the Claim Company of Northbrook, a 180-seat "informal dinner house," and Errant's pilot restaurant for expansion in suburban shopping centers. Cost: $500,000.

The knight Errant charges ahead, and he does not tilt at windmills.

Left, Jim Errant, determined young entrepreneur stands before his monument; below, slightly dazed Chicago Claim Company patrons await the appearance of "The Motherlode."

Proprietor Errant displays his "mining-pan menu" to veteran Chicago diner–out Fred Magel.

BARLEY MUSHROOM SOUP

Chicago Claim Company

Ingredients:

Yield: 1 gallon

Water	1 gallon
Soup Bone with Marrow and 4 to 8 ounces Beef	1
Salt	$1\frac{1}{2}$ teaspoons
Seasoned Salt	$2\frac{1}{4}$ teaspoons
Pepper	$\frac{3}{4}$ teaspoon
Bay Leaf	1
Celery Rib, minced	1
Leek, small, minced	1
Turnip, small, minced	1
Onion, medium, minced	1
Cabbage, finely chopped	6 ounces
Mushrooms, fresh, thinly sliced	$1\frac{1}{2}$ pounds
*Barley	4 to 8 ounces
Garlic, minced	2 cloves
Basil, dried, leaves	1 teaspoon
Sage, dried, leaves	1 teaspoon

Procedure:

1. Combine water, soup bone, salt, seasoned salt, pepper, and bay leaf. Cover and simmer for 3 hours, skimming as necessary.
2. Remove bone, cool, and strip off meat. Dice meat and return to kettle.
3. Cook barley separately, using as needed for desired thickness, then add to kettle. Add remaining ingredients and simmer for 1 hour or longer to desired thickness.

*Note:

Uncooked barley may be added directly to kettle. In this case, additional water will be necessary.

MINESTRONE

Chicago Claim Company

Ingredients: Yield: 1 gallon

Dried Beans, white, pink, or cranberry	4 ounces
*Water	$1\frac{1}{2}$ quarts
Soup Bone with Marrow, medium	1
Salt Pork, 1-inch square	2
Onion, small, chopped	1
Carrots, diced, large	$\frac{3}{4}$ cup
Celery, diced, large	$\frac{3}{4}$ cup
Garlic, minced	1 clove
Parsley, chopped	2 tablespoons
Basil Leaves, dried	1 tablespoon
Tomatoes, canned, chopped, undrained	8 ounces
Potato, medium, raw, diced	1
Green Beans, fresh, cut in half	2 ounces
Zucchini, sliced	4 ounces
Cabbage, shredded	6 ounces
Macaroni Shells	4 ounces
Salt	$1\frac{1}{2}$ teaspoons
Parmesan Cheese, grated	as needed

Procedure:

1. Rinse beans, add water, and boil for 5 minutes. Cover and let stand for 1 hour.
2. Add soup bone and simmer for 2 hours.
3. Remove bone. Mash $\frac{1}{2}$ cup of the cooked beans and return to kettle.
4. Heat salt pork in covered fry pan until melted. Add onion and cook slowly until soft.
5. Add carrots, celery, garlic, parsley, and basil and cook 5 minutes more. Add this mixture and tomatoes to stock and simmer 30 minutes.
6. Add potatoes and green beans and cook 10 minutes.
7. Add zucchini, cabbage, salt, and macaroni and cook 10 minutes or until macaroni is done.
8. Top each serving with a sprinkling of Parmesan cheese.

*Note:

This is a thick soup. Adjust water as needed as soup cooks.

VEGETABLE BEEF SOUP

Chicago Claim Company

Ingredients:

Yield: 1 gallon

Water	1 gallon
Soup Bone, containing 4 ounces beef	1
Salt	$\frac{3}{4}$ teaspoon
Pepper	$\frac{1}{4}$ teaspoon
Garlic Powder	$\frac{1}{2}$ teaspoon
Seasoned Salt	$2\frac{1}{4}$ teaspoons
Tomatoes, canned	4 ounces
Corn, canned	2 ounces
Peas, canned	2 ounces
Oil	$1\frac{1}{2}$ teaspoons
Catsup	3 ounces
Onion, white, small, chopped	1
Celery, sliced	$\frac{1}{4}$ cup
Potato, raw, diced	1 medium
Salt	as needed

Procedure:

1. Combine water, soup bone, salt, pepper, garlic powder, and seasoning salt. Cover, bring to boil, reduce heat, and simmer $2\frac{1}{2}$ hours or until meat is tender.
2. Remove bone, cool, and strip off meat. Dice meat and return to kettle. Add tomatoes, corn, and peas.
3. Combine oil and catsup; add onion and celery. Cover and cook over low heat for 10 minutes. Add potato and cook 5 minutes more. Add this mixture to soup kettle and simmer 15 minutes.
4. Add salt to taste and serve.

SNAPPER SOUP

Chicago Claim Company

Ingredients: Yield: 4 gallons

Water	1½ gallons
Burgundy	2 quarts
Carrots, diced	8
Pepper, black, ground	1 tablespoon
Celery Tops, chopped	4
Celery, chopped	½ cup
Bay Leaves	4
Parsley, chopped	¼ bunch
Red Snapper, skinned, diced	8 pounds
Butter	12 ounces
Onion, diced	2 cups
Celery, chopped	4 cups
Green Pepper, chopped	4½ cups
Butter	4 ounces
Flour	1 cup
Beef Stock	1 gallon
Worcestershire Sauce	1 tablespoon
Butter	4 ounces
Tomato Paste	4 ounces
Lemon Juice	3 lemons
Salt	2 tablespoons
Butter	1½ pounds
Tomatoes, fresh, peeled, diced	5
Sherry, individual decanters	as needed

Procedure:

1. Combine water, Burgundy, carrots, pepper, celery tops, chopped celery, bay leaves, and parsley and simmer 10 minutes.
2. Add red snapper and simmer 10 minutes. Strain and set fish and garni aside. Add more Burgundy to stock if necessary to make 2 gallons.
3. Using 12 ounces butter, saute onion, celery, and green pepper. Add to stock and simmer 20 minutes.
4. Make a brown sauce by melting 4 ounces butter stirring in flour to make a thick roux. Slowly stir in beef stock and cook until thickened. Simmer 10 minutes.

MOTHERLODE
(the special house hamburger)

Chicago Claim Company

Ingredients:

Yield: 1 portion

Ground Beef, 16% fat	7 ounces
Cheese, slices, (American, mild cheddar, bleu or Swiss), 1 ounce each	1½ to 2
Bread (rye, black bread, or steamed hamburger egg bun)	as needed
Topping—sauteed mushrooms or onions, fried onions, teriyaki sauce, or "Claim Sauce" (see recipes)	

Procedure:

1. Place meat patty on grill, then turn 90 degrees to give it a characteristic criss-cross pattern. Cook until half done.
2. Turn over gently and repeat 90-degree turning process.
3. Cook to desired degree of doneness.
4. Add cheese, remove from grill, and place in salamander to melt cheese.
5. Place patty on bread or bun and add choice of topping. (See topping recipes following for sauteed mushrooms or onions, fried onions, teriyaki sauce, and "Claim Sauce.")

SNAPPER SOUP *(cont'd.)*

5. Combine 4 ounces butter, tomato paste, lemon juice, and salt. Cook to a smooth consistency, then mix into the brown sauce. Add all to the soup kettle.
6. Melt 1½ pounds butter, add fresh tomatoes and fish/garni mixture and saute for 10 minutes. Add to kettle and simmer 1 hour.
7. Serve with individual decanters of sherry containing ½ ounce per serving.

TOPPING RECIPES
(for use as topping for "Motherlode" Patty)

1. Sauteed Mushrooms or Onions

Ingredients: Yield: 7½ quarts

Butter, melted	¾ pound
Mushrooms or Onions, sliced	20 pounds
Soy Sauce, Japanese	2 cups
Sherry	2 ounces
Seasoned Salt	2 tablespoons

Procedure:

1. Saute half the mushrooms or onions in ¼ pound of the melted butter until slightly soft.
2. Mix together the remaining butter, soy sauce, sherry, and seasoned salt. Add half this mixture to the pot, add remaining mushrooms or onions, and pour the rest of the soy mixture over all.
3. Cook until slightly soft, stirring occasionally. Cook mushrooms 10 to 15 minutes; onions, 15 to 20 minutes.
4. Serve warm over "Motherlode" patty.

2. Fried Onions

Ingredients: Yield: 100 portions

Onion, white, thinly sliced	5 pounds
Flour	6 cups
Seasoned Salt	1 tablespoon

Procedure:

1. Rinse onions in cold water and shake well to remove excess water. Separate into rings.
2. Mix flour and seasoned salt thoroughly.
3. Add drained onions and toss until onion slices are evenly coated.
4. Fry in deep fat at 375°F. about 2 to 3 minutes or until crisp and golden.

3. *Teriyaki Sauce*

Ingredients: Yield: 3 quarts

Soy Sauce, Japanese	1 quart
Brown Sugar	2 pounds
Onion Salt	$\frac{1}{2}$ teaspoon
Garlic Powder	1 teaspoon
Worcestershire Sauce	$1\frac{1}{2}$ teaspoons
Jamaican Ginger	2 teaspoons
Sweet Vermouth	2 ounces
Hot Water	2 quarts

Procedure:

1. Mix all ingredients together except hot water. Blend well, then stir in hot water.
2. Heat and stir until all sugar is dissolved.
3. Serve warm over "Motherlode" patty.

4. *Claim Sauce*

Ingredients: Yield: $\frac{3}{4}$ cup

Catsup	6 ounces
Barbecue Sauce, Open Pit, mild	4 ounces
Dark Brown Sugar	$\frac{1}{4}$ cup
Lemon Juice	1 tablespoon

Procedure:

1. Mix ingredients well.
2. Serve as topping for "Motherlode" patty.

CHICKEN TERIYAKI

Chicago Claim Company

Ingredients: Yield: 25 portions

Chicken Breasts, boneless, skin on, 12-ounce	8
Teriyaki Sauce (see "Motherlode" Topping Recipes)	3 quarts
Pineapple Juice, canned	6 ounces
Maraschino Cherry Juice (optional)	4 ounces
Green Pepper, large pieces, blanched	25
Onion Slices, raw	25
Tomato Wedges	25
Orange Sections	25
Pineapple Slices, canned	25

Procedure:

1. Make marinade by combining teriyaki sauce, pineapple juice, and cherry juice. Reserve 1 quart for basting.
2. Put chicken breasts into remaining marinade and refrigerate for 6 to 8 hours.
3. Remove chicken breasts from marinade and cut into quarters. Fold chicken quarters and place on skewers in alternating pattern of piece of chicken, piece of green pepper, chicken, onion slice, chicken, tomato wedge, chicken, orange section.
4. Place on open broiler, turning occasionally. Heat reserved marinade and baste chicken frequently as it cooks.
5. Serve skewer on bed of rice. Garnish with pineapple slice and accompany with small souffle cup of hot marinade.

FRENCH FRIED ZUCCHINI

Chicago Claim Company

Ingredients: Yield: 24 portions ($2\frac{3}{4}$ quarts batter)

Eggs, large	1 dozen
Flour	4 cups
Beer	5 cups
Bread Crumbs, dry, fine	$1\frac{1}{2}$ pounds
Seasoned Salt	2 tablespoons
Zucchini	24 portions

BOOT HILL OMELETTE

Chicago Claim Company

Ingredients: Yield: 1 portion

Eggs	3
Butter	2 tablespoons
Tomato Slices, grilled	2
Pineapple Slice, grilled	1
Spinach, cooked or canned	$\frac{1}{4}$ cup
Zucchini, thinly sliced, quartered	$\frac{1}{4}$ cup
Seasoned Salt	$\frac{1}{2}$ teaspoon
Sour Cream	$\frac{1}{4}$ cup
Swiss Cheese Slices, 1 ounce each	2

Procedure:

1. Spread butter over hot grill, covering an area approximately 9 by 12 inches. Blend eggs well and pour slowly back and forth onto grill to cover buttered area.
2. When omelette becomes slightly firm and bubbles appear, press juice out of spinach and spread the spinach diagonally across the middle of omelette.
3. Place zucchini on spinach and sprinkle with seasoned salt. Spread with sour cream.
4. Chop 1 slice of cheese and place on sour cream. Top with tomato slices.
5. To form omelette, slide long spatula under one side and fold over middle. Fold other side. Place on plate, folded side down.
6. Cut second slice of cheese down the middle and arrange both pieces lengthwise on top of omelette. Place in salamander to melt cheese.
7. Top with pineapple slice with a dash of sour cream in its center.

FRENCH FRIED ZUCCHINI *(cont'd.)*
Procedure:

1. Beat eggs. Add flour slowly, beating constantly to make a smooth paste. Beat in beer.
2. Mix bread crumbs with seasoned salt.
3. Cut off ends of zucchini and peel. Score each with a fork. Cut in half, lengthwise, and, if large, cut in quarters. Cut into $\frac{5}{8}$-inch slices.
4. Coat zucchini evenly with flour, dip into batter, then into seasoned crumbs.
5. Fry in deep fat at 360°F. until golden, about 4 minutes.

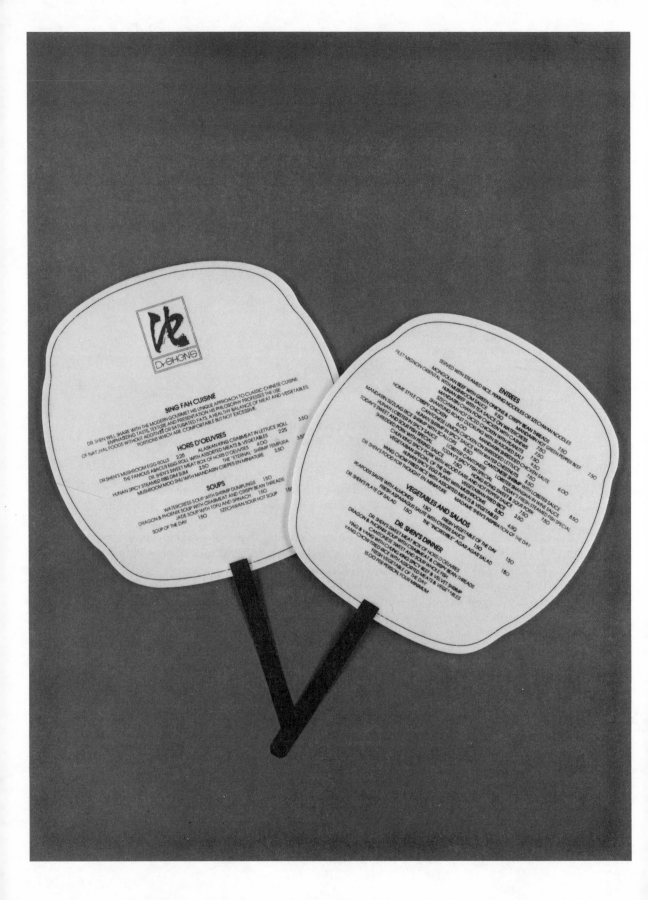

Dr SHEN'S
All This and Sing Fah Too

Dr. Shen's
1050 N. State Street,
Chicago, Illinois.

Phil Shen is a man with a mission. He may also be a prophet, or something of a gambler. Drawing on his considerable experience as successful restaurateur, cook, teacher, menu-merchandiser, and food chemist (in which field he has a Ph.D.), Shen has single-handedly taken on the challenge of organizing and modernizing Chinese cooking methods.

And he's doing it in a setting of lavish high style.

Since 1973, Shen has been the proprietor of Chicago's distinguished Abacus Restaurant. Now, in addition to that establishment, he recently opened (May 1978), "Dr. Shen's" an oppulent $1.2 million, 300-seat eating emporium in the heart of Chicago's near north side. It is here that Shen is offering his "Sing Fah" (or "new method") style of Chinese cooking.

There is nothing quite like Dr. Shen's in the US—not in Chicago, or in New York, or San Francisco, the bastions of Chinese restaurantdom. Dr. Shen's is luxurious with a vengeance, a design product of decorator Richard Himmel. The restaurant—rich, dark, spacious, and quite beautiful—encloses three sides of a well-planted atrium, which, from a second floor vantage point, it shares with Arnie's restaurant directly below. (See chapter on Arnie's.) The focus of the dining area is a white-tiled exhibition kitchen. Although this kitchen is used around the clock for barbecuing and fashioning hors d'oeuvres, it becomes a "theatre" twice an evening when Shen's chefs demonstrate the highly dramatic art of Chinese noodle making. Regular patrons refer to the demonstration as the "nightly noodle show."

If the front of Dr. Shen's Restaurant combines showmanship and visually arresting decor, the back of the house is equally lavish. There is a wide, service corridor from the main

Part of Phil Shen's inscrutable merchandising "savy" is Dr. Shen's menu printed on handsome lucite fans. Alas, they disappear into the pockets of collectors even before he can change the prices.

kitchen to the exhibition kitchen that runs the length of the restaurant, and comfortably holds two waiter stations, a large service bar, electronic cash registers, and pre-check machines. Thus, there is very little clutter in the various dining rooms. Dr. Shen's main kitchen is unusually large, air-conditioned, and bright—with artificial as well as natural, light from a bank of windows. In addition to the latest standard equipment, including a dish line system with a circulating-water scrapping trough, the kitchen has a variety of especially built pieces: a convection oven with overhead hanging racks for roasting ducks; a custom-designed bank of stainless steel drawers for a multitude of Chinese spices and herbs; and a unique rice station that combines the functions of storage, washing, cooking, and pick-up—a unit that nicely smooths out peak-time congestion.

This contemporary setting is the birthplace of Phil Shen's unique Sing Fah cuisine. If Dr. Shen's is a "gourmet restaurant that just *happens* to be Chinese," in the proprietor's words, then the Sing Fah method is a modern way of preparing food that just *happens* to be Chinese in origin. Dr.

Shen's menu is Western in form, offering fare that is Eastern in content. The emphasis is on natural foods, no saturated fats, no additives—not even monosodium glutamate, that flavor-enhancing but tongue-twisting chemical standby of traditional Chinese cooking. Another classic standby: dried ingredients—from black mushrooms to sea cucumber—are used in the Sing Fah method, but in balance with fresh fish and vegetables. Fewer meat dishes and high cholesterol items are offered. Drawing on his background as a food chemist, Shen is juggling carbohydrates, protein, and cellulose on a menu that is irrevocably "health oriented." Examples of the orientation: vegetarian fare is offered in all menu categories from starters and soups through entrees and salads; all salads are made fresh at tableside; desserts feature soft-serve yogurt and fresh fruit—mangos and papayas when available.

Other innovations on the menu (which includes items from all regions of China—Canton, Hunan, Szechwan, and Peking): no dish, from hors d'oeuvre to entrees, is served in the familiar Chinese "family style." All portions including Dr. Shen's soups—from Jade Soup with Tofu and Spinach to Dragon and Phoenix Soup with (crabmeat and crispy bean threads)—are prepared for one person. And all portions are smaller than the public expects from traditional Chinese restaurants. Smaller servings at a higher tab? Yes, because Shen's prices must cover the higher food cost of all those "fresh, natural" foods. (Single-serving entrees, including a choice of vegetable or salad, and rice or "pasta," range from $7.50 for Szechwan Hot Diced Chicken with Peanuts, to $13.50 for Peking Duck with Mandarin "crepes.") The higher-than-usual menu prices must also cover the restaurant's three-ring circuses: the labor-intensive kitchen staff, the dining room servers who offer individual attention, and the initial cost and maintenance of a very expensive decor.

Left, a view of Dr. Shen's dining room, often referred to as a "gorgeous hunk of Oriental onge-potchket."

Shen believes that the public wants to eat less food, but *better quality* food. He holds that people are appalled "by our waste of food and natural resources," that they realize "we eat too much food." Shen maintains that *his* customer will want to "eat healthy Chinese foods, without chemical additives," and will welcome "the freedom and individualism" of single portions and personal service.

Prophet or gambler, Phil Shen is a crusader and he wants to educate the public. Fortunately he believes that his crusade can be accomplished entertainingly, with the education given painlessly. Dr. Shen's menu, printed on lucite "fans" may be intended for the "health-conscious modern gourmet" but it is not without merchandising pizzazz. There is careful thought to the sensuality of traditional Chinese food—a juggle of taste, texture, color, presentation—innovation: the use of fresh mushrooms, cucumbers often replacing water chestnuts, king crab wrapped in romaine lettuce, Hunan five-spiced beef presented as a "sandwich" with a steam roll (*dim sum*), steamed ribs in chili bean sauce, Cantonese lemon chicken on shredded lettuce, and filet mignon "Oriental."

How has Chicago—and the world—reacted to Phil Shen's "new method"? Cautiously at first. But as the early months passed, the reception became increasingly enthusiastic, and business mounted around the clock. (Dr. Shen's is open lunch, through *dim sum*-tea-and-cocktail time, to dinner, and after-theatre supper.) The public now seems to be enjoying its "education" at the unique Dr. Shen's. And the honorable prophet, Phil Shen, is being repaid for the risk he took, by turning a tidy and honorable profit indeed.

STEAMED FISH WITH BLACK BEAN SAUCE

Dr. Shen's

Ingredients: Yield: 4 servings

Walleye Pike, fresh	1 whole
Black Beans, salted, minced	4 ounces
Fresh Ginger Root, shredded	2 tablespoons
Garlic Clove, finely chopped	1
Salt	$\frac{1}{2}$ teaspoon
Soy Sauce ($\frac{1}{2}$ light, $\frac{1}{2}$ dark)	$\frac{1}{2}$ cup
Sesame Oil	1 tablespoon
Chinese Rice Wine (or Pale Dry Sherry)	3 tablespoons
Sugar	$\frac{1}{2}$ teaspoon
Pepper	pinch
Green Onions, shredded	2
Vegetable Oil	$\frac{1}{2}$ cup

Procedure:

1. Slash both sides of the fish four times, about $\frac{3}{4}$ inch deep, slashing across the body at slight slant.
2. Mix black beans, ginger root, garlic, salt, soy sauce, sesame oil, rice wine (or sherry), and sugar, and brush mixture over the entire fish, inside and out.
3. Steam for fifteen minutes, then sprinkle with pepper and green onions.
4. Heat vegetable oil to about 350°F., then splash over fish. Ready to serve.

SWEET AND SOUR PORK

Dr. Shen's

Ingredients: Yield: 4 servings

Boneless Pork, lean	6 ounces
Rice Wine (or Pale Dry Sherry)	3 tablespoons
Light Soy Sauce	1 teaspoon
Egg	1
Salt	1 teaspoon
Cornstarch	$\frac{1}{4}$ cup
Flour	$\frac{1}{4}$ cup
Chicken Stock	$\frac{1}{4}$ cup
Oil	$\frac{1}{2}$ teaspoon
Green Pepper	1
Tomato, large	1
Oil for Frying	3 cups
Oil	1 tablespoon
Garlic, minced	$\frac{1}{2}$ teaspoon
Chicken Stock	$\frac{1}{2}$ cup
Sugar	$\frac{1}{4}$ cup
Vinegar	$\frac{1}{4}$ cup
Tomato Catsup	2 tablespoons
Light Soy Sauce	1 tablespoon
Cornstarch Paste	
(2 parts cornstarch to 1 part water)	1 tablespoon

Procedure:

1. Cut pork into 1-inch cubes. Marinate in rice wine (or sherry) and light soy sauce about 20 minutes.
2. Mix egg, salt, cornstarch, flour, chicken stock, and oil in a bowl to make a smooth batter.
3. Cut green pepper and tomato into bite-size wedges.
4. Preheat oven to 200°F.
5. Heat frying oil in a wok or deep fryer to a temperature of 375°F. Coat each cube of pork with batter and drop one by one into hot oil, frying until they are crisp and golden brown. Drain, and transfer to warm oven.
6. Preheat a wok or frying pan. Add oil and garlic and heat until the oil is hot, but not smoking. Add green pepper and tomato, stirring for 30 seconds.
7. Pour in chicken stock, sugar, vinegar, catsup, and soy sauce and bring to a boil, stirring to dissolve the sugar.
8. Add cornstarch paste, stirring constantly to form a smooth clear glaze, then toss in the reserved pork, coating it well and serve.

MONGOLIAN BEEF

Dr. Shen's

Ingredients: Yield: 4 to 6 servings

Flank Steak	1 pound
Baking Soda	$\frac{1}{2}$ teaspoon
Sugar	1 teaspoon
Light Soy Sauce	1 tablespoon
Cornstarch	1 tablespoon
Water	1 tablespoon
Oil	2 tablespoons
Sesame Oil	$\frac{1}{2}$ teaspoon
Green Onions	1 bunch
Ginger	3 slices
Oil	1 tablespoon
Oyster Sauce	2 tablespoons
Sugar	1 teaspoon
Rice Wine (or Pale Dry Sherry)	1 tablespoon
Dark Soy Sauce	1 tablespoon
White Pepper, ground	1 dash
Salt	1 teaspoon
Oil	$\frac{1}{4}$ cup

Procedure:

1. Slice the flank steak with the grain into $1\frac{1}{2}$-inch wide slices. Cut slices into $\frac{1}{4}$-inch pieces across the grain.
2. Marinate with baking soda, sugar, light soy sauce, cornstarch, water, oil, and sesame oil for at least 15 minutes (preferably an hour).
3. Cut green onions into $1\frac{1}{2}$-inch lengths.
4. Cut the ginger slices into shreds.
5. Heat the wok to almost red hot.
6. Pour in oil and heat it until it is about 350° (just before it starts to smoke).
7. Toss in the shredded ginger and stir it for about half a minute.
8. Add the beef and stir quickly for about half a minute.
9. Add the green onions and stir for another half a minute.
10. Stir in the seasonings: oyster sauce, sugar, rice wine, dark soy sauce, ground white pepper, salt and oil for 10 seconds and serve immediately.

LEMON CHICKEN

Dr. Shen's

Ingredients: Yield: 4 servings

Chicken Breasts, boned, skinned	2 whole
Light Soy Sauce	2 tablespoons
Sesame Oil	$\frac{1}{4}$ teaspoon
Salt	1 teaspoon
Pale Dry Sherry	1 tablespoon
Flour, sifted	$1\frac{1}{2}$ cup
Water, ice cold	$1\frac{1}{2}$ cup
Baking Powder	1 tablespoon
Vegetable Oil, for frying	
Cornstarch Paste	
(2 parts cornstarch to 1 part water)	2 tablespoons
Sugar	$\frac{3}{4}$ cup
Vinegar, white	$\frac{1}{2}$ cup
Chicken Broth	1 cup
Lemon Juice	`1 lemon
Head Lettuce, finely shredded	$\frac{1}{4}$ head
Crushed Pineapple, drained	$\frac{1}{2}$ cup
Raw Carrot, minced	2 tablespoons
Green Pepper, minced	1 tablespoon
Lemon Rind, minced	2 tablespoons
Green Onion, minced	1 tablespoon

Procedure:

1. Place chicken breasts, light soy sauce, sesame oil, salt, and pale dry sherry in a shallow bowl. Toss to coat well, let marinate 30 minutes.
2. Drain chicken and discard marinade. Pat chicken with paper towel to absorb excess moisture.
3. Combine flour, water, and baking powder in a bowl and mix just until lumps disappear.
4. Heat oil in a wok or deep fryer to 375°F. Dip chicken breast into prepared batter and slide into hot oil. Fry 1 piece, repeat process. Keep warm in 350°F. oven.
5. Combine cornstarch paste, sugar, vinegar, broth, and lemon juice in a saucepan over moderate heat, stirring until mixture thickens. Keep warm.
6. Cut chicken in 1-inch crosswise slices, and arrange on top of lettuce shredded on platter.
7. Mix pineapple, carrot, green pepper, lemon rind, and green onion and sprinkle over chicken. Pour lemon sauce over chicken.

SZECHWAN HOT DICED CHICKEN

Dr. Shen's

Ingredients:

Yield: 4 servings

Chicken Breast	1 pound
Soy Sauce	1 tablespoon
Cornstarch	1½ tablespoons
Peanut Oil	4 tablespoons
Red Pepper, dry	8 pieces
Ginger, chopped	1 teaspoon
Light Soy Sauce	2 tablespoons
Wine	1 tablespoon
Brown Vinegar	½ tablespoon
Sugar	1 tablespoon
Cornstarch	1 teaspoon
Salt	½ teaspoon
Sesame Oil	1 teaspoon
Peanuts, without skins	½ cup

Procedure:

1. Cut chicken into 1-inch cubes.
2. Add soy sauce and cornstarch to chicken cubes, stir, and soak for a half hour.
3. Heat 4 tablespoons oil to fry dry red pepper until it turns black.
4. Add ginger and chicken cubes; stir quickly.
5. Next combine light soy sauce, wine, brown vinegar, sugar, cornstarch, salt, and sesame oil and add to chicken mixture, stirring until thickened and heated thoroughly.
6. Turn off fire.
7. Add the peanuts; mix well just before serving.

MANDARIN HOT GREEN PEPPER BEEF

Dr. Shen's

Ingredients: Yield: 4 servings

Flank Steak	4 ounces
Baking Soda	$\frac{1}{4}$ teaspoon
Sugar	$\frac{1}{4}$ teaspoon
Soy Sauce, dark	1 teaspoon
Cornstarch	$\frac{1}{2}$ teaspoon
Water	1 teaspoon
Oil	1 tablespoon
Sesame Oil	$\frac{1}{4}$ teaspoon
Cornstarch Paste	
(2 parts cornstarch to 1 part water)	2 tablespoons
Green Pepper	1
Bamboo Shoots, shredded	1 cup
Oil	$\frac{1}{4}$ cup
Chicken	$\frac{1}{4}$ cup
Wine	1 tablespoon
Vinegar	1 tablespoon
Sugar	1 teaspoon
Hot Bean Paste with Garlic	1 teaspoon
Soy Sauce, light	1 tablespoon

Procedure:

1. Slice the flank steak with the grain into $1\frac{1}{2}$-inch wide strips, then cut into $\frac{1}{4}$-inch pieces across the grain. Cut the small pieces again into halves lengthwise to produce shreds of beef. Combine baking soda, sugar, dark soy sauce, cornstarch, water, oil, and sesame oil and marinate beef in mixture.
2. Cut the green pepper into narrow strips.
3. Combine 2 parts cornstarch and 1 part water to make 2 tablespoons cornstarch paste. Place ingredients in jar and shake well.
4. Heat the wok until almost red hot.
5. Pour in oil and heat until it is about 350°F. (just before it starts to smoke.)
6. Add the beef and stir quickly for about half a minute.
7. Stir in green pepper, bamboo shoots, oil, chicken, wine, vinegar, sugar, hot bean paste with garlic, and light soy sauce.
8. Thicken with cornstarch paste and serve.

HUNAN SPICY EGGPLANT

Dr. Shen's

Ingredients: Yield: 4 servings

Eggplant	2
Oil	4 cups
Pork, shredded	4 ounces
Ginger, chopped	$\frac{1}{2}$ teaspoon
Garlic, chopped	$\frac{1}{2}$ teaspoon
Hot Bean Paste	1 tablespoon
Light Soy Sauce	1 tablespoon
Dark Soy Sauce	1 tablespoon
Vinegar	$\frac{1}{2}$ tablespoon
Sugar	1 teaspoon
Salt	$\frac{1}{2}$ teaspoon
Sesame Seeds	$\frac{1}{2}$ teaspoon
Soup Stock	$\frac{1}{2}$ cup
Cornstarch Paste	
(equal parts of cornstarch and water)	1 tablespoon

Procedure:

1. Choose firm eggplants; remove stalk and peel.
2. Cut into square strips, lengthwise.
3. Heat oil in wok until very hot.
4. Place eggplant in wok. Turn heat to low, fry for about 2 minutes. Remove from wok, drain, and set aside.
5. Remove oil from wok. Heat wok and add 4 tablespoons of the oil used previously. Heat oil to 350°F. or until just before smoking.
6. Place shredded pork in wok along with ginger, garlic, hot bean paste, light and dark soy sauce, vinegar, sugar, salt, and sesame. Stir 15 seconds.
7. Add soup stock and stir another 15 seconds.
8. Add eggplant and cook about $\frac{1}{2}$ minute.
9. Stir in cornstarch paste and serve.

SUGAR SPUN APPLES

Dr. Shen's

Ingredients: Yield: 16 sugar spun apples

Egg	1
Cold Water	½ cup plus 2 tablespoons
All-Purpose Flour	1 cup
Apples, firm, medium	2
Vegetable Oil	3 cups
	1 tablespoon
Sugar	1 cup
Cold Water	¼ cup
Sesame Seeds	1 teaspoon

Procedure:

1. Beat egg and cold water together and add to flour, stirring constantly with a large spoon. Stir until you have a fairly smooth batter.
2. With a small, sharp knife, cut the apples into quarters. Peel off the skin and cut away the cores. Then cut the quarters into eighths.
3. Arrange your ingredients—the batter, apples, vegetable oil, sugar, cold water, and sesame seeds—within easy reach and set out a large serving plate lightly greased with oil and a large bowl containing 1 quart water plus 1 dozen ice cubes.
4. In 2- to 3-quart sauce pan, heat 3 cups of oil until a haze forms above it or it reaches 375°F. At the same time, in a 12-inch wok or 10-inch skillet, heat 1 teaspoon oil with sugar and cold water. Bring sugar and water to a boil over high heat, stirring only until sugar dissolves. Cook mixture briskly without stirring until syrup registers 300°F. on thermometer.
5. Stir in sesame seeds; turn heat down to lowest point.
6. Drop 8 of the wedges into the batter, stirring them about to coat them thoroughly. With slotted spoon, transfer wedges to heated oil and deep-fry them for one minute, or until they turn light amber. Immediately lift them out of oil and put them into the skillet of hot syrup. Stir wedges to coat them thoroughly with syrup, then using slotted spoon, drop them one at a time into the bowl of cold water. The syrup coating will harden instantly and enclose each piece of apple in a clear, brilliant glaze. Transfer the finished spun apples to the lightly greased serving plate and repeat with next 8 wedges. Serve as soon as possible. The delicate candy glaze will soften if they are allowed to stand for long.

Griglia
BROILER

Entrecote Ai Ferri 10.50
New York Cut Sirloin.

Costolette Vitello 8.25
Veal Chops.

Costolette D'Agnello
Ai Ferri 8.50
French Cut Lamb Chops.

Fegato Ai Ferri 7.50
Calf's Liver.

Filet Mignon
Maitre D'Hotel 10.50

Chateaubriand, For 2
Salsa Bearnaise 23.00

Pollo Alla Griglia 5.75
Broiled Chicken.

Vitello
VEAL

Piccata Lombarda 7.50
Scaloppine Sauted With White Wine, Lemon And Butter.

Scaloppini Alla
Sorrentina 8.
Scaloppine Sauted With Eggplant, Prosciutto And Cheese.

Scaloppine Saute
Florio 8.00
Scaloppine Sauted With Mushrooms And Marsala.

Costoletta
Parr

Bracioline Di
Vitello 8.00
Veal Birds Stuffed With Cheese And Prosciutto.

Saltimbocca Alla
Romana
Scaloppine Sauted With Prosciutto, Sage And White Wine.

Fegato Alla Veneta
Calf's Liver Sauted With Onions And White Wine.

Costoletta Di Vitello
Alla Milanese
Breaded Veal Chop Sauted.

Pollo
FOWL

Suprema Di Pollo
Gismonda 7.50
Breast Of Chicken With Spinach And Mushrooms.

Suprema Di Pollo
Castello 8.
Chicken Breast. Fettuccine. Cream Sauce.

Suprema Di Pollo
Rossini 8.25
Breast Of Chicken With Pate.

Giambonetto Alla
Doros 7.
Boneless Stuffed Chicken On Rice Pilaf.

Suprema Di Pollo
Bolognese 8.00
Breast Of Chicken With Prosciutto And Cheese.

Spezzatino Di Pollo
Piemontese 7.
Chicken Tidbits Sauted With White Wine And Peppers.

Fegatini Di Pollo
Pilaf 7.00
Chicken Livers Sauted With White Wine, Sage, Rice.

Spezzatino Alla
Cacciatora 7.
Chicken Tidbits With Mushrooms And Tomatoes.

Suprema Di Pollo 7.75
Marechale
Breast Of Chicken With Asparagus.

Manzo
BEEF

| | 11.50 |
| | 11.50 |

Entrecote Nicoise 11.
New York Sirloin Sauted With Anchovies And Olives.

Entrecote All'
Italiana 11.
New York Sirloin Sauted With Peppers, Mushrooms And Onions.

Steak Au Poivre Flambe 11.

Rue En Flambe 11.25

DORO'S
RESTAURANT
871 N. Rush St., Chicago, Illinois 60611
Ph. (312) 266-1414

DORO'S
RESTAURANT

DORO'S
RESTAURANT

DORO'S

All That Glitters Is More Than Gold

Doro's
871 North Rush Street,
Chicago, Illinois.

Doro's arrived on the Chicago scene in May 1974,—unknown, unproven, and offering an unfamiliar, high-priced Northern Italian cuisine. In four years however, the restaurant has overcome its obscurity to become a permanent fixture in the city's culinary establishment. At present, seventy percent of Doro's business is repeat.

Located on Rush Street, Chicago's traditional Glitter Gulch, Doro's is close by the smart shops, hotels, and offices of the city's Magnificent Mile area. Thus it is convenient to a variety of customers, all of them necessary to support an expensive restaurant at lunch and dinner. Doro's *is* expensive. Dinner checks average $22 to $24 per person; and the twenty-five to thirty cases of wine, mostly fine Italian, sold by the restaurant each week add considerably more to that figure.

Doro's is a Chicago original. It bears little resemblance to, and has no association with, another distinguished restaurant, Doro's of San Francisco. The name itself is an adaptation of *d'oro*, an Italian construction meaning "of gold." And there certainly is a lot of *oro* at Doro's, from the gold and ivory wallpaper, to the glistening gilt upholstery on banquettes and chairs, all amplified by numerous crystal chandeliers and sconces. But surprisingly perhaps, this glitter isn't gauche.

The restaurant, which seats 130, is large in area and generous in space between tables, offering the kind of elbow-room privacy that its customers expect. The layout also provides an excellent service run for all tables from the kitchen, where Doro's real treasure is found.

There was no Chicago restaurant specializing in Northern Italian cookery before Doro's consortium of owners put their

Beyond its nouveau glitter, Doro's offers an impeccable menu
of Northern Italian cookery.

shrewdness and imaginations together. The major partners, Frank Scoby, Herbert Schelly, and Harry Menick, are long-time friends and former associates in a liquor and beer distributing company, Better Brands of Illinois. Although inexperienced in the foodservice business, the partners brought considerable management expertise to their new venture. As distributors, they were able to observe the workings of a variety of restaurants in Chicago and New York. It was their intelligent gamble that a first-class, Northern Italian restaurant could be marketed in Chicago. Until the advent of Doro's, Italian *cucina* Chicago-style offered the familiar dishes of Southern Italy and Sicily—all of them hearty, most of them redolent with garlic, awash with olive oil, and generously embraced by the tomato. Doro's Italy (north from Rome to Piedmont and centering in Tuscany) features a different kind of cooking: lighter and more dependent on cream, butter, and other dairy products. Geographically, this is the area where most of Italy's beef and veal come from, where rice and lighter pastas are favored; historically, this is the region of Catherine de Medici, an important figure in culinary annals. When the fourteen-year-old Catherine married Henry II of France in 1533, she took her Florentine cooks, recipes, and kitchen secrets to her husband's "less than civilized" court. Thus, the beginning of French *haute cuisine*, based on Northern Italian cookery.

True to tradition, Doro's food is delicately prepared, much of it in individual portions, cooked on order. Table-side service, used to prepare many main courses, as well as most desserts, is a familiar sight at Doro's. A particular favorite in the latter category is Doro's Zabaglione, served over a small portion of ice cream and fresh stawberries. Popular entrees include Fegato Saltato al Burro (calf liver sauteed with white wine, butter, and lemon), Servella Burro Nero (calf brains with black butter and capers), sweetbreads, and of course, superb veal in a dozen different guises.

Although Doro's forty-six employees work in a happy house, the one who should be the happiest is the restaurant's leading man, Chef Armando Massimini. It was to Massimini that Doro's owners turned when searching for someone to implement their concept. The chef's credentials are impressive. He comes from a family of three generations of Northern Italian chefs. He was head of the kitchen at the Excelsior Hotel in Rome at the age of twenty-seven. Then from 1962 until 1974 he was chef at New York's renowned Giambelli's Restaurant. Massimini had a great deal to say about the design of Doro's kitchen facilities. The meticulous kitchen is beautifully equipped for ease of movement and efficient food preparation. Extensive range area was provided. Because most is sauteed, there is only one broiler. Separate refrigerated drawers under the counters were designed to hold meat and other perishable items at proper individual temperatures until the moment of preparation. An entire wall of the kitchen holds a bank of separate coolers and refrigerators for vegetables, meat, veal, and fish. Massimini also requested, and received, a $4,000 pasta-making machine which prepares a variety of pasta types, with the potential to turn out 10,000 ravioli an hour (pictured below).

Lavish attention to detail in both back and front of the house, a type of cuisine inimitably special, and a flair for personal service have made Doro's an "event" establishment. There are only two sittings at lunch and dinner because patrons frequently take more than two hours to enjoy their experience. Doro's success—its high repeat business and its growing patronage—has depended largely on word-of-mouth, although the restaurant maintains a schedule of dignified advertisements in local magazines and concert or opera programs.

This specialty restaurant's quiet move into a position of pre-eminence proves that Chicago has room for novel, expansive (and expensive) foodservice operations—when they deliver what they promise. For all the allure of its surface glitter, Doro's offers even more substance. And solid 14K value.

For all its *chatchke–svelte*, Doro's is a casual place. "Let them eat pasta," Marie Antoinette might well have said, after a visit to this esteemed eatery on Chicago's Glitter Gulch.

ZUPPA DI PESCE
(Fish Soup)

Doro's

Ingredients: Yield: 6 portions

Fish, ready to cook, diced (sole, turbot, anchovies, squid, cockle, etc.)	2 pounds
Onion, chopped	1 medium
Salt	as needed
Pepper	as needed
Bouquet Garni (celery, parsley, bay leaf)	1 small
Dry White Wine	2 tablespoons
Garlic, minced	1 clove
Parsley	2 tablespoons
Olive Oil	2 ounces
Water	to cover
Croutons	as needed

Procedure:

1. Cut squid into finger length pieces and put into pot with onion, salt, pepper, and bouquet garni.
2. Cook until squid is almost done, then pour in wine.
3. Reduce wine and add anchovies. Add less-tender fish and cook 5 minutes, then add the more-tender fish.
4. Combine garlic, parsley, and olive oil and saute. Remove garlic and pour oil with parsley over fish and add water.
5. Cook 10 minutes. Remove bouquet garni, garnish with croutons, and serve.

COSTOLETTA VALTOSTANA
(Stuffed Veal Chop)

Doro's

Ingredients: Yield: 2 portions

Veal Rib Chops, frenched and butterflied	2
Cheese, Muenster or Mozzarella, thin slices	2
Prosciutto, thin slices	2
Parmesan Cheese, grated	2 tablespoons
Flour	as needed
Eggs, well beaten	1 or 2
Oil	2 tablespoons
Butter	2 tablespoons
White Wine	1 or 2 ounces
Parsley, minced	1 teaspoon
Butter	3 tablespoons
Chicken Stock	2 ounces
Brown Gravy or Beef Stock	2 ounces
Salt	$\frac{1}{8}$ teaspoon

Procedure:

1. Slice veal chops to bone, open out, cover with waxed paper, and pound flat. Remove paper.
2. Place a slice of cheese, a slice of prosciutto, and a sprinkle of Parmesan on one half of chop. Fold over the other half and pat down.
3. Dust chops well with flour and dip into beaten egg.
4. Combine oil and 2 tablespoons butter in pan over medium heat. Add chops and cook until brown, about 2 minutes. Turn and cook 1 minute more.
5. Place in oven at 400°F. for 20 minutes.
6. Pour off liquid and place pan over medium heat.
7. Add white wine, parsley, 3 tablespoons butter, brown gravy, chicken stock, and salt. Simmer 2 minutes.

VEAL SORRENTINA

Doro's

Ingredients: Yield: 2 portions

Eggplant, thin slices	6
Butter	6 ounces
Veal, thin slices	6
Flour	as needed
Shallots, chopped	1 teaspoon
White Wine	2 ounces
Brown Stock	2 ounces
Prosciutto, thin slices	6
Cheese, Muenster, thin slices	6
Parmesan Cheese, grated	as needed
Parsley, chopped	as needed

Procedure:

1. Saute eggplant in 2 ounces butter until tender. Set aside.
2. Dust veal lightly with flour and saute in 2 ounces butter about 2 minutes, turning once.
3. Add shallots and cook until golden.
4. Add wine and brown stock. When hot, add 2 ounces butter to thicken. Cook 1 or 2 minutes.
5. Remove pan from heat. Top each veal slice with a slice of eggplant, 1 slice prosciutto, then a slice of mild cheese.
6. Sprinkle Parmesan over all. Bake in oven at 400°F. for 2 minutes until cheese is melted.
7. Sprinkle with parsley and serve.

FEGATO ALLA VENEZIANA
(Calf Liver Venetian-Style)

Doro's

Ingredients:

Yield: 4 portions

Calf Liver	2 pounds
Onion, thinly sliced	1½ pounds
Olive Oil	3 tablespoons
Butter	¼ cup
Salt	as needed
Pepper	as needed
Sage, powdered	a pinch
Parsley Sprigs, chopped	2 or 3
Polenta	as needed

Procedure:

1. Cut liver into very thin slivers, about the thickness of thinly sliced bacon.
2. Saute onion in oil and butter until soft.
3. Add liver and cook about 2 minutes, turning to brown all sides.
4. Season with salt, pepper, and sage.
5. Sprinkle with parsley and serve with hot polenta cut into thick slices.

PETTO DI POLLO ALLA GISMONDA

Doro's

Ingredients: Yield: 1 portion

Chicken Breast, deboned	1 large
Egg, beaten	1
Flour	as needed
Butter	3 tablespoons
White Stock	2 ounces
Brown Stock	1 ounce
Mushrooms, fresh, sliced	$\frac{1}{4}$ cup
Spinach, cooked	$\frac{1}{2}$ cup

Procedure:

1. Dip chicken in egg, then in flour. Cook slowly in 2 tablespoons butter until tender, about 45 minutes.
2. Pour off pan juices, add 1 tablespoon butter, white stock, brown stock, and mushrooms.
3. Simmer 3 or 4 minutes.
4. Place cooked spinach on platter, top with chicken breast and pour sauce over it.
5. Garnish with parsley.

RISOTTO CON SCAMPI E BISI
(Rice with Scampi and Peas)

Doro's

Ingredients: Yield: 2 or 3 portions

Shrimp, diced	$\frac{1}{2}$ to 1 pound
Garlic, minced	1 teaspoon
Oil	2 tablespoons
White Wine	2 ounces
White Stock	4 to 6 ounces
Rice, cooked in broth	4 to 6 cups
Parmesan Cheese, grated	6 to 8 table spoons
Peas	1 cup

SPAGHETTI ALLA CARBONARA

Doro's

Ingredients:　　　　　　　　　　　　　　　Yield: 2 portions

Italian Bacon, diced	2 ounces
Prosciutto, diced	2 ounces
Oil	1 tablespoon
Onion, chopped	$\frac{1}{4}$ cup
Shallots, minced	1 teaspoon
White Wine	1 ounce
White Stock	3 to 4 ounces
Pasta, cooked *al dente*	2 servings
Egg Yolk	1
Half and Half	6 ounces
Parmesan Cheese, grated	as needed
Parsley, chopped	as needed

Procedure:

1. Cook bacon and prosciutto in oil; add onions and shallots, and cook until brown.
2. Pour off grease. Add wine, stock, and cooked pasta.
3. Mix well and remove from heat.
4. Add egg yolk and half and half. Cook 1 minute.
5. Sprinkle with cheese, garnish with parsley, and serve.

RISOTTO CON SCAMPI E BISI *(cont'd.)*

Procedure:

1. Saute shrimp and garlic in oil until shrimp are done.
2. Add wine, 3 ounces stock, rice, and grated cheese. Toss together gently.
3. Add peas and toss gently until hot. Add more stock if necessary.

CARCIOFINI DORATI
(Baby Artichoke Hearts)

Doro's

Ingredients:

Yield: 2 portions

Baby Artichoke Hearts	8
Eggs, beaten	2
Flour	as needed
Butter, clarified	3 tablespoons
Salt	as needed
Parsley, minced	as needed

Procedure:

1. Cut artichoke hearts in half from top to bottom. Dip in egg, then dredge well in flour.
2. Saute quickly on all sides in hot butter, about 1 or 2 minutes.
3. Drain well and serve sprinkled with parsley.

ASPARAGI ALLA PARMIGIANA

Doro's

Ingredients:

Yield: 6 portions

Asparagus	2 pounds
Water, boiling, salted	as needed
Butter	$\frac{1}{4}$ pound
Parmesan Cheese, grated	$\frac{1}{2}$ cup

Procedure:

1. Cook asparagus three-fourths done in boiling water.
2. Cut off tough part of stems.
3. Place in one layer in baking dish with heads pointed towards center.
4. Dot with butter and sprinkle with Parmesan.
5. Place under broiler until butter melts.

FETTUCCINE ALFREDO

Doro's

Ingredients: Yield: 2 portions

Butter	2 ounces
Noodles, cooked	2 servings
Chicken Stock	1 ounce
Cream	6 ounces
Parmesan Cheese, grated	2 ounces
Pepper, black, ground	as needed

Procedure:

1. Melt butter, add noodles, stock, and cream. As mixture approaches boiling point, add cheese.
2. Cook over medium heat until mixture starts to thicken.
3. When desired thickness is reached, remove from heat. (Sauce will thicken more as mixture is served and starts to cool.)
4. Sprinkle with pepper to taste and serve.

ZABAGLIONE

Doro's

Ingredients: Yield: 2 portions

Egg Yolks	3
Sugar, granulated	2 tablespoons
Marsala Wine	$\frac{1}{4}$ cup
Vanilla Ice Cream	2 scoops
Fruit, fresh, preferably strawberries	as needed

Procedure:

1. Combine eggs, sugar, and wine in top of double boiler.
2. Beat vigorously with whip until very thick.
3. Spoon fruit over ice cream and top with warm sauce.

The Drake

A Special Recipe for Success

The Drake Hotel
Lake Shore Drive and
Upper Michigan Avenue,
Chicago, Illinois.

Americana Room
Avenue One
Cape Cod Room
Club International
Coq d'Or
Raleigh Rooms
Drake Hotel Room Service

Prestigious from the day it opened in 1921, The Drake has always been regarded as a luxury hotel. So it is, fifty-eight years later, with two footnotes: The Drake has now earned its title as Chicago's _most_ prestigious hotel; and "luxury" it remains, even though the word has a different meaning from what it had in the 1920s when the carriage trade unloaded their steamer trunks for a three- or four-month stay. Since those halcyon days, The Drake's luxury status has been redefined by the changing market, and by the lessons learned over five-and-a-half decades of depression, war, and post-war dislocation.

How is The Drake able to stand against its latest competition—almost 2000 _new_ hotel rooms within the immediate area of the Magnificent Mile? The Drake's president, Edwin L. Brashears, Jr., whose family has managed the hotel since 1930, answers that "The Drake can profitably maintain its high quality and compete with a broad range of hotels and rate structures because it doesn't have the tremendous mort-gage-interest burden of the newer properties."

The Drake has invested over $26 million since 1945 to maintain the quality of its property and services, but the hotel's first mortgage is completely paid, so that it can continue its program of upgrading while advancing the rate structure very moderately in today's competitive market. Some of The Drake's competition is asking $50 to $60 for an average room, but The Drake's current price is $45, and the hotel is enjoying over seventy percent occupancy in its 660 rooms.

95

The Drake's foodservice operation includes six restaurant areas ranging from coffeeshop to cocktail lounge to formal dining room.

An "incomparable" hotel, however, is more than mortgages and finance. At The Drake, it is people: the family who runs it as management, and the family who runs it as employees; and 450 of The Drake's nearly 1000 employees have been there an average of 14 years.

The incomparable hotel has elevator operators as a matter of hospitality, but also security; windows that can be opened despite fully modern air conditioning; new plumbing fixtures as well as new pipes in the walls to make them function; coat room attendants who wouldn't think of charging for the "privilege" of checking guests' coats.

An incomparable hotel is also one that offers excellent food and makes professional foodservice a large part of its business. At The Drake, the sale of food and liquor accounts for sixty percent of the hotel's revenue.

The Drake's foodservice department includes six restaurant areas plus room service. The best known restaurant is the much-admired and much-awarded Cape Cod Room, which began its existence during the 1933 Chicago World's Fair. It is the home of excellent fish, with Dover Sole Sautee Meuniere, Bouillabaisse, and Pompano en Papillote being

particular favorites; it is also the home of sometimes imperious service, as restaurant essayists will remind us. The Cape Cod Room, like most of The Drake, has not changed much in the forty-five years of its existence. There is a new (but not too shiny) clam and oyster bar at the Cape Cod entrance, but aside from that, the checkered tablecloths and captain's chairs, a few fish nets, copper pots, chowder kettles, lobster traps, a display of old bottles remain as they always have. Repeat customers want continuity; The Drake wants them to be happy; and since happiness means volume, the Cape Cod Room is the hotel's most profitable foodservice area.

Left, The Drake Hotel, still Queen of all she surveys in an expanding–diminishing cityscape. Right and below, two views of America's oldest theme restaurant, the nautical Cape Cod Room.

Beyond the Cape Cod Room, which always draws the sea lion's share of attention, there are other restaurants that are every bit as interesting to the customer and to the professional. The Raleigh Rooms are an example. With a total of 225 seats, these adjoining rooms do 1000 covers a day. Traditionally furnished, and overlooking the Avenue and the Lake, the Raleigh Rooms could be considered the hotel's coffee shop because of the big breakfast business; but their pleasant decor, moderate prices and good food keep the rooms busy at lunch and dinner. Over one third of the Raleigh customers are from outside the hotel. These are nearby residents, shoppers, and businessmen who regard it as a fine restaurant. Time-established favorites in the Raleigh Rooms are French crepes filled with seafood, "Mardi Gras," a tuna *poulette* on toast in casserole, and roast Chicken Bourgeoise.

The Drake has another, more informal coffee shop—fifty-three seats and twelve stools located next to the hotel drug store, off the Arcade. This hurry-up-and-eat operation is called the Americana Room, and even though it serves the hotel, eighty percent of its customers are from outside. Favorite foods are a very moderately priced Chili con Carne and an excellent Tuna Fish Salad Sandwich.

Many members and guests think that the private Club International is one of the top places to eat in the city. It follows then that the Club's hamburger steak with chopped onions and green peppers is one of the most respected hamburgers around town. The International is, essentially, a simple but splendid meat-and-potatoes place with beautiful fish, vegetables, and salads. The room has its own distinguished, relatively heavy character, something that once wanted to be referred to as "masculine."

Dowdy, frumpish, or top drawer, the Drake's Raleigh Rooms, left, are big-biz with value; below, the Drake never pours a miserly drink at any of its bars.

Aside from the large drinks that the bartenders always pour (at The Drake nothing is chintzily measured), another surprising thing about the Coq d'Or cocktail lounge off the Arcade is the amount of food business the 100-seat room does. Light but hearty meals are served at noon—perhaps tartar steak, an Oxford sandwich, or a broiled tenderloin of beef on toast. The room is a jewel, the lighting level is right, and there is plenty of space. To The Drake's delight, Coq d'Or's newest clientele is made up of women shoppers who come in about 2 pm, picking up the late lunch business considerably.

In the fall of 1977 The Drake's long-time supper club, The Camellia House, (originally designed by Dorothy Draper in 1940), gave way to "progress" and became a restaurant called Avenue One, featuring regional American cooking. Its menu lists over thirty entrees including New Orleans "Carpet Bag" steak (with oysters), pheasant, Florida stone crab, and a calf liver pepper steak. To date, Avenue One is The Drake's most venturesome foodservice operation.

The Drake is justly proud of its 7 am-to-midnight room service. It is an expensive operation but one that Drake guests expect, especially at breakfast when twenty percent of them order by phone. The Drake's special continental breakfast is served directly from The Drake breakfast kitchen in twenty minutes flat, utilizing a freight elevator fitted out with toasters, heaters, and coffee urns, to make the quick run to all floors.

If you add catering volume to room service, plus the volume of the five restaurants discussed, The Drake serves 4000 to 6000 meals a day. Its food and beverage costs are the highest in the city, over $3 million annually. The hotel purchases only top quality fresh meat and fish, produce, and dairy products. The hotel does its own butchering of primal cuts; it makes its own bread, rolls, and pastries; ages its beef at least three weeks. From its own Scotch whisky label to its own garbage disposal system, The Drake goes about foodservice in its own incomparable way.

"Continuity is a way of life at The Drake," remarks former vice president and general manager, DW Schuler, "in some ways. In matters of guest convenience and comfort, The Drake was the first to change; in many other ways, like taking shortcuts, it will be the last to change."

The Drake Hotel's efficient room service offers boiled eggs and *blanc de blanc* bubbly with equal fervor. Here's to romance!

BOUILLABAISSE, MARSEILLAISE

The Drake

Ingredients: Yield: 1 portion

Lobster Tail	2 ounces
Oil	as needed
Leeks, julienne	$\frac{1}{4}$ cup
Onion, julienne	$\frac{1}{4}$ cup
Tomatoes, fresh, peeled, chopped	$\frac{1}{4}$ cup
Pike	1 ounce
Halibut	1 ounce
Red Snapper	1 ounce
Scallops	4 pieces
Clams	2
White Wine	2 ounces
Water	6 ounces
Saffron	pinch
Parsley, chopped	pinch

Procedure:

1. Cut lobster tail in pieces and saute in hot oil. Simmer for 3 minutes.
2. Add remaining ingredients except parsley. Simmer for 20 minutes.
3. To serve, sprinkle with chopped parsley and accompany with garlic french bread.

PRIME AGED SIRLOIN STEAK, BORDELAISE

The Drake

Ingredients: Yield: 1 portion

From an 18- to 20-pound sirloin strip
(aged 3 weeks) cut a 14-ounce steak.

Procedure:

1. Broil to taste.
2. Serve with button mushrooms and Bordelaise sauce.

RAW TARTAR STEAK, GARNI

The Drake

Ingredients: Yield: 4 portions

Beef Tenderloin Tips	2 pounds
Salt	as needed
Pepper	as needed
Worcestershire Sauce	1 teaspoon
Onion, finely chopped	1 ounce
Capers	1 ounce
Egg Yolk, raw	1

Procedure:

1. Put beef through chopper blade of grinder twice. Add seasoning and mix in onion and capers. Thoroughly blend in egg yolk.
2. Serve 8-ounce portion on bed of bibb lettuce with sliced pumpernickel bread.

CHATEAUBRIAND FOR TWO, BEARNAISE SAUCE

The Drake

Ingredients: Yield: 2 portions

Heart of Prime Tenderloin	14 ounces
Button Mushrooms, sauteed	2
Bearnaise Sauce (Hollandaise sauce with chopped tarragon leaves)	8 ounces

Procedure:

1. Broil double filet mignon for 12 minutes each side.
2. Slice and serve with button mushrooms and Bearnaise sauce.

ESCALOPINE OF VEAL, MARSALA

The Drake

Ingredients: Yield: 1 portion

Leg of Veal Slices, 4 ounces each	2
Butter	1 ounce
Mushroom Caps, sliced	2
Marsala Wine	1 ounce

Procedure:

1. Saute veal slices in butter for 5 minutes each side.
2. Add sliced mushrooms and simmer for 5 minutes.
3. De-glaze in pan with wine.

CHILI CON CARNE

The Drake

Ingredients: Yield: 12 portions, 8 ounces each

Beef, ground	2 pounds
Onions, medium, chopped	2
Chili Beans, cooked	4 pounds
Chili Powder	4 teaspoons
Chicken Broth	6 ounces
Tomato Puree	12 ounces

Procedure:

1. Brown meat with onions. Add remaining ingredients and cook for 15 minutes.

CLUB INTERNATIONAL HAMBURGER STEAK

The Drake

Ingredients: Yield: 1 portion

Beef Chuck	10 ounces
Onion, chopped	$\frac{1}{2}$ ounce
Green Pepper, chopped	$\frac{1}{2}$ ounce
Water	1 ounce
Salt	as needed
Pepper	as needed

Procedure:

1. Grind meat. Add green pepper, onion, and water. Season with salt and pepper.
2. Form into patty and broil for 5 minutes each side.

CALF LIVER STEAK

The Drake

Ingredients: Yield: 1 portion

Calf Liver Steak, center cut, 7 ounces	1
Oil	1 ounce

Procedure:

1. Brush calf liver with cooking oil.
2. Broil 3 minutes each side for medium rare steak.
   Do not salt.

BREAST OF TURKEY

The Drake

Ingredients: Yield: 6 portions

Mushrooms, fresh, sliced	$\frac{1}{2}$ ounce
Butter	as needed
Roux	2 ounces
Chicken Broth	1 pint
White Wine	1 ounce
Salt	as needed
Pepper, white	as needed
Poached Breast of Turkey Slices, 6 ounces each	6
Noodles, cooked	as needed

Procedure:

1. Saute mushrooms in butter, add roux, and blend in chicken broth. Stir until thickened. Add wine and seasoning.
2. Place each turkey slice on a bed of noodles and top with sauce.

ROAST WISCONSIN DUCKLING, BIGARADE SAUCE

The Drake

Ingredients: Yield: 2 portions

Wisconsin Duck, 5 pounds	1
Orange Juice	2 ounces
Currant Jelly	1 ounce
Brown Sauce	1 cup
Orange Sections	6

Procedure:

1. Roast duck in oven at 375°F. for $1\frac{1}{2}$ hours.
2. Cut duck in half and de-bone.
3. To pan drippings add brown sauce, orange juice, and jelly and cook for 5 minutes.
4. Serve in individual shirred egg casserole, garnishing with orange sections.

CHICKEN BOURGEOISE

The Drake

Ingredients: Yield: 6 portions

Frying Chickens, disjointed	3
Fat	as needed
Sherry	1 ounce
Chicken Broth	6 ounces
Brown Sauce	8 ounces
Carrot Balls, cooked, parisian scoop size	24
Potato Balls, cooked, parisian scoop size	24
Button Mushrooms, fresh	24
Pearl Onions, cooked	24

Procedure:

1. Brown chicken pieces in fat. Cook in oven at 375°F. for 20 minutes.
2. To the browning pan, add sherry, chicken broth, and brown sauce.
3. Add vegetables and simmer for 5 minutes.
4. Serve one half chicken in casserole with vegetables and sauce.

WHOLE IMPORTED DOVER SOLE, SAUTE MEUNIERE

The Drake

Ingredients: Yield: 2 portions

Dover Sole, whole	$2\frac{1}{2}$ pounds
Milk	8 ounces
Flour	8 ounces
Oil	2 ounces
Brown Butter	2 ounces

Procedure:

1. Remove skin from sole.
2. Dip in milk, then in flour.
3. Saute in oil for 5 minutes each side.
4. Bone and serve at table with brown butter.

LOBSTER THERMIDOR

The Drake

Ingredients: Yield: 1 portion

Lobster Meat, cooked, diced	4 ounces
Butter	1 ounce
Mushrooms, fresh, sliced	1 ounce
Shallots, chopped	$\frac{1}{4}$ teaspoon
Salt	as needed
Pepper	as needed
Cayenne Pepper	pinch
Mustard, dry, English	$\frac{1}{4}$ teaspoon
White Sauce	4 ounces
Egg Yolk, beaten	1
Parmesan Cheese, grated	as needed
Butter, melted	as needed

Procedure:

1. Saute lobster in butter with shallots, mushrooms, salt, pepper, cayenne pepper, and mustard.
2. Add white sauce and beaten egg yolk. Simmer until thickened.
3. Pour into a half lobster shell. Sprinkle with grated cheese and brush with melted butter.
4. Brown in oven at 400°F. before serving.

POMPANO EN PAPILLOTE

The Drake

Ingredients: Yield: 6 servings

Butter	2 tablespoons
Shallots, chopped	$\frac{1}{2}$ teaspoon
Mushrooms, fresh, sliced	$\frac{1}{2}$ cup
Lobster, cooked, diced	$\frac{1}{2}$ cup
Pompano Fillets, 7 ounces each	6
Red Wine	6 ounces
Water	6 ounces
Worcestershire Sauce	$\frac{1}{2}$ teaspoon
Salt	$\frac{1}{2}$ teaspoon
Parchment paper, heart-shaped	6 sheets
Oil	as needed

Procedure:

1. Saute shallots, mushrooms, and lobster in butter for 5 minutes.
2. Place fillets of pompano evenly over sauteed ingredients in pan. Add remaining ingredients and poach for 20 minutes.
3. From parchment paper cut 6 large valentine hearts 22 by 14 inches. Place individual paper hearts on work table and brush lightly with oil.
4. On the left section of each valentine, place one fillet of pompano. Cover with proportionate amount of sauce from cooking pan. Fold right side of paper heart over the fillet, turning all edges to form a tight seal, thus preventing air from escaping from the bag. Place bags, sealed edge down, on baking sheet. Place in oven at 350°F. until each bag begins to puff up.

FRENCH CREPES FILLED WITH SEAFOOD, MORNAY SAUCE

The Drake

Ingredients: Yield: 6 portions

Butter	as needed
Mushrooms, sliced	2
Shrimp Petite, cooked, chopped	4 ounces
King Crab, cooked, chopped	2 ounces
Red Snapper, cooked, flaked	8 ounces
French Pancakes	12
Cream Sauce	8 ounces
Parmesan Cheese, grated	1 cup

Procedure:

1. Saute mushrooms in butter. Add shrimp, crab, and snapper. Blend in cream sauce.
2. Fill individual french pancakes with mixture. Roll and top with cream sauce.
3. Sprinkle with Parmesan cheese and glaze in oven at 400°F. before serving.

MARDI GRAS
(a tuna casserole)

The Drake

Ingredients: Yield: 6 portions

Butter	as needed
Mushroom Caps, sliced	2
Tuna Fish, shredded	10 ounces
Chives, chopped	½ cup
Cream Sauce	16 ounces
Parmesan Cheese, grated	½ cup
Toast	as needed

Procedure:

1. Saute mushrooms in butter, add tuna, then mix in cream sauce and chives.
2. Place in individual shirred egg casseroles.
3. Top with cheese and bake in oven at 375°F. for 3 minutes.
4. Serve toast points with each portion.

CLUB INTERNATIONAL SPECIAL SALAD

The Drake

Ingredients: Yield: 2 portions

Garlic Clove	1
Olive Oil	4 tablespoons
Wine Vinegar	1 tablespoon
Worcestershire Sauce	dash
Salt	as needed
Pepper, whole, ground	as needed
Bibb Lettuce	2 heads
Artichokes, cut in half	2
Heart of Palm, 1-inch slices	4
Avocado Wedges	4
Tomato Wedges	4
Hard-Cooked Egg, quartered	1

Procedure:

1. Rub salad bowl with garlic clove. Blend oil and vinegar; add Worcestershire sauce, salt, and pepper.
2. Add remaining ingredients and toss lightly.
3. Serve on individual chilled salad plates.

HOLLANDAISE SAUCE

The Drake

Ingredients: Yield: 8 ounces

Egg Yolks	4
Water	2 tablespoons
Lemon Juice	1 tablespoon
Butter, melted	$\frac{1}{2}$ cup
Cayenne Pepper	dash

Procedure:

1. Beat egg yolks with water and lemon juice over hot water until thickened.
2. Remove pan from hot water and add melted butter slowly, using wire whip until blended. Add salt, pepper, and cayenne pepper. Serve warm.

TUNA FISH SALAD SANDWICH

The Drake

Ingredients: Yield: 6 sandwiches

    Tuna, shredded   12 ounces
    Celery, diced   3 ounces
    Mayonnaise   9 ounces

Procedure:

1.   Blend all ingredients.

COLE SLAW

The Drake

Ingredients: Yield: 20 portions

    Cabbage, shredded   4 pounds
    Sour Cream   1 cup
    Mayonnaise   2 cups
    Olive Oil   1 cup
    Salt   as needed
    Pepper   as needed

Procedure:

1.   Combine all ingredients and toss lightly to mix.
2.   Serve in individual vegetable dish on bed of lettuce.

RICE PUDDING

The Drake

Ingredients: Yield: 8 to 10 portions

Rice, raw	1 cup
Milk	1 pint
Half and Half	3 cups
Sugar	$\frac{1}{2}$ cup
Salt	pinch
Vanilla	$\frac{1}{2}$ teaspoon
Liquid Egg Custard (see recipe)	1 pint
White Raisins	1 cup

Procedure:

1. Cook rice in double boiler with milk. Remove from heat and mix in cream, sugar, salt, vanilla, and custard.
2. Sprinkle raisins on bottom of baking casserole. Add pudding mix.
3. Bake in a hot water bath in oven at 375°F. for 45 minutes or until set.

LIQUID EGG CUSTARD
(for use in Rice Pudding)

The Drake

Ingredients: Yield: $1\frac{1}{2}$ quarts

Milk	1 quart
Eggs	12 ounces
Sugar	6 ounces
Coffee Cream	10 ounces
Salt	as needed
Vanilla	as needed
Yellow Food Color	as needed

Procedure:

1. Mix all ingredients together and whisk to blend well.

APPLE SOUFFLE PUDDING, SABAYON SAUCE

The Drake

Ingredients: Yield: 6 portions

Pudding
Butter	as needed
Sugar	as needed
Apples, freshly cooked, diced	2
Butter	1 ounce
Flour	1 ounce
Milk	1 cup
Vanilla	$\frac{1}{2}$ teaspoon
Salt	$\frac{1}{4}$ teaspoon
Egg Yolks, beaten	4
Egg Whites	5
Sugar	2 ounces
Cornstarch	$\frac{2}{3}$ ounce

Sauce
Egg Yolks	5
Sugar	4 ounces
White Wine	2 tablespoons
Vanilla	$\frac{1}{2}$ teaspoon
Whipping Cream	6 ounces

Procedure:

To make pudding:

1. Line pudding molds with butter, dust with sugar, then line with diced apple.
2. Melt 1 ounce butter and add flour. Combine and bring to a boil the milk, vanilla, and salt. Remove from heat and slowly stir into the roux. Add 4 beaten egg yolks.
3. Beat egg whites until fluffy. Mix sugar and cornstarch and beat into egg whites. Fold into first mixture.
4. Fill molds three-fourths full. Bake in *bain marie* for 35 to 40 minutes.

To make sauce:

1. Beat 5 yolks and sugar in deep saucepan with wire whisk until light. Add wine.
2. Cook over hot water, beating constantly, until thickened. Add vanilla and whipping cream.
3. Pour over turned-out pudding just before serving.

The Indian Trail

Owned and operated by the Klingeman family since 1934.

In the 1700's Indians established a trail extending from the shore of Lake Michigan to the site of an Indian village to the West of our present location. The Indians bent saplings and fastened them so that they became permanently contorted. A long line of similarly bent trees could thus be followed along the Indian trail.

The Indian Trail

Winnetka   Illinois

The Indian Trail   WINNETKA, ILLINOIS

The Indian Trail
Winnetka, Illinois

Sunday Dinner   October 15, 1978

                              Vegetable Soup
Frosted Fruit Juice   Chilled Tomato Juice
              Chilled Rhubarb & Raspberry Cup
              Herring in Sour Cream

BROILED TENDERLOIN STE...

BROILED CLUB STEAK wit...

ROAST BEEF TENDERLOIN...
ROAST YOUNG DUCKLING...
BAKED BONELESS BREAST...
ONE-HALF FRIED CHICKEN...
ROAST LEG OF LAMB -- M...
POT ROAST OF BEEF...
FRICASSEE OF BREAST C...
BAKED WHITEFISH -- Lem...

BROILED BOSTON SCROD...
BREADED VEAL CUTLET --...
FRIED JUMBO SHRIMP wit...

Choice of Two:

Brussel Sprouts

Choice of One:
                              Peach...
                              Headlet...

Apricot Lattice Pie

Chilled Cantaloupe We...
              Apple...

Coffee Ice Cream
Vanilla Ice Cream

Chocolate Sundae
Strawberry Sundae
Butterscotch Sundae

Coffee   Sanka
Coca-Cola   Seven'u...
                       Ki...

The Indian Trail
Winnetka, Illinois

Friday Dinner   October 13, 1978

                    Cream of Mushroom Soup
Frosted Fruit Juice   Chilled Tomato Juice
              Chilled Rhubarb & Raspberry Cup
          Turkey Salad Appetizer with Capers & Pecans
              ------*****------
Broiled Tenderloin Steak with Sauteed Onions, Mushrooms or
                                      Gorgonzola Cheese $7.75
Broiled Club Steak with Sauteed Onions, Mushrooms or
                                      Gorgonzola Cheese   7.75
One-Half Fried Chicken with Gravy   5.90
Pot Roast of Beef   6.00
Braised Lamb Shank Seasoned with Vegetables   6.20
Roast Loin of Pork -- Apple Sauce   6.00
Fricassee of Breast of Turkey with Toasted Almonds   6.10
Filet of Sole with Tartar Sauce   6.00
Baked Whitefish -- Lemon Wedge   **Center Cut $6.10
                                  ****Tail Cut $6.30
Baked Halibut au gratin   5.90
King Crabmeat Salad Bowl   7.10
Turkey Salad Bowl   5.60

Choice of Two:
                    Whipped Potatoes
Creamed Spinach   New Peas
                    Buttered Carrots
              ------*****------
Choice of One:
              Pear Salad with Honey Dressing
          Headlettuce Salad with Choice of Dressing
Cottage Cheese   Pineapple Sherbet
              ------*****------
Lemon Meringue Pie   Blueberry Tart
              Double Fudge Layer Cake
              Chilled Cantaloupe Wedge
              Tia Maria Crumble Whip
Coffee Ice Cream   Chocolate Ice Cream
Vanilla Ice Cream   Peppermint Ice Cream
              Butter Pecan Ice Cream
Chocolate Sundae   Caramel Sundae
Butterscotch Sundae   Strawberry Sundae
              Pineapple Sundae
              a la mode 45¢
   Coffee   Sanka   Tea   Milk   Skim Milk
Coca-Cola   Seven'up   Root Beer Tab   Fresca   Lemonade
Salad Plate: Turkey Salad - Melba Peach Salad - Cottage Cheese -
              Rolls and Beverage $4.15
              King Crabmeat Salad Plate as above   6.15
              Minimum Charge Per Person 65¢

The Indian Trail
The Restaurant that Answers the Question, "Can a Tea Room Over 40 be Exciting?"

The Indian Trail
507 Chestnut Street,
Winnetka, Illinois.

The French adage, "All that changes remains the same," gains new meaning at Winnetka's The Indian Trail. Despite the tumultuous changes during the four decades the restaurant has been operating, the high quality of food and service at The Indian Trail has stayed "the same." While "doing their best daily" remained the constant, The Indian Trail has experienced the variabilities of success: the restaurant's capacity has enlarged from an original forty-eight seats to over 300, while the restaurant's volume has climbed from approximately $12,000 in 1934 to over $1.5 million in 1977.

All the while, The Indian Trail has satisfied the changing demands of changing generations. This impressive steady growth is all the more remarkable because the village of Winnetka has been, and remains, dry. To say that The Indian Trail is "food oriented," as do the restaurant's owners, is something of an understatement. But then, understatement, a lively dignity, as well as constancy of quality and effort, are intrinsic to The Indian Trail.

The Indian Trail's thorough knowledge of its market dictates pricing. Lunch and dinner tabs have always been moderate. A 1934 Thanksgiving Day dinner was offered for $1. In 1978 the Thanksgiving meal cost $7.50, and 1,485 were served. Still moderate, to say the least. At present most luncheons are under $4; most dinners under $7.

The Indian Trail prints its own menus a few hours before each meal, giving the planners the flexibility to anticipate the day's weather or other conditions affecting the volume of their business—a great aid in controlling food costs and maintaining moderate pricing.

Maintaining the same location, The Indian Trail Tea Room opened on September 12, 1934, under the ownership of Har-

117

At Indian Trail, "the same old thing" takes on new meaning.

vey and Clara Klingeman and Elizabeth Struve. It is interesting to note that five previous restaurant owners had failed there during the years of the Depression.

"Actually, our three-year lease was 'the first long-term lease' negotiated in the village for several years. Our $24-a-day break-even point seemed astronomical, especially when we sold roast beef sandwiches for 15 cents and all five-course dinners were 80 cents or less," recalls Clara Klingeman today.

Perhaps fear of failure inspired success. The owners knew they had to do their best, and their operating principle has always been stated "to maintain, at all times, a high standard of appetizing dishes, nicely served, at modest prices."

The contemporaneity of the restaurant is based on an ever-alert merchandising program directed at its market: an increasingly young, but basically middle-aged-and-older group, in the mid- and upper-income range. These are people from all over the Chicago metropolitan area and from neighboring states as well; people who expect to receive extraordinary value and will travel far to get it.

Over the decades the restaurant has attempted to promote good will and customer interest, rather than promote a specific increase in sales. People still talk about how The Indian Trail picked up the check for men and women in military uniform during World War II, or about the restaurant's twenty-fifth anniversary celebration which was staged for three days under a giant marquee, complete with free cocktails, hors d'oeuvre, and members of the Chicago Symphony playing.

Other promotions that have worked for The Indian Trail have included an amusing St. Patrick's Day menu, and a Halloween menu rewritten to celebrate that occasion. Halloween is a special event at The Indian Trail when the restaurant becomes a "home party" with all eighty-five employees dressed in costume.

Another promotion geared to make better use of facilities during traditionally slow winter months is a series of travel programs. Speakers and movies cover a variety of tour areas, from Russia to the South Seas, with the restaurant providing dinners corresponding to each area. The response has been a sellout, with each program repeated, and sold out again. It is little wonder that The Indian Trail has a repeat business of over eighty percent.

The restaurant gives fresh definition to the phrase "homelike." Its three bright rooms are friendly, informal, and comfortable. The food is sometimes simple, sometimes sophisticated, often elegant, and *consistently* good. Consistency!—the basic reason why The Indian Trail is one of the best restaurants in the Chicago area.

"We know that our type of menu is the key to success. Our real competition comes from the home, not from other restaurants which rely on showmanship, atmosphere, or a specialty theme," notes Harry Klingeman, the restaurant's vice president and son of the founders.

Beneath the facade of "Suburban Tudor" Indian Trail lives!

The Indian Trail customers realize that the owners are involved and concerned, "never operating by remote control." To the Klingemans, "our restaurant must have one certain quality above all else—a consistent and honest character. That character must be earned and re-earned, at all costs, daily."

But the cost of consistency and honesty is not dullness. The Indian Trail's character, deservedly earned (and "re-earned") daily, is a lively one. Never dependent on fads and flights of fancy, the restaurant generates day-to-day excitement clearly based on an enduring professional romance.

Opposite and below, the various dining rooms at Indian Trail seem to wander on endlessly with their various neat, quaint "decors," but wherever customers sit, the food is familiar. And good!

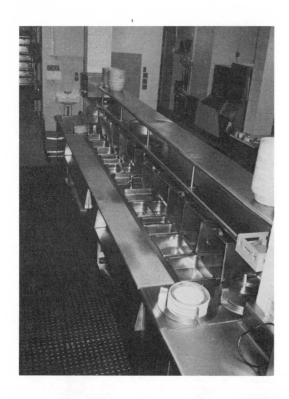

The busy heart of Indian Trail is its gleaming,
efficient kitchen—the vegetable prep and beverage areas.

GLAZED CHICKEN LIVER PATE

The Indian Trail

Ingredients: Yield: 30 to 36 servings

Chicken Livers, fresh	2 pounds
Salted Water or Chicken Stock	as needed
Butter	as needed
Salt	as needed
Onion Juice	as needed
Garlic Salt	as needed
Pepper	as needed
Condensed Beef Consomme, canned	1 can (10¾ ounce)
Water	½ cup
Bay Leaf	1
Salt	1 teaspoon
Pepper	dash
Gelatin, lemon-flavored	3 ounces
Dry Sauterne	2 tablespoons
Lemon Juice	1 tablespoon
Tarragon Vinegar	1 teaspoon
Stuffed Olives, thinly sliced	as needed
Egg, hard-cooked, sliced	as needed

Procedure:
1. Cook chicken livers in simmering salted water or stock until tender. Cool.
2. Put livers through the fine knife of a food chopper 2 or 3 times.
3. Combine with enough butter to make a smooth paste and season well with salt, onion juice, garlic salt, and pepper.
4. Press pate into a small buttered mold and chill.
5. Combine consomme, water, bay leaf, salt, and pepper in a small saucepan. Cover and simmer 5 minutes. Remove bay leaf. Dissolve gelatin in hot liquid.
6. Add sauterne, lemon juice, and vinegar, and chill until syrupy.
7. Unmold pate and garnish with olive and egg slices.
8. Pour a thin layer of gelatin over the top and chill until almost firm. Pour a second layer of gelatin over and chill again. Add a third layer and chill until set.

Note:

Prepared chicken liver pate may be used in place of fresh chicken livers. In this case omit procedures 1, 2, and 3.

BEET BORSCHT COCKTAIL

The Indian Trail

Ingredients: Yield: 4 portions

Beet Juice, from 1 pound jar beets	1 cup
Tomato Juice	1 cup
Monosodium Glutamate	$\frac{1}{4}$ teaspoon
Onion Juice	1 teaspoon
Lemon Juice	1 lemon
Sugar	$\frac{1}{2}$ teaspoon
Sour Cream	$\frac{1}{2}$ cup
Salt	as needed
Pepper	as needed
Horseradish, grated	as needed
Sour Cream	as needed

Procedure:

1. Blend all ingredients, except second amount of sour cream, salt, pepper, and horseradish. Chill.
2. Serve in cocktail glasses, topping each with 1 tablespoon sour cream seasoned to taste with salt, pepper, and horseradish.

JELLIED BEET BORSCHT

The Indian Trail

Ingredients: Yield: 30 portions

Jellied Consomme, canned	2 cans($10\frac{3}{4}$ ounces each)
Gelatin, unflavored, dissolved	4 tablespoons
Tomatoes, fresh, peeled, chopped	4 medium
Green Onions, finely chopped	8
Parsley, chopped	2 teaspoons
Beets, canned or cooked, finely chopped	4 cups
Salt	as needed
Pepper	as needed

CANADIAN CHEESE SOUP

The Indian Trail

Ingredients:

Yield: 70 portions

Onion, finely chopped	1 quart
Butter	2 cups
Flour, sifted	2 cups
Cornstarch	$\frac{3}{4}$ cup
Milk	2 gallons
Stock	2 gallons
Carrots, fresh, diced	1 quart
Celery, fresh, diced	1 quart
Paprika	$1\frac{1}{3}$ teaspoons
Salt	as needed
Cheese, sharp cheddar, cubed	2 quarts
Parsley, chopped	as needed

Procedure:

1.   Saute onion lightly in melted butter.
2.   Mix sifted flour and cornstarch and add to butter. Stir to a smooth paste.
3.   Add milk and stock gradually; stir and cook to make a smooth sauce.
4.   Add vegetables, sauteed onions, seasonings, and cheese. Bring to simmer and cook for 15 minutes. Do not overcook.
5.   Add chopped parsley just before serving.

JELLIED BEET BORSCHT *(cont'd.)*

Procedure:

1.   Heat 1 can consomme.
2.   Add dissolved gelatin.
3.   Combine with remaining ingredients. Pour into individual molds or a shallow pan.
4.   Chill until set.
5.   To serve, unmold or cut into small squares.

WAX BEANS ALBERT

The Indian Trail

Ingredients: Yield: 315 portions

Bacon, diced	2 pounds
Onions, medium, chopped	4
Wax Beans, frozen, cooked, drained	48 pounds
Cream Sauce, thick	1½ gallons
*Fricassee of Chicken Sauce	1½ gallons
Parmesan Cheese, grated	2½ quarts

Procedure:

1. Saute bacon and onion until bacon is crisp. Discard fat.
2. Combine with beans, cream sauce, and fricassee sauce. Mix well.
3. Turn into steamtable pans and top with grated cheese.
4. Bake in oven at 350°F. for 20 minutes or until bubbly hot.

*Note:

A cream sauce made with chicken broth instead of milk.

SWEET POTATOES AND APRICOTS

The Indian Trail

Ingredients: Yield: 14 portions

Sweet Potatoes, cooked	2 quarts
Apricot Halves, frozen	2 cups
Cornstarch, clear jell	3 tablespoons
Sour Cream	2 cups
Salt	½ teaspoon
Cinnamon	½ teaspoon

Procedure:

1. Cut sweet potatoes into ¾-inch slices. Arrange in shallow pan.
2. Drain apricots well. Thicken juice with cornstarch and pour over sweet potatoes.
3. Blend sour cream, salt, and cinnamon and pour over sweet potatoes.
4. Arrange apricot halves on top. Bake in oven at 350°F. for 20 minutes.

CASSEROLE OF TUNAFISH AND RICE IMPERIAL

The Indian Trail

Ingredients: Yield: 30 to 40 portions

Butter	as needed
Onion, chopped	4 cups
Green Pepper, chopped	2 cups
Celery, chopped	6 cups
Mushrooms, fresh, chopped	4 cups
Rice, raw	2 cups
*Tuna Fish, 1-inch cubes	$2\frac{1}{2}$ quarts
Parsley, chopped	1 cup
Pimiento, chopped	$\frac{1}{2}$ cup
Mayonnaise	2 cups
Salt	as needed
Pepper	as needed
Buttered Crumbs	as needed

Procedure:

1. Saute onion, green pepper, celery, and mushrooms very lightly. Add pimiento and chopped parsley.
2. Cook rice and allow to cool. Add to sauteed mixture.
3. Add tuna, mayonnaise, salt, and pepper. Toss lightly to mix.
4. Place mixture into a steamtable pan 20 by 12 by $2\frac{1}{2}$ inches or into individual flat casseroles. Top with buttered crumbs. Bake in oven at 350°F. for 30 minutes.

*Note:

Diced turkey may be substituted.

WILD RICE INDIAN TRAIL

The Indian Trail

Ingredients: Yield: 320 portions

Rice, long grain	8 pounds
Wild Rice	7 pounds
Onion, minced	1 pound
Mushrooms, fresh, sliced	3 pounds
Celery, chopped	1 pound
Butter	2 pounds
Ham, minced	3 pounds
Chicken Base	$\frac{1}{2}$ pound
Monosodium Glutamate	2 ounces

Procedure:

1. Steam white rice and wild rice separately.
2. Saute onion, mushrooms, and celery in butter. Add ham.
3. Combine with both kinds of rice and toss lightly.
4. Add chicken base and monosodium glutamate. Mix well.
5. Serve hot.

HOT GREEN BEANS CAESAR

The Indian Trail

Ingredients: Yield: 15 portions

Green Beans, frozen, cooked and drained	2 pounds
Onion, minced	2 tablespoons
Oil	2 tablespoons
Vinegar	2 tablespoons
Salt	as needed
Bread Cubes, $\frac{1}{2}$-inch	$1\frac{1}{2}$ cups
Oil	$\frac{1}{4}$ cup
Parmesan Cheese, grated	6 tablespoons

MOLDED TOMATO SALAD

The Indian Trail

Ingredients:

Yield: 360 portions

Tomato Juice, canned	2 #5 cans
Gelatin, unflavored	6¼ ounces
Tomatoes, canned, strained	3 #10 cans
Tomato Puree	1 #10 can
Sugar	1 quart
Salt	5 tablespoons
Celery Salt	1 tablespoon
Pepper, black	1 teaspoon
Onion, grated	1¼ tablespoons
Vinegar	1 cup

Procedure:

1. Dissolve gelatin in tomato juice in steamer. Add remaining ingredients and mix well.
2. Pour into individual molds and chill until firm.
3. Serve with cucumber dressing or Green Goddess dressing.

HOT GREEN BEANS CAESAR *(cont'd.)*
Procedure:

1. Place beans in shallow pan.
2. Saute onion lightly in 2 tablespoons oil. Add vinegar and salt. Mix with beans.
3. Saute bread cubes in ¼ cup oil until golden brown and crisp. Sprinkle over beans. Top with grated cheese.
4. Heat through and serve.

GENOISE CAKE

The Indian Trail

Ingredients: Yield: 10 2-layer, 9-inch cakes. 14 to 16 servings per cake.

Cake
Eggs, beaten light and fluffy	2½ quarts
Sugar	2½ quarts
Salt	5 teaspoons
Vanilla	5 teaspoons
Sifted Cake Flour	12½ cups

Filling
Sugar	7½ cups
Cornstarch	1¼ cups
Egg Yolks	5 dozen
Milk	3¾ quarts
Vanilla	3 tablespoons
	plus 1 teaspoon
Butter, creamed	5 cups

Frosting
Butter	2 tablespoons
Confectioners' Sugar	2½ quarts
Eggs	10
Chocolate, melted	10 ounces
Vanilla	5 teaspoons

Procedure:

To make cake:
1. Beat all ingredients except flour together until thick and lemon colored. Fold in flour, a little at a time, gently but thoroughly. Pour into 10 greased 9-inch layer pans. Bake in oven at 350°F. for 25 to 30 minutes. Cool and split each layer.

To make filling:
1. Combine sugar and cornstarch. Add egg yolks and beat until fluffy. Stir in milk and cook until thick. Add vanilla and cool. Blend in creamed butter.
2. Spread over one cake layer. Top with another layer.

To make frosting:
1. Cream butter. Blend in sugar. Add eggs and beat well. Blend in chocolate and vanilla. Beat until smooth.
2. Spread carefully over cake.

DANISH RUM PUDDING

The Indian Trail

Ingredients: Yield: 120 portions

Pudding
Gelatin, unflavored	$2\frac{1}{2}$ ounces
Water	$2\frac{1}{2}$ cups
Milk	$7\frac{1}{2}$ cups
Egg Yolks, beaten	40
Sugar	$7\frac{1}{2}$ cups
Rum	10 tablespoons
Vanilla	as needed
Salt	as needed
Whipped Cream	$1\frac{1}{2}$ quarts

Sauce
Boysenberry Juice	2 gallons
Cornstarch, clear jell	$3\frac{1}{4}$ cups
Cold Water	as needed
Sugar	8 cups
Salt	as needed

Procedure:

1. Dissolve gelatin in water.
2. Mix beaten egg yolks with 3 cups sugar.
3. Scald milk and stir into eggs. Add gelatin and allow to cool.
4. Add rum and vanilla.
5. Beat egg whites until fluffy, beat in remaining sugar. Fold into cool mixture.
6. Fold in whipped cream. Pour into molds and chill until set.
7. To make sauce, bring boysenberry juice to a boil.
8. Mix cornstarch with cold water as needed. Slowly stir into hot juice. Cook and stir until thickened.
9. Add sugar and salt. Cool.
10. Serve over molded pudding, using about $\frac{1}{3}$ cup sauce per serving.

HAZELNUT RUM WHIPPED CREAM ROLL

The Indian Trail

Ingredients: Yield: 36 portions

Egg Yolks	16
Sugar	20 ounces
Bread Crumbs	$\frac{3}{4}$ cup
Rum	2 teaspoons
Salt	$\frac{1}{2}$ teaspoon
Egg Whites, stiffly beaten	16
Hazelnuts, shelled, coarsely ground	$1\frac{1}{4}$ pounds
Whipping Cream	2 quarts
Rum or Vanilla	as needed
Powdered Sugar	as needed

Procedure:

1. Mix egg yolks with sugar until light and lemon colored.
2. Add bread crumbs, rum, and salt.
3. Alternately fold in beaten egg whites and nuts.
4. Pour into 3 shallow, well-greased and floured 12- by 18-inch baking sheets. Bake in oven at 350°F. for 15 to 20 minutes.
5. Remove from pan at once into a cloth dusted generously with powdered sugar. Cut off crisp edges of cake and roll up while hot. Allow to cool.
6. Whip cream and flavor to taste with rum or vanilla.
7. Unroll cakes, spread with whipped cream, and roll again. Sprinkle roll with powdered sugar. Chill.
8. Slice each roll into 12 servings.

In summer, the Indian Trail's outdoor dining terrace provides sun and fun for longtime customers.

dinner

Jimmy's Place
3420 n. Elston
Chicago
tel. 539-2999

JAPANESE STYLE FISH 3.25
(Fresh raw marinated fish of the day)
  FRESH BLUE POINTS, COCKTAIL SAUCE 3.50
    LOBSTER MOUSSE, FRESH CRAYFISH SAUCE 3.75
      HOT DUCK PATE IN PASTRY CRUST, MADEIRA
      WINE AND TRUFFLE SAUCE 3.75

SOUP OF THE DAY 1.75
    FRENCH ONION SOUP 2.50
    COLD SPANISH GAZPACHO 2.25

MIXED GREEN SALAD WITH DRESSING OF THE DAY
(Included with your entree)
  "JIMMY'S PLACE" SALAD + 1.75
  (Fresh spinach, three types of lettuce, lemon dressing,
  bacon, croutons and fresh Japanese mushrooms)

* FRESHLY PREPARED FISH OF THE DAY 10.00-11.50
  (YOSHI'S BOUILLABAISSE, when available 12.50)

* "JIMMY'S PLACE" VEAL 12.00
  (Scallopine of veal sauteed in butter with white wine and
  cream sauce with fresh Japanese mushrooms)

* FRESH CALVES BRAINS, GRENOBLE STYLE 9.50
  (Sauteed in butter with lemon, capers and croutons)

* ROAST LEG OF LAMB, GARLIC SAUCE 11.00

* SAUTEED FILET OF BEEF 12.50
  (Red wine sauce with shallots and marrow)

* OUR DAILY SPECIAL(S)

(All entrees served with Yoshi's special potatoes)

CARAMEL APPLES WITH RUM AND ICE CREAM 2.50
  ASSORTMENT OF HOMEMADE PASTRIES 2.00-3.00
    FRESH PEAR IN RED WINE WITH CINNAMON 2.00
      CARAMEL CUSTARD 1.75
        ICE CREAMS AND SHERBETS 1.50

COFFEE, TEA AND SANKA .75
  FILTER COFFEE 1.50

We accept Master Charge and Visa credit cards.

closed
mon. and tues.

---

brunch

Jimmy's Place
3420 n. Elston
Chicago 60618
tel. 539-2999

1st course   TOASTS, CROISSANTS AND
                 HOMEMADE SWEET BRIOCHE WITH
                 BUTTER, JAMS AND MARMALADES

2nd course   INDIVIDUAL APPETIZER PLATES

3rd course   CHOICE OF EGG DISH:
                 1) POACHED EGG "FLORENTINE"
                 2) EGG "COCOTTE"
                 3) COLD POACHED EGG "NICOISE"

4th course   CHOICE OF ENTREE:
                 1) FRESHLY PREPARED FISH
                    OF THE DAY
                 2) ROAST LOIN OF PORK
                    "AU JUS"
                 3) CHICKEN CREPE WITH CREAM
                    SAUCE AND MUSHROOMS

5th course   FRESH FRUIT SALAD WITH
                 KIRSCHWASSER

and   INDIVIDUAL POTS OF COFFEE
             ON YOUR TABLE

$ 9.50

We accept Master Charge and Visa credit cards.

HOURS
lunch
wed. thru sat.
11:30-2:00
dinner
wed. and thurs.
5:30-9:30
fri. and sat.
5:30-10:30
sun.
3:00-8:00
brunch
sun.
noon-3:00
closed
mon. and tues.

Jimmy's Place
3420 n. Elston
Chicago 60618
tel. 539-2999

Jimmy's Place
a fine restaurant

3420 n. elston
chicago
539-2999

Jimmy's Place

"The New Hospitality"—
Value for Today and Tommorrow

Jimmy's Place
3420 N. Elston Avenue,
Chicago, Illinois.

The first sign of Jimmy Rohr's bright "new hospitality" is a crisp, green-and-yellow striped awning that might seem incongruous on Elston Avenue, one of Chicago's drab industrial byways. On the awning are the simple words, "Jimmy's Place—A Fine Restaurant." A curiosity! But, then, one must come to terms with a number of curious things about this out-of-the-way and out-of-the-ordinary restaurant: it's small (46 seats), fairly expensive (dinner averages $22), and it features the largely unfamiliar "international style" cookery of French-trained Japanese chef Yoshi Katsumura . . . yet the restaurant is neither French nor Japanese! However, the most curious thing about Jimmy's Place is that it should be in business at all. Only a year or so ago, solid and conservative Chicago diners-out wouldn't have tolerated it. The trend-setters were belatedly reveling in the culinary joys of the "French Revolution," in any of its manifestations, from the heavily sauced classics to the manicured julienne presentations of *nouvelle cuisine.* Until recently, Chicago wouldn't have bothered with a place in the midst of an un-chic blue collar neighborhood where light, health-conscious natural foods are offered at high tariffs . . . simply broiled, grilled items served with sauce on the side, or without sauce on request. But, onward and upward! It's a credit to Chicago tastes that Jimmy's Place is a smash hit.

In the short time since its opening in July 1978, Rohr's tiny establishment has come to be regarded as one of Chicago's finest restaurants. It has consistently attracted a discriminating clientele who knows the secret of the "new hospitality"—that there's something special, and personal, about the quality of food and service in a small, professionally run restaurant in which the proprietor insists on taking every order himself.

135

Jimmy's Place is an out-of-the-way "In" establishment, where the attractive menu changes monthly, with specials daily.

Located on Chicago's northwest side, six miles from the busy-ness of downtown restaurant activity, Jimmy's Place is a lively monument to the determination of proprietor Rohr who took a great professional gamble on the urbanity of the Chicago appetite. Still, Rohr is a shrewd man who realizes that his establishment will draw the in-city crowds, hungry for fine food (and easy parking). And he knows that he can count on the appetites of Chicago's north-suburbanites on their way to downtown symphony, opera, or theatre pleasures, because Jimmy's Place is only minutes from the major Chicago north-south expressway.

There's no question that Jimmy Rohr knows something about Chicago geography and a great deal about Chicago palates. Having observed the city's increasing gastro-urbanity over the past ten years at two distinguished French restaurants—as waiter at L'Escargot (see chapter about L'Escargot) and as maitre d' at La Reserve—Rohr felt that Chicago was ready for something else: "The last thing this city needs is another French restaurant. It needs more *good*, imaginative restaurants." Rohr had this in mind when he opened his own restaurant, the culmination of a decade of dreaming and planning. And he wanted to have it his way entirely.

In a widely published letter of introduction to Jimmy's Place, Rohr defined the essence of his "new hospitality" as "superior food, very personal service, and sparkling cleanliness."

Rohr's low-rent location meant that he could lavish his money on necessarily expensive fresh foods (he's content with a 40-45% food cost, and delighted with a 37% liquor cost). Being out-of-the-way also meant that Rohr could buck the trend toward expensive, glitzy, front-of-the-house decoration and put his money where he knew it belonged—in the kitchen. Thus, Jimmy's place was built on a 10-to-1 kitchen vs. dining room cost ratio. And the former is 410 square feet; the latter, 400 square feet—a rare situation. However, this does not mean that Rohr's dining room is spartan. It *is* clean as well as inviting and cordial, with good lighting, mirror-topped tables, and modern fixtures. The dining room also has eye-level windows that look into the bright, busy kitchen. That's the way that Rohr wanted it; he was sure that only by emphasizing the kitchen could the kitchen product be superior, and a superior chef be contented.

Opposite and below, the long, narrow dining room at Jimmy's Place, with high windows overlooking the kitchen. "Wow," said one customer, "I feel like I'm on a train!"

Rohr's "superior chef," and partner, is one of Chicago's truly imaginative, young cooks—at the age of 29. In his menu creativity, Yoshi Katsumura goes beyond his own Japanese background, French training, and kitchen experience at Jean Banchet's Le Francais restaurant (see chapter about Le Francais). In devising an amalgam of dishes in the "international style," Katsumura borrows from cooking *procedures* as well as preparations and presentations from around the world . . . whether they be French, Japanese, Moroccan, Spanish, or regional American. (Jimmy's Place is anything but a palid "continental" restaurant.) The frequently changing menu (always with daily specialties) includes appetizers ranging from Yoshi's duck pate and chicken liver mousse to oriental raw fish and South American marinated scallops. Soups may be French, Andalousian, or Creole. Entrees, always based on market availability, might vary from roasted calf's liver with avocado to Katsumura's fish stew, reminiscent of both Marseilles *and* the China Seas. Other memorable dishes which combine the traditions of east and west include Jimmy's Place Veal, Japanese-Style Marinated Salmon, Grilled Striped Sea Bass with Pernod Sauce, and Yoshi's Fresh Sea Scallops served in pastry (see recipes).

If the key to Jimmy's Place is the "new hospitality," the "Open Sesame" to its success is prompt word-of-mouth affirmation and reaffirmation. Also, Chicago's increasingly important, if ascerbic, (restaurant) critical-fraternity has praised Jimmy's Place as "the most exciting new restaurant in town," and "a mecca for appreciators of fine cuisine." Other newspaper comments: "It delivers a great value of outstanding food and fine service," "It's my favorite kind of restaurant—small, unpretentious but charming, and dedicated to the proposition that the main thing people want when they dine is top-quality food."

If Jimmy's Place were located in New York's east fifties, or slightly west, it would be regarded as knockout. That this "international style" restaurant has comfortably settled in Chicago's boonies is no small credit to the imagination of Jimmy Rohr and Yoshi Katsumura—or to Chicago. Jimmy's Place bears its own distinct identity, but shares with other top Chicago restaurants a high degree of foodservice professionalism, civilized service, and style in presentation. Rohr's restaurant may, or may not be, the wave of the future, but it is here to stay, because it's run by people who *know*. And care.

JAPANESE-STYLE MARINATED SALMON

Jimmy's Place

Ingredients: Yield: 6 portions

Salmon, small side, very fresh	
White Wine, dry	2 cups
Wine Vinegar, white	2 cups
Bay Leaves	2
Pepper corns, black, whole	$\frac{1}{2}$ teaspoon
Onion	1 medium
Carrots	2
Capers	1 small jar
Lemons	6 wedges
Tomatoes	6 wedges
Radishes, whole	6
Leaf Lettuce	1 head
Parsley Sprigs	6 small clusters
Salt	2 tablespoons

Procedure:

1. Salt salmon, remove bones (leaving skin), and refrigerate for half a day.
2. Make marinade in shallow pan using 2 cups dry white wine, 2 cups white wine vinegar, 2 bay leaves, $\frac{1}{2}$ teaspoon whole black pepper corns, 1 onion, sliced, and 2 carrots, sliced.
3. Place salmon in marinade and marinate $\frac{1}{2}$ hour on each side. Remove from marinade and towel dry. Retain marinade.
4. Clean lettuce, drain, and arrange bed of lettuce on large plates.
5. Slice salmon very thin, as with a smoked salmon, and arrange slices neatly on top of lettuce leaves. Top salmon slices with onions and carrots from marinade.
6. Decorate plates with tomato wedges, radishes, lemon wedges, capers, and parsley sprigs.

JIMMY'S PLACE SALAD

Jimmy's Place

Ingredients:

Yield: 6 portions

Spinach, fresh	2 bunches
Head Lettuce	1
Boston Lettuce	1
Romaine	1
Enoki (Japanese) Mushrooms	1 package
Tomatoes	12 wedges
Bacon, cubed and fried crisp	6 slices
Croutons	1 cup
Lemons	6 wedges
Radishes, whole	6

Dressing

Lemon juice, fresh	$\frac{1}{4}$ cup
Dijon Mustard	$\frac{1}{4}$ cup
Vegetable Oil, pure	$1\frac{1}{2}$ cups
Salt	dash
Pepper, white	dash

Procedure:

1. Make dressing: in blender, place lemon juice and Dijon mustard; add salt and pepper, and mix well.
2. While mixer is running, slowly add vegetable oil, not allowing the dressing to break. Refrigerate.
3. Clean lettuces and spinach separately. Drain well or dry in towel.
4. Break lettuces into bite-size pieces and mix in bowl with half of dressing. Arrange lettuce neatly on large plates.
5. Break spinach leaves and mix in bowl with remaining dressing. Arrange spinach leaves neatly on top of lettuce leaves.
6. Garnish sides of plates with Japanese mushrooms (*enoki*), and 2 tomato wedges and 1 lemon wedge per plate. Sprinkle top of salad with bacon bits, radish slices, and croutons. Top with fresh ground pepper if desired.

YOSHI'S FRESH SEA SCALLOPS

Jimmy's Place

Ingredients: Yield: 6 portions

Puff Pastry
Butter, very soft	1 pound
Flour (plus flour for rolling)	1 pound
Water	1 cup
Salt	dash
Egg, beaten	1

Scallops and Vegetables
Spinach (fresh or frozen)	2 cups cooked
Butter, sweet	1 teaspoon
Leek (white only)	1
Carrot, small	1
Celery	1 stalk
White Wine, dry	1 quart
Shallots	3
Butter, very soft	3 sticks
Lemon Juice, fresh	$\frac{1}{2}$ lemon
Salt	to taste
Pepper, cayenne	to taste
Milk	1 cup
Water	2 quarts
Salt	1 teaspoon
Pepper, white	dash
Sea Scallops, fresh	3 pounds

Note:

Prepare puff pastry dough one day in advance, or use frozen puff pastry dough.

YOSHI'S FRESH SEA SCALLOPS *(cont'd.)*

Procedure:

1. In mixer, place $\frac{1}{4}$ pound soft butter, 1 pound flour, 1 cup water, and a dash of salt. Mix well; dough should not stick to fingers. Place dough in bowl and let rest in refrigerator for 2 hours.
2. Remove dough from refrigerator and roll out on floured board or marble. In center of dough, spread remaining soft butter ($\frac{3}{4}$ pound). Fold edges to center over butter, completely covering butter. Let rest in refrigerator for 1 hour. Remove from refrigerator and let rest at room temperature for $\frac{1}{2}$ hour.
3. Roll out dough lengthwise, fold in thirds, and return to refrigerator, covered with a wet towel for 20 minutes.
4. Repeat step 3, folding dough in fourths, then in thirds, then again in fourths, allowing dough to rest 20 minutes in refrigerator, between rollings.
5. On floured board, roll out dough $\frac{1}{4}$- to $\frac{1}{3}$-inch thickness, and cut six $3 \times 5''$ rectangles. Place rectangles on baking sheet. Brush edges of rectangles with water and make $\frac{1}{2}$-inch wide strips of dough all around rectangles. Press down strips lightly with a fork. Brush rectangles with a beaten egg mixed with a drop of water, and bake at 375° for approximately 10-15 minutes. Keep warm.
6. Cook spinach in salted water. Drain. Season to taste and add 1 teaspoon sweet butter. Keep warm.
7. Peel and julienne leek, carrot, and celery. Cook in salted water for 3 minutes. Drain and keep warm.
8. Reduce 1 quart white wine with 3 minced shallots in large saucepan until liquid barely covers bottom of pan.
9. Slowly, using a wire whip add 3 sticks very soft butter beating constantly over a low fire. Add juice of $\frac{1}{2}$ lemon, salt and cayenne pepper to taste. Keep warm.
10. In large sauce pan add 1 cup milk, 2 quarts water, 1 teaspoon salt, and a dash of white pepper. Bring to boil. As soon as mixture comes to a boil, add scallops; cook until liquid returns to a boil, plus one minute. Remove and drain scallops.
11. Put a pastry shell on each plate. Make bed of spinach in bottom of each pastry shell, top with scallops and julienne of vegetables, and cover with sauce.
12. Serve boiled small potatoes, sprinkled with chopped parsley, on the side.

YOSHI'S SPANISH GAZPACHO

Jimmy's Place

Ingredients: Yield: 6 portions

Green Peppers	2 medium
Onion	1 small
Tomatoes, ripe	2
Cucumber	1 small
Garlic	3 cloves
Tomato Juice	1 quart
Lemon Juice	1 lemon
Salt	to taste
Tabasco Sauce	to taste
Olive Oil	2 tablespoons

Procedure:

1. Remove seeds from green peppers. Very finely dice green peppers and onion, set aside.
2. Peel tomatoes and cucumber, remove the seeds, and dice very fine; set aside.
3. Mince 3 garlic cloves; set aside.
4. In bowl, add tomato juice: and lemon juice, mix well.
5. Combine ingredients in bowl; mix well.
6. Add salt and Tabasco to taste, and 2 tablespoons olive oil; mix well.

Note:

If soup is too thick you may add cold water.

GRILLED STRIPED SEA BASS WITH PERNOD SAUCE

Jimmy's Place

Ingredients: Yield: 6 portions

White Wine, dry	1 quart
Shallots	3
Spinach (fresh or frozen)	3 cups cooked
Salt	as needed
Pepper, white	to taste
Butter, sweet	1 teaspoon
Butter, very soft	3 sticks
Lemon Juice	$\frac{1}{2}$ lemon
Pepper, cayenne	to taste
Pernod Liqueur	$\frac{1}{4}$ cup
Sea Bass fillets, 8-10 ounces each	6 fresh
Vegetable Oil	2 tablespoons

Procedure:

1. Reduce 1 quart white wine with 3 minced shallots in large saucepan until liquid barely covers bottom of pan.
2. While liquid is reducing, cook spinach in salted water. Drain; season with salt, white pepper, and 1 teaspoon sweet butter. Keep warm.
3. When liquid has reduced, slowly, using a wire whip, add 3 sticks very soft butter, beating constantly over low heat. Add juice of $\frac{1}{2}$ lemon, salt and cayenne pepper to taste, and $\frac{1}{4}$ cup of Pernod. Keep warm.
4. Heat broiler until very hot. Season fish fillets with salt and white pepper. Brush fillets with a very small amount of vegetable oil and place on broiler. Broil for 2 minutes. Twist fillets halfway (not turning over) to make criss-cross grill lines on the fillets; broil for 2 more minutes.
5. Turn over fillets and cook until done, approximately 1-2 minutes.
6. On plates, make a bed of spinach, top with fillets, and cover with sauce. Serve with boiled potatoes or white rice.

JIMMY'S PLACE VEAL

Jimmy's Place

Ingredients: Yield: 6 portions

Spinach (fresh or frozen)	4 cups cooked
Salt	to taste
Pepper, white	to taste
Butter, sweet	1 tablespoon
Veal Chops, lean	12
Flour	$\frac{1}{2}$ cup
Butter, clarified	$\frac{1}{3}$ cup
White Wine, dry	$\frac{1}{2}$ cup
Whipping Cream	2 cups
Enoki (Japanese) Mushrooms	1 package
Parsley, chopped	1 teaspoon

Procedure:

1. Cook spinach in salted water. Drain; season to taste and add 1 tablespoon sweet butter. Keep warm.
2. Lightly season and flour chops.
3. Sautee veal chops in hot clarified butter until cooked and slightly browned on each side. Remove from pan and empty out the grease. Keep warm.
4. In the same pan, add $\frac{1}{2}$ cup dry white wine and reduce until wine barely covers bottom of pan. Add 2 cups whipping cream and bring to boil. Add salt and white pepper to taste. Continue cooking until slightly thickened.
5. In separate pan, sautee Japanese mushrooms (*enoki*) in clarified butter for $\frac{1}{2}$ minute. Drain and add to cream sauce.
6. Make beds of spinach on plates, top with 2 veal chops, and cover with sauce. Sprinkle with chopped parsley. Serve with buttered egg noodles or white rice.

SWEETBREADS WITH MADEIRA WINE
AND TRUFFLES

Jimmy's Place

Ingredients: Yield: 6 portions

Sweetbreads, fresh	5 pounds
Peppercorns, black, whole	10
Bay Leaves	3
Lemon, whole	$\frac{1}{4}$
Sauce	
Madeira or Port Wine	1 bottle
Truffle Peelings	$1\frac{1}{2}$ ounces
Veal Stock (canned or frozen)	2 cups
Spinach (frozen or fresh)	4 cups cooked
Butter, sweet	2 tablespoons
Salt	to taste
Pepper, white	to taste
Flour	$\frac{1}{2}$ cup
Butter, clarified	$\frac{1}{2}$ cup

Procedure:

1. Soak sweetbreads in cold water for 3 hours.
2. Remove sweetbreads from water; drain. Bring 5 quarts water to boil in a large pot. Add salt to taste, black peppercorns, bay leaves, and $\frac{1}{4}$ lemon. Add sweetbreads, let water return to boil, and boil for 3 minutes. Place pot in sink and allow cold water to run slowly into the pot for 15 minutes. While water is running, make sauce.
3. In pot reduce 13 ounces of Madeira (or Port) until liquid barely covers bottom of the pan. Add chopped truffle peelings and veal stock. Reduce heat and let boil until sauce appears shiny and smooth. Keep warm.
4. Cook spinach in salted water. Drain. Add 1 tablespoon sweet butter and season with salt and pepper to taste. Keep warm.
5. Remove sweetbreads from water and dry well on a towel. Remove membrane. Sprinkle sweetbreads with salt and white pepper to taste, and lightly flour on all sides. In pan, sautee sweetbreads in clarified butter until lightly browned on all sides.
6. Skim grease from pan, leaving sweetbreads in pan. Add 1 cup Madeira (or Port) wine and reduce until wine barely covers bottom of pan. Add sauce and cook for 5 minutes over low heat, turning sweetbreads occasionally. Add 1 tablespoon sweet butter. Season to taste.
7. Make a bed of spinach on each plate and cover with sweetbreads and sauce. Serve with one or two boiled potatoes.

ROAST LEG OF LAMB WITH GARLIC SAUCE

Jimmy's Place

Ingredients: Yield: 6 portions

Lamb leg, whole, 10- to 12-pound	1
Salt	to taste
Pepper, white	to taste
Thyme	1 teaspoon
Vegetable Oil	½ cup
Onion	1 medium
Carrots	2 medium
Celery	2 stalks
Garlic cloves	10
Garlic, whole	3
White Wine, dry	2 cups
Water	2 quarts
Butter, sweet	2 tablespoons
Corn Starch	if needed

Procedure:

1. Bone lamb (reserve bones), keeping meat in one piece. Remove fat and nerves. Season inside of lamb leg with salt, white pepper, and thyme. Insert 7 cloves of garlic in leg cavity, and tie roast in leg-shape with string. Season outside with salt and white pepper.
2. Break up bones into smaller pieces.
3. On top of stove heat vegetable oil in roasting pan until hot. Add lamb and brown on all sides. Remove from heat. Add to roasting pan 1 medium onion, quartered, 2 medium carrots, 2 celery stalks, and 3 whole garlic. Bake in preheated 375° oven for 25-30 minutes (less for rare lamb).
4. Remove leg of lamb (keeping warm), leaving vegetables and bones. Skim grease.
5. On top of stove add 2 cups dry white wine and 2 quarts water, and reduce to about 4 cups of liquid. Strain liquid, reserving garlic. Mash the garlic through a strainer into sauce. Season to taste and add 2 tablespoons sweet butter. (If sauce is too thin, thicken slightly with corn starch mixed with a little water.)
6. Thinly slice lamb and serve on plates covered with sauce. Cooked spinach and white beans or white rice are recommended accompaniments.

CARAMEL APPLES WITH RUM AND ICE CREAM

Jimmy's Place

Ingredients: Yield: 6 portions

Apples, baking	6 small or
	4 large
Butter, sweet	1½ sticks
Sugar	1⅓ cups
Lemon Juice	1 teaspoon
Rum, dark	1½ tablespoon
Coffee Ice Cream	12 scoops

Procedure:

1. Peel, core, and slice apples fairly thin.
2. Melt butter in skillet and add sugar and lemon juice.
3. Cook over medium heat until sugar turns to a light brown caramel.
4. Add peeled sliced apples and cook 2 to 3 minutes.
5. Add rum and serve immediately in bowls over two scoops of ice cream.

FLOATING ISLANDS WITH ENGLISH SAUCE

Jimmy's Place

Ingredients: Yield: 6 portions

English Sauce
Egg Yolks   8
Sugar $\frac{1}{2}$ pound
Milk $\frac{1}{2}$ quart
Vanilla Extract $\frac{1}{2}$ tablespoon

Floating Islands
Egg Whites   2 cups
Salt   dash
Lemon Juice, fresh   1 teaspoon
Sugar $\frac{1}{2}$ cup
Almonds, sliced $\frac{1}{3}$ cup

Caramel
Water $\frac{1}{2}$ cup
Sugar $\frac{1}{2}$ cup
Lemon Juice, fresh $\frac{1}{4}$ teaspoon

FLOATING ISLANDS WITH ENGLISH SAUCE *(cont'd.)*
Procedure:

1.   Make English Sauce first so it can cool while Floating Islands are being made. In a stainless steel bowl mix well 8 egg yolks and $\frac{1}{2}$ pound of sugar. In a saucepan, heat $\frac{1}{2}$ quart milk almost to the boiling point. Pour hot milk into the bowl and mix well with egg yolks and sugar. Return to saucepan, add $\frac{1}{2}$ tablespoon vanilla, and cook, stirring constantly, until mixture lightly covers a wooden spoon. Remove mixture from heat and strain into a cool bowl set in ice water. Stir occasionally. (If sauce appears too thick, add one or two scoops of vanilla ice cream.)

2.   Fill large, rectangular cake pan almost to capacity with water and bring to a boil. Set aside and beat egg whites.

3.   In mixer, beat 2 cups egg whites with a dash of salt and 1 teaspoon fresh lemon juice until whites begin to stiffen. When they start to stiffen, slowly add $\frac{1}{2}$ cup sugar and continue beating until whites form soft peaks. Do not overbeat! Using two large spoons, form $3 \times 6''$ egg-shapes of meringue and place on surface of hot water in cake pan; allow to sit for 15 minutes. After 15 minutes, turn meringues over, and again allow to sit for 15 minutes. (This is all that is required to cook meringues.)

4.   Remove meringues from water and space neatly in a rectangular glass cake pan. Sprinkle tops with sliced almonds.

5.   Make a caramel in saucepan using $\frac{1}{2}$ cup water and $\frac{1}{2}$ cup sugar with lemon juice. Cook to a light brown color. Spoon lines of caramel over tops of almond-covered meringues.

6.   Spoon cooled English Sauce *around* meringues, but do *not* cover meringues with sauce. Serve in bowls. (Let dessert sit at room temperature until ready to serve; do not refrigerate or caramel will run.)

LE FRANCAIS

LES HORS D'OEUVRE FROIDS

L'ESTURGEON FUME A LA RUSSE LE SAUMON FUME	4.00
LE JAMBON DE CAMPAGNE ET MELON (Prosciutto ham)	3.00
L'AVOCAT FARCI AU CRABE (Avocado with crab meat)	3.25
LE CAVIAR BELUGA (for 2) (Fresh Iranian Beluga caviar)	21.00
LE COCKTAIL DE CREVETTES (Shrimp cocktail)	3.00
LES PATES ET TERRINES MAISON	3.50
LES HUITRES PLEINE MER	2.50
LA BALLOTINE DE SAUMON FROID EN CROUTE	3.50

NOS HORS D'OEUVRES CHAUDS

LA MOUSSELINE DE GRENOUILLES CHAMPENOISE (Frog legs mousse with champagne sauce)	3.25
LE CROUSTADE DE CRAB ET CREVETTES THERMIDOR	3.50
LES COEURS D'ARTICHAUTS "SOPHIE" (Fresh artichokes buttoms with goose liver) An Bearnaise sauce	3.50
LA QUICHE ALSACIENNE	1.75
LA TIMBALE D'ESCARGOTS CHABLISIENNE	3.00
LA CASSEROLETTE DE SCAMPIS PROVENCALE	3.25

NOS POTAGES

LA MARMITE DE CONSOMME MAISON	1.75
LA GRATINEE LYONNAISE (Baked onion soup)	1.50
LE BISQUE DE HOMARD (Lobster bisque)	1.95

LES DELICES DES GOURMETS

LES ROSETTES DE BOEUF MARCHAND DE VIN (Beef medaillon with bordelaise sauce)	9.50
LE CARRE D'AGNEAU PERSILLE BONNE BOUCHE (Lamb rack roast with herbs)	23.00
LE GRENADIN DE VEAU SAUTE AUX CHANTERELLES (Veal steak with special cream sauce and mushrooms)	10.50
LES BLANCS DE FAISAN "BELLE EPOQUE" (Breast of pheasant with morrells for two)	24.00
LE FILET DE BOEUF EN CROUTE "BRILLAT SAVARIN" (Beef wellington for two and with goose liver and truffles sauce)	24.00

NOS ENTREES

LE TOURNEDOS ROSSINI (Filet mignon with goose liver perigueux sauce)	10.50
LE FILET AU POIVRE DES ILES (Filet mignon with fresh green pepper corn)	10.50
LES ROGNONS DE VEAU SAUTES BERICHONNE (Veal kidney with shallots in white wine)	8.50
L'ENTRECOTE A LA MOELLE (Sirloin steak with marrow and red wine sauce)	10.50
LA COTE DE VEAU PRINCE ORLOFF (Veal chop with puree of mushroom soubise sauce)	10.50
LE POUSSIN ALSACIENNE	8.50
LE CANETON BIGARRADE (With orange sauce and wild rice)	8.50
L'ESCALOPE DE RIS DE VEAU CLAMART	10.50

NOS GRILLADES

L'ENTRECOTE DOUBLE BEARNAISE (Broiled double sirloin for two)	21.00
LE FILET GRILLE MAITRE D'HOTEL (Filet mignon with herb butter)	10.50
LE CHATEAUBRIANT BOUQUETIERE (Sauce foyot - sauce bordelaise - for 2)	23.00
LES COTES D'AGNEAU VERT PRE (French lamb chop)	11.00
LA SALADE SPECIALE (Endives - waiteress - avocado - boston - ...t of palm eggs)	2.50

— SUR COMMANDE —
(Order Week before) for 6 Minimum

CONSOMME' DE FAISAN SIBERIEN

LA BARQUETTE DE MOULES PYRAMIDE (in Saison)

L'ASPIC DE FOIE GRAS TRUFFE

LE PATE DE CAILLES LUCCULUS

LE CARRE D'AGNEAU EN CHEMISE DOREE

LE SAUMON EN CROUTE "PAUL BOCUSE"

LE PERDREAUX AUX CHOUX VERTS

LE GRATIN DE QUEUE D'ECREVISSES (in Saison Only)

LE FEUILLETE DE RIS DE VEAU A L'ANCIENNE

LA COTE DE BOEUF AUX CEPES

LA 'ROGNONNADE DE VEAU POELEE A LA JUDIC (for 8)

LE FILET DE BOEUF MARINE EN CHEVREUIL

...ETON FARCI AUX NAVETS
...IX OLIVES

LE FRANCAIS

LE FRANCAIS
The Suburban Phenomenon

Le Francais
269 S. Milwaukee Avenue,
Wheeling, Illinois.

Honored for his culinary imagination and the consistent quality of his food by *Maitre Cuisinier* of France and America, thirty-nine-year-old Chef Jean Banchet has risen, phoenix-like, from the ashes of the 1975 fire that destroyed his first Le Francais in suburban Wheeling. The Banchet establishment was, and is, the Chicago area's premiere French restaurant. It has succeeded famously by word of mouth, and because of showman-chef Jean Banchet's publicity efforts. He is treated by the press and his peers as a culinary genius. Le Francais does not need to advertise for customers. Well-heeled regulars flock to the place as if it were their private club, and new customers wait their turn.

The new restaurant, opened in June 1976, is similar to the old except for some external French Provincial hokeries. Inside, there is the same comfortable seating for patrons (90), but with more elbow room between tables. The main dining room is bright with old copper and fresh flowers.

Also new, but hewing to Banchet's original concept are the service from carts, dramatic presentation of fresh foods, and a bright, brand new kitchen the chef designed from(and with much) scratch.

Tariffs at Le Francais average $45 at dinner and more than $25 at lunch. At these prices, Banchet neither needs nor desires large volume; his 120 to 140 guests per night have made reservations well in advance.

There are sixteen employees at Le Francais providing the gracious service that the food deserves.

Banchet wants to serve "only the best." "I have never prepared uninspired French meals, and never will," says Banchet. What the proprietor-chef will do, however, is pre-

153

Creative menus from Le Francais, one of America's most honored restaurants.

pare any dish in the French epicurean literature, if ordered seven days in advance, for a minimum of four people.

Banchet belongs to the new generation of French chefs which includes Paul Bocuse, Michel Guerard of *cuisine minceur* fame, and Freddy Girardet. One of Banchet's most popular dishes at Le Francais is his Salmon with Sorrel Sauce, originally created by the Troisgrois brothers. Two celebrated inventions of his own include Quiche of Sweetbreads and Mushrooms with spinach, and lobster tail covered with a lobster mousse and baked in puff pastry, served with a Pernod and tarragon sauce.

A native of Roanne, the site of the Troisgrois brothers' restaurant, Banchet apprenticed at the highly regarded Pyramide in Vienne. After a post in London, he came to the Playboy Club in Lake Geneva, Wisconsin, as Executive Chef. Talented Jean Banchet soon had an understandable "consuming desire" to have his own establishment.

"I saw too many things in many of the places where I worked," said the chef. "Too many shortcuts, too much emphasis on cost accounting. I began to put my money aside, and when the moment came, my wife and I scouted all over the Chicago area."

The Wheeling location of Le Francais, forty miles north of Chicago's downtown, was partly determined by Banchet's German-born wife who shrewdly knew "that in America, the customers of French restaurants live in the suburbs."

Banchet refers to his kitchen presence, not immodestly, as "masterful of the mousse." Its proprietor is also masterful of the marketplace. He has firmly ingratiated himself with the culinary establishment. Banchet is "enormously innovative," writes influential *The New York Times* critic Craig Claiborne, who traveled to Wheeling to visit the restaurant: "Le Francais would rank on almost any count with the finest French restaurants in America." And says Mimi Sheraton in *Esquire* Magazine, "Le Francais is little short of a gastronomic miracle . . [and] has to be considered a wonder, and considering Jean Banchet's youth, ability, and dedication, it is likely to remain so."

Left, an idealized drawing of Le Francais. Right, the master himself, Jean Banchet, a terror in the kitchen, pursuing the righteousness of quality, and a public relations dumpling pursuing the right encomium.

SOUPE DE MOULES AU BASILIC
(Mussel Soup with Basil)

Le Francais

Ingredients: Yield: 3 quarts

Mussels, fresh	3 quarts
Shallots, chopped	10
Parsley, chopped	$\frac{1}{4}$ cup
Celery, chopped	2 stalks
Dry White Wine	1 pint
Salt	as needed
Pepper	as needed
Fish Stock (see recipe)	1 quart
Basil Leaves	1 tablespoon
Heavy Cream	1 quart
Egg Yolks	2
Butter, melted	$\frac{1}{2}$ pound
	as needed

Procedure:

1. Wash and clean mussels well. Cook in covered pan with shallots, parsley, celery, wine, salt, and pepper for about 6 minutes or until mussels are open.
2. Pass through a fine strainer, return liquid to saucepan, and reduce to 1 quart.
3. Add fish stock and basil leaves and 3 cups of the cream.
4. Simmer for 3 or 4 minutes and season with salt and pepper. Remove basil leaves.
5. At the last moment add remaining cream mixed with egg yolks and butter. Garnish with mussels and sprinkle with additional basil.
6. Serve very hot.

FISH STOCK

Le Francais

Ingredients:

Yield: 8 to 10 cups

Fish Bones (may include heads with gills removed)	2½ pounds
Celery, chopped	2 cups
Onions, thinly sliced	2 cups
Garlic Clove, sliced	1
Leeks, green part, chopped	2 cups
Thyme, fresh	3 sprigs
Bay Leaf	1
Water	2 quarts
Dry White Wine	¾ cup
Peppercorns	¼ teaspoon
Salt	as needed

Procedure:

1. Combine all ingredients.
2. Bring to a boil and simmer about 20 minutes. Strain.

CLARIFIED BUTTER

Le Francais

Procedure:

1. Place butter in a heat-proof glass measuring cup and let it melt slowly in an oven at 200°F.
2. Do not stir. Pour off the clear liquid, leaving the white substance at the bottom. The clear liquid is clarified butter.

BISQUE DE HOMARD AU SAFRAN
(Lobster Bisque with Saffron)

Le Francais

Ingredients:

Yield: 1 gallon

Lobsters, live	2 large
Butter, clarified	as needed
Cognac	4 ounces
Onion, medium, minced	1
Carrots, medium, diced	2
Leek, medium chopped	1
Shallots, chopped	6
Celery Stalk, large, chopped	1
Tomatoes, fresh, chopped	6
Tomato Paste	$\frac{1}{4}$ cup
Thyme, leaf	$\frac{1}{2}$ teaspoon
Bay Leaf	1
Pepper, cayenne	$\frac{1}{4}$ teaspoon
Tarragon	$1\frac{1}{2}$ teaspoons
Saffron	$\frac{1}{2}$ teaspoon
Fish Stock	2 quarts
White Wine	1 pint
Roux	10 to 12 ounces
Heavy Cream	1 quart

Procedure:

1. Cut lobsters in small pieces, saute in butter, and flambe with half the cognac.
2. Remove from heat and add onion, carrots, leeks, shallots, celery, tomatoes, tomato paste, and seasonings, except tarragon and saffron.
3. Cook 3 or 4 minutes, add tarragon, saffron, fish stock, and wine.
4. Cook for 20 minutes. Add enough roux to thicken slightly. Simmer for 2 minutes.
5. Strain and add cream.
6. Garnish each order with remaining cognac and some diced lobster.

CONSOMME DE FAISAN SIBERIEN
(Pheasant Consomme)

Le Francais

Ingredients:

Yield: 2 quarts

Chicken Bones	1 pound
Pheasant Bones	2 pounds
Beef Knuckles	1 pound
Leeks, medium	2
Carrots, medium	2
Celery, rib, large	1
Egg Whites	2
Chervil Leaves	1 tablespoon
Salt	as needed
Chicken Broth	2 quarts
Pheasant Meat, cooked	1 pound
Egg White	1
Cream	1 quart
Salt	as needed
Pepper	as needed
Truffles, canned, chopped	as desired
Goose Liver, julienne	as needed
Celery Heart	as needed

Procedure:

1. Put bones and vegetables through a grinder.
2. Mix with 2 egg whites, chervil leaves, salt, and chicken broth. Simmer for $1\frac{1}{2}$ hours.
3. Strain through cheesecloth. Reserve.
4. Grind pheasant meat very finely, mix with 1 egg white, and chill for 1 hour.
5. Slowly add cream, salt, pepper, and chopped truffles to pheasant mixture. Refrigerate for 30 minutes.
6. With a teaspoon make small dumplings of chilled mixture and poach them in the consomme.
7. Garnish the consomme with pheasant dumplings, julienne of goose liver, truffles, and celery heart.

QUICHE OF SWEETBREADS AND MUSHROOMS

Le Francais

Ingredients:

Yield: 6 portions

Sweetbreads, 1 small pair	$\frac{3}{4}$ pound
Water	as needed
Salt	as needed
Pepper	as needed
Spinach, fresh	$\frac{1}{2}$ pound
Mushrooms, fresh, sliced	$\frac{1}{2}$ pound
Butter	6 tablespoons
Eggs	4
Heavy Cream	$1\frac{1}{2}$ cups plus $\frac{1}{3}$ cup
Nutmeg, grated	$\frac{1}{8}$ teaspoon
Dry White Wine	$\frac{1}{4}$ cup
Pastry	6 individual pies or 1 10-inch pie

QUICHE OF SWEETBREADS AND MUSHROOMS *(cont'd.)*

Procedure:

1. Soak sweetbreads for several hours in cold water to cover. Drain.
2. Cover again with cold water, bring to a boil and simmer 5 minutes. Drain, run under cold water, and let cool. Chill well.
3. Place sweetbreads in a dish and cover them with a weight. Weight down, refrigerated, at least six hours.
4. Trim off outside membranes and veins. Cut into 1-inch cubes. Sprinkle with salt and pepper. Set aside.
5. Sprinkle mushrooms with salt and pepper and set aside.
6. Cook spinach about 1 minute. Drain and run under cold water. Squeeze out moisture. Chop coarsely, sprinkle with salt and pepper, and set aside.
7. Heat 2 tablespoons butter in each of three skillets.
8. Cook sweetbreads in one skillet, stirring and tossing about 5 minutes.
9. Cook spinach about 2 minutes in second skillet. Set aside.
10. Combine eggs, $1\frac{1}{2}$ cups cream, salt, pepper, and nutmeg. Beat well.
11. Cook mushrooms in third skillet about 3 minutes. Add sweetbreads and any pan juices to mushrooms. Cook together about 1 minute.
12. Scoop out sweetbread mixture and set aside. Add wine and cook until almost totally reduced. Add $\frac{1}{3}$ cup cream and cook, stirring, 1 minute. Add this to the egg and cream mixture.
13. Line pans with pastry.
14. Place spinach in pie shell. Cover with sweetbread-mushroom mixture. Pour in egg mixture.
15. Place pans on a baking sheet. Put an oven rack on floor of oven and set baking sheet on rack. Bake in oven at 450°F. for 20 minutes for individual pies or 30 minutes for large pie.
16. Reduce heat to 350°F. and bake 10 or 15 minutes longer.

SALMON WITH SORREL SAUCE

Le Francais

Ingredients: Yield: 4 to 6 portions

Fillet of Salmon or Striped Bass	3 to $3\frac{1}{2}$ pounds
Shallots, chopped	$\frac{1}{4}$ cup
Fish Stock (see recipe below)	4 cups
Dry Vermouth	$1\frac{1}{2}$ cups
Dry White Wine	1 cup
Heavy Cream	$2\frac{1}{4}$ cups
Salt	as needed
Pepper	as needed
*Fish Glaze (optional)	3 tablespoons
Sorrel or Spinach, fresh, finely shredded	$\frac{1}{4}$ pound
Egg Yolks	4
Butter	2 tablespoons
Lemon Juice	$\frac{1}{2}$ lemon
Flour	as needed
Butter, clarified	$\frac{1}{2}$ cup

Procedure:

1. Cut fish on bias into $\frac{1}{4}$-inch slices. Flatten gently with mallet. Refrigerate.
2. Combine shallots, fish stock, vermouth, and white wine. Cook about 45 minutes until liquid is reduced to about one half cup.
3. Add 2 cups cream, salt, and pepper. Bring to a boil and stir in fish glaze, if used. Cook about 2 minutes.
4. Add sorrel or spinach and bring to a boil. Remove from heat.
5. Beat egg yolks and $\frac{1}{4}$ cup heavy cream together. Add to above mixture. Stir in 2 tablespoons butter and lemon juice. Keep hot but do not allow to boil.
6. Dredge fish slices in flour and cook in clarified butter until golden brown, about 1 minute per side.
7. Spoon sauce over fish and serve.

*Note:

Fish glaze is a long-simmered reduction of fish stock. The stock is cooked many hours until it becomes a thick, gelatinous, brown mass like thick, smooth caramel.

COUPE NORMANDE

Le Francais

Ingredients: Yield: 6 portions

Apples, cooking, firm	4
Butter	$\frac{1}{4}$ cup
Sugar	$\frac{1}{2}$ cup
Calvados or Applejack	$\frac{1}{4}$ cup
Vanilla Ice Cream	6 portions

Procedure:

1. Core and peel apples. Cut into quarters and then into slices. This should make about 4 cups.
2. Heat butter in a heavy skillet and add apples.
3. Cook, stirring gently, about 6 to 10 minutes. The slices should remain firm and not become mushy.
4. Add sugar and cook 2 minutes, stirring and tossing gently.
5. Sprinkle with calvados and ignite.
6. Serve hot or warm over ice cream.

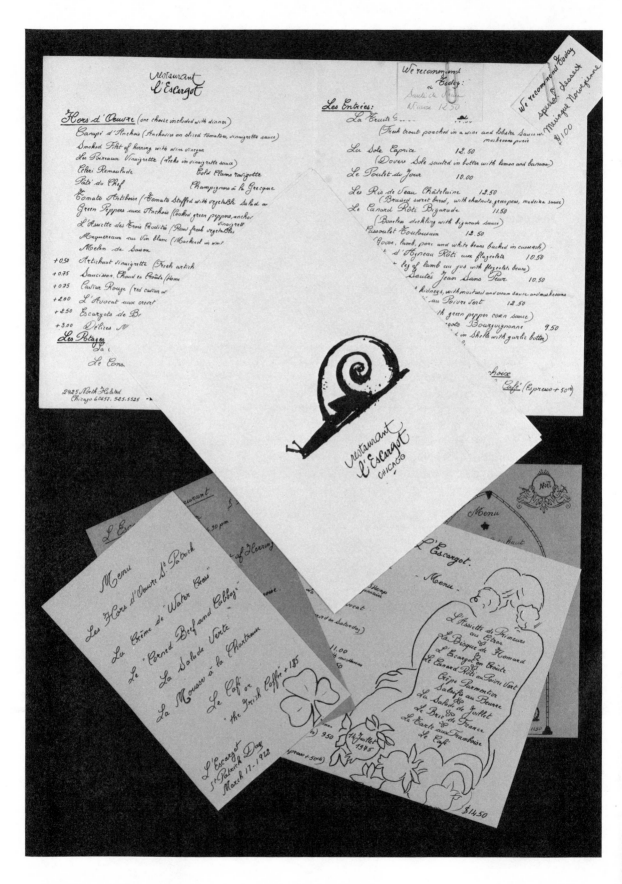

L'Escargot

French Provincial Cooking, the New Chicago Tradition

L'Escargot
2925 North Halsted Street
Chicago, Illinois.

A few minutes by cab from the near north side, and Chicago's New Town, nestles the unpretentious French Provincial restaurant, L'Escargot. In just over ten years, the restaurant has become a Chicago tradition, and perhaps more than a tradition since its reputation for excellence approaches the legendary.

When L'Escargot opened in 1968, its fringe location might have remained a problem. Happily, today it is in the heart of one of the city's newest smart neighborhoods, the site of abundant renovation projects.

Just as L'Escargot broke ground with its location, the restaurant also pioneered more important areas of cuisine and presentation. Owner Alan Tutzer recalls that a decade ago, his home town did not have a Provincial French restaurant. Chicago had versions of expensive New York-style French restaurants, but Tutzer had something else in mind. "An honest establishment" that offered "authentic fare of the French provinces." In other words, small-town cooking, but *French* small-town cooking, which is a cuisine unto itself.

Tutzer was joined in this venture by Lucien Verge, a young French chef whose background included an apprenticeship at L'Ecole Profesionnelle de Cuisine de Lyon. Verge's professional experience is interesting and particularly relevant to his present position of Chef de cuisine at L'Escargot. Drafted into the French army, Verge became food manager for a paratroop unit and sky patrol unit in Grenoble. It was valuable experience, for in the armed forces of France, food means more than nourishment. Imaginative good food is a serious matter of morale. The chef learned a great deal.

After serving, Verge went to the Hotel Crillon in Paris and later to the Plaza Athenee. He came to the United States as

165

For eleven years, L'Escargo has been the benchmark of French cookery in Chicago. Its criteria: consistently good food, great comfort and informality.

sous chef at New York's famous Veau d'Or where he worked
for six years. Then Alan Tutzer persuaded Verge to come to
Chicago and thus began their successful collaboration.

If L'Escargot's unassuming exterior is "Chicago Bungaloid"
in style, its understated interior is sheer *a la Lyonnaise.* It
took considerable effort on Tutzer's part to renovate and
"purify" the interior. What he achieved is as authentically
French Provincial as a re-creation would allow. Although the
restaurant is small (two rooms seating ninety-seven), it has
an expansive feeling. Open, bright, simple, cheerful,
L'Escargot has a special quality, a *sourire certaine* unique in
Chicago. There are comfortable booths, or white-clothed
tables with bentwood chairs, French posters—from Lucien
Verge's own collection—and street signs from France that are
decorative and unobtrusive. An area held in great affection
by many is the bar/dining room with its long, dark oak bar,
and display tables of hors d'oeuvre and fresh fruit.

In one sense, L'Escargot is a "no nonsense" kind of restaurant
where food is all-important. On the other hand, the am-
biance and service are so cheerful that "no nonsense" seems
misleading.

Certainly L'Escargot is not for everyone, but the restaurant's success is based on the fact that it does not try to be. More than three-quarters of its patrons are regulars, about twenty percent from out of the city. New customers are just as likely to be from New York or San Francisco as from Chicago. Probably they learn about L'Escargot from friends, or perhaps they read United Airlines' magazine where the restaurant often receives "Excellence in Dining" Awards.

Ninety percent of L'Escargot's clientele order wine, whether it is a bottle of French regional at $7.00, *vin ordinaire* by the glass ($1.50), or a 1969 Chateau Cheval Blanc St. Emillion at $42.50.

Two etchings (by Anita E. Alexander) capture the naive charm of L'Escargot's exterior (opposite) and bar seating area (right).

L'Escargot's twenty employees serve eighty to 100 customers on a weekday night and up to 200 customers on weekends. The restaurant's overall check average is $21, a figure that includes liquor or wine, and takes into account the restaurant's *prix fixe* ($7.50) *petit diner,* now called the "Early Special Plan." This dinner is a merchandising concept of owner Alan Tutzer to build business in the otherwise slow hours between 5 and 6:15 p.m. Considering the quality of food and variety of offerings, this four course meal, with coffee, is quite a bargain.

All the recipes prepared at L'Escargot are favorites of Lucien Verge, although he admits that "some are more favorite than others." Among them, his Gateau de Foie (liver souffle) or the stunning Feuillete de Cervelle (veal brains in pastry with tomato sauce) requires time-consuming preparation and are available only by advance order.

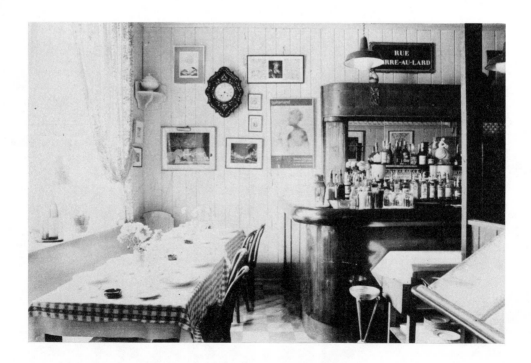

Neither drawings, however quaint, nor photographs do justice to the cozy welcome of L'Escargot; the hospitality has to be experienced. The photo on page 170 attempts to show the informal graciousness of L'Escargot's main dining room.

There is also a difference between L'Escargot's weekday and weekend menu. Because of greater volume, the latter emphasizes simpler preparation. There is no boning of fish, and the duck offering is limited to *a l'orange;* whereas, during the week, duck might be prepared with a variety of three sauces. Also, throughout the week there is more emphasis on kidneys and sweetbreads, steak au poivre, and the restaurant's famous baked onion soup. Always available is the city's best cassoulet (it takes three days to prepare): white beans, salt pork, sausage, goose, served in an earthenware pot. The price of $15.50 includes appetizer, soup, salad, dessert, and coffee.

Chef Verge is a proud man who maintains not only an authentic menu of the French provinces, but one unavailable anywhere else in the city.

"The important thing is not to have just an authentic restaurant, or a money making one, or a popular one . . . the significant professional thing is to have a combination of all three," states Alan Tutzer. L'Escargot succeeds in these goals. In fulfilling a need, it has helped create a new market of sophisticated diners. Any other serious French restaurant in the Chicago area is in its debt.

ESCARGOTS FORESTIERE

L'Escargot

Ingredients: Yield: 6 portions

Butter, sweet	$\frac{3}{4}$ pound
Parsley, small bunch, chopped	1
Garlic, minced	1 clove
Shallots, chopped	4
Salt	as needed
Pepper, white	as needed
Pernod Liqueur	1 tablespoon
Mushroom Caps	18
Butter, sweet	as needed
Salt	as needed
Pepper, white	as needed
Snails	36
White Wine	1 ounce

Procedure:

1. Soften butter and add parsley, garlic, shallots, salt, pepper, and Pernod. Mix thoroughly.
2. Place mushroom caps on a dish, cavity side up. Dot each with a little sweet butter and sprinkle with salt and pepper. Bake in oven at 450°F. for about 10 minutes. Let cool.
3. Place 2 snails on each mushroom cap. Spoon enough butter mixture over each to cover the snails. Put back in oven and heat until butter is melted.
4. Sprinkle with white wine just before serving.
5. Accompany with french bread and white Burgundy.

CREME D'AVOCAT
(Cream of Avocado Soup)

L'Escargot

Ingredients:

Yield: 8 portions

Butter	4 ounces
Leeks, sliced	2
Onion, chopped	1 large
Chicken Bouillon Cubes	3
Water	2 quarts
Salt	as needed
Pepper	as needed
Potatoes, raw, medium, peeled, diced	4
Avocados	3
Whipping Cream	1 pint
Light Cream	1 cup
Milk	1 cup
Worcestershire Sauce	as needed
Small Croutons	as needed

Procedure:

1. Simmer butter, leeks, and onions for 5 minutes.
2. Add chicken bouillon cubes, water, salt, and pepper and simmer 15 minutes.
3. Add potatoes and cook 15 minutes more. Strain through a vegetable mill and let cool completely.
4. Peel and cut avocados. Put into a blender and fill the blender, half with strained soup and half with cream and milk. Blend well. Mix with any remaining soup, milk, or cream. Add Worcestershire sauce to taste.
5. Serve well chilled with small croutons.

FEUILLETE DE CERVELLE
(Veal Brains in Pastry with Tomato Sauce)

L'Escargot

Ingredients:

Yield: 6 portions

Veal Brains	3
Vinegar	$\frac{1}{3}$ cup
Bay Leaves	2 or 3
Celery Rib	1
Salt	as needed
Flour	as needed
Butter	4 ounces
Oil	2 ounces
Mushrooms, fresh, sliced	1 pound
Puff Pastry	2 pounds
Egg Wash	as needed
Tomato Sauce	as needed

Procedure:

1. Soak brains in cold water for one or two hours. Pull off the covering membrane by sliding fingers under the skin and around cavities. (Working under running water makes it easier to remove membrane and blood clots.)
2. Place brains in water to cover, add vinegar, bay leaves, celery, and a little salt. Simmer for 10 minutes. Allow brains to cool in this broth.
3. Cut brains in half lengthwise. Season with salt and pepper, dust with flour, and place in skillet with butter and oil. Allow them to color but not cook on both sides. Remove and let cool.
4. Saute mushrooms lightly and allow them to cool.
5. Roll half the puff pastry dough into a rectangle 24 by $5\frac{1}{2}$ inches, $\frac{1}{4}$ inch thick. Arrange brains on dough and put mushrooms on top of them.
6. Roll out second half of dough the same way. Fold it in half lengthwise but do not press together. With a knife, cut slits $\frac{1}{2}$ inch apart from the folded center to within one inch of the edge.
7. Working with the brain-covered dough, wet the edges well. Place the slit piece over it, unfolding it to cover completely. Seal edges well by pressing together with a fork.
8. Brush with egg wash. Bake in an oven at 375°F. for 35 to 40 minutes.
9. Slice and serve hot with tomato sauce around the pastry.

GATEAU DE FOIE
(Liver Souffle)

L'Escargot

Ingredients: Yield: 4 portions

Butter	$\frac{1}{4}$ cup
Flour	3 tablespoons
Milk	2 cups
Worcestershire Sauce	dash
Salt	1 teaspoon
Pepper, white	dash
Egg Yolks, beaten	2
Chicken Livers, raw, finely chopped	6
Parsley, chopped	8 sprigs
Garlic, minced	3 cloves
Cream of Tartar	pinch
Egg Whites	2
Tomato Sauce	as needed

Procedure:

1. Make a roux of butter and flour. Heat milk to boiling and stir slowly into roux. Cook and stir about one minute or until thickened. Remove from heat.
2. Add Worcestershire sauce, salt, pepper, and egg yolks. Put mixture into a large bowl and add livers, parsley, and garlic.
3. Cover the entire inside surface of a 1-quart souffle mold with butter. Dust well with flour. Put mold in refrigerator to preserve coating until ready for use.
4. Add cream of tartar to egg whites and beat until very firm. Add 2 tablespoons of whipped whites to the liver mixture and mix in. Gently fold in the remainder of the egg whites.
5. Pour into souffle mold. Bake on center rack of oven at 400°F. for 25 minutes.
6. Serve immediately with tomato sauce around it.

CORNISH HEN GRANDMERE

L'Escargot

Ingredients:

Yield: 8 portions

Cornish Hens and Giblets	8
Salt	as needed
Pepper	as needed
Celery Rib, chopped	1
Carrots, medium, diced	2
Onion, large, diced	1
Dry White Wine	2 cups
Veal Stock or Consomme	1 pint
Cornstarch	as needed
Mushrooms, fresh, diced, sauteed	2 pounds
Onions, small, glazed	32
New Potatoes, medium, rissole	16
Salt Pork, diced, blanched, sauteed	1 pound

Procedure:

1. Salt and pepper hens. Roast them on a bed of celery, carrots, onion, and giblets for about 25 minutes in the oven at 350°F. Remove and keep warm.
2. De-glaze pan with wine. Add veal stock or consomme and simmer 10 or 15 minutes. Strain liquid. Thicken with a little cornstarch, cooking and stirring until desired thickness is reached. Strain.
3. Serve hens garnished with mushrooms, onions, potatoes, and salt pork, basted with gravy.

TRUITE AU BEAUJOLAIS

L'Escargot

Ingredients: Yield: 6 portions

Butter, melted	2 ounces
Carrot, medium, diced	1
Onion, medium, diced	1
Bay Leaf, small	1
Celery Rib, chopped	1
Parsley Sprigs, chopped	2 to 3
Garlic Clove	1
Thyme	pinch
Fish Stock	1 quart
Red Wine	$1\frac{1}{2}$ cup
Salt	as needed
Peppercorns, whole	6
Mushrooms, fresh	12
Brook Trout, fresh	6
Whipped Cream	$\frac{1}{2}$ cup
Mayonnaise	$\frac{1}{2}$ cup
Horseradish, grated	1 teaspoon

Procedure:

1. Combine and saute in butter the carrot, onion, bay leaf, celery, parsley, garlic, and thyme.
2. Add fish stock, wine, salt, and peppercorns. Add mushroom stems. Simmer 1 hour. Strain and cool.
3. Place trout in deep pan, add mushroom caps and strained sauce. Cook slowly for 8 minutes. Allow broth and trout to cool, then strain the broth. Skin and dry trout carefully. Skim grease from broth.
4. Arrange trout on platter and garnish with mushroom caps. Cover with broth which should, at this point, be slightly gelatinous.
5. Serve cold with a side sauce made of whipped cream, mayonnaise, and a dash of horseradish.

ENDIVES FLAMANDE

L'Escargot

Ingredients: Yield: 5 portions

Belgian Endive	10
Lemons	$1\frac{1}{2}$
Salt	as needed
Sugar	pinch
Ham, thin slices	10
Bechamel Sauce, thick	1 pint
Whipping Cream	1 pint
Swiss Cheese, grated	as needed
Clarified Butter	as needed

Procedure:

1. Make a cross-shaped incision in the stem end of each endive. Sprinkle with lemon juice. Place in a pan and cover with water. Add salt and a pinch of sugar. Cook at least 45 minutes or until tender. Allow to cool.
2. Dry endive well. Wrap each in a thin slice of ham and place in a buttered baking dish.
3. Cover each with a generous portion of Bechamel sauce and cream.
4. Sprinkle with cheese, then with clarified butter.
5. Bake in oven at 350°F. for 15 minutes.

TRUITE PAIVA

L'Escargot

Ingredients: Yield: 4 portions

Brook Trout, boned, cleaned, scales and fins removed	4
Butter	$\frac{1}{5}$ pound
Flour	5 tablespoons
Milk or Light Cream	1 cup
Salt	as needed
Pepper, white	as needed
Mushrooms, fresh	$1\frac{1}{2}$ pounds
Butter	as needed
Shallots, chopped	4
Carrot, medium	$\frac{1}{2}$
Celery Rib	$\frac{1}{2}$
Leek	$\frac{1}{4}$
Small Bouquet Garni, parsley, bay leaf	1
Dry White Wine	$\frac{1}{5}$ gallon
Water	1 cup
Whipping Cream	$2\frac{1}{2}$ pints
Egg Yolks	2

Procedure:

1. Make roux of $\frac{1}{5}$ pound butter and the flour. Heat milk or light cream and thicken with 2 tablespoons of the roux. Cook until thickened, stirring constantly. Season with salt and pepper.
2. Reserve 4 mushroom caps for garnish. Chop remainder very fine and saute with onion in a little butter for about 10 minutes. Stir in the white sauce.
3. Open each trout flat, season with salt and pepper. Spoon mushroom mixture on the trout and fold closed.
4. Sprinkle chopped shallots in a shallow baking dish. Lay trout on top of shallots. Cut carrot, celery, and leek into julienne strips, sprinkle over trout and add bouquet garni.
5. Add wine and water, cover with aluminum foil and simmer 7 minutes. Let stand 10 minutes. Carefully remove trout, cover, and keep warm.

SALADE DE CHICOREE AVEC CHAPON
(Chicory Salad with Garlic Bread)

L'Escargot

Ingredients: Yield: 8 portions

Chicory Heads (not too green)	2
Heels of French Bread	4
Garlic Cloves	2
French Mustard, prepared	1 teaspoon
Wine Vinegar, red	2 tablespoons
Olive Oil	$\frac{1}{2}$ cup
Salt	as needed
Pepper	as needed

Procedure:

1. Wash chicory and dry well.
2. Rub bread heels all over well with garlic. The result is a *chapon*. Cut into small cubes.
3. Tear chicory and toss with bread cubes.
4. Mix mustard, vinegar, oil, salt, and pepper. Add chicory mixed with bread cubes and toss lightly.

TRUITE PAIVA *(cont'd.)*

6. Pour off liquid in pan, leaving $\frac{1}{5}$ of it to make sauce. Add 2 pints of whipping cream to pan and reduce to about 4 cups. Add enough roux to reach the desired thickness, about $2\frac{1}{2}$ tablespoons. Cook about 5 minutes, stirring constantly.
7. Make Sabayon sauce by whipping $\frac{1}{2}$ pint of cream, then fold in beaten egg yolks.
8. Remove skin and heads of trout. Place trout on buttered serving dish. Garnish with sauteed mushroom caps. Pour cream sauce over trout. Spread Sabayon sauce over all and glaze in oven.

CELERI REMOULADE

L'Escargot

Ingredients: Yield: 6 portions

Celery Root	2 pounds
Lemon	1
Salt	$\frac{1}{2}$ teaspoon
Pepper, white	dash
Egg Yolks	6
French Mustard, prepared	$\frac{1}{4}$ cup
Red Wine Vinegar	1 tablespoon
Oil	3 cups
Salt	as needed
Pepper	as needed

Procedure:

1. Cut off both ends of the celery root. Stand it on a cutting board and peel by slicing the skin down all around the sides. Lay the root on its side and cut slices about $\frac{1}{8}$ inch thick. Lay each slice flat and cut into julienne strips.
2. Put strips into a bowl and add juice from 1 lemon to prevent discoloration. Add $\frac{1}{2}$ teaspoon salt and dash of pepper.
3. Mix egg yolks and mustard vigorously. Slowly beat oil into the mixture. Beat in vinegar and add salt and pepper. Check seasonings.
4. Add celery root strips and toss lightly to mix.
5. Serve with thinly sliced Italian salami or prosciutto ham or serve on a Boston lettuce leaf.

POIRES VALENTIN

L'Escargot

Ingredients:　　　　　　　　　　　　　　　　Yield: 6 portions

Pears, whole, peeled, stem preserved, poached in light sugar, syrup, lemon, and vanilla	6
Egg Yolks	4
Milk, scalded	2 cups
Sugar	2 ounces
Flour	2 ounces
Vanilla	few drops
Whipping Cream	2 cups
Gelatin, softened	$\frac{1}{2}$ teaspoon
Kirsch	2 ounces
Meringue Shells	6
Raspberry Sauce or Melba Sauce	2 ounces
Vanilla Sauce	as needed

Procedure:

1. Mix sugar and flour, beat in egg yolks. Slowly add hot milk. Cook and stir until thickened. Add vanilla and softened gelatin. Strain if necessary and allow to cool.
2. Whip cream and add 1 cup of it and 1 ounce of the kirsch to the cooked and cooled custard.
3. Fill meringue shells with the mixture. Place a dry, cold pear, upright, on top. Decorate with the remaining whipped cream.
4. Lace with raspberry sauce mixed with remaining kirsch. Pour a little vanilla sauce around the meringue.

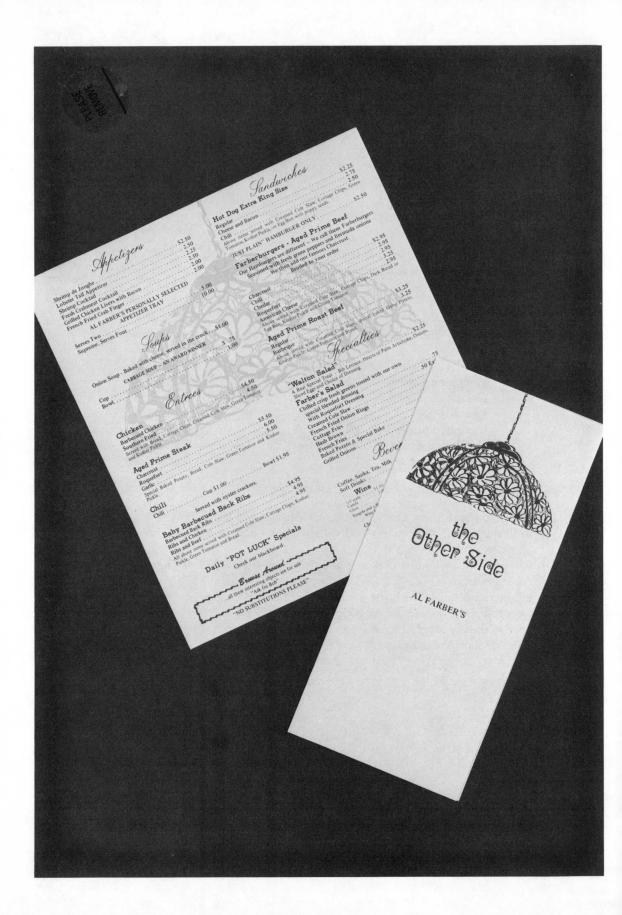

Sandwiches

Hot Dog Extra King Size
Regular $2.25
Cheese and Bacon 2.75
Chili 2.50
Above items served with Creamed Cole Slaw, Cottage Chips, Green
Tomatoe, Kosher Pickle, on Egg Bun with poppy seeds. $2.50

"JUST PLAIN" HAMBURGER ONLY

Farberburgers - Aged Prime Beef
Our flamburgers are different — We call them Farberburgers
Seasoned with fresh green peppers and Bermuda onions
We then add our famous Charcrust.
Broiled to your order

Charcrust $2.95
Chili 2.95
Chedar 2.95
Roquefort 3.25
American Cheese 2.95
Above served with Creamed Cole Slaw, Cottage Chips, Dark Bread or
Egg Bun, Kosher Pickle and Green Tomatoe.

Aged Prime Roast Beef
Regular $3.25
Barbeque 3.25
Above served with Creamed Cole Slaw, special Baked Idaho Potato,
Kosher Pickle, Green Tomatoe and Bread.

Appetizers

Shrimp de Jonghe $2.50
Lobster Tail Appetizer 2.25
Shrimp Cocktail 2.50
Fresh Crabmeat Cocktail 2.00
Grilled Chicken Livers with Bacon 2.00
French Fried Crab Finger 5.00
AL FARBER'S PERSONALLY SELECTED
APPETIZER TRAY 10.00

Serves Two
Supreme, Serves Four

Soups

Onion Soup - Baked with cheese, served in the crock $1.00
CABBAGE SOUP — AN AWARD WINNER
Cup .... $.75
Bowl 1.00

Entrees

Chicken
Barbecued Chicken $4.50
Southern Fried 4.50
Served with Bread, Cottage Chips, Creamed Cole Slaw, Green Tomatoe
and Koshel Pickle.

Aged Prime Steak
Charcrust $5.50
Roquefort 6.00
Garlic 5.50
Special Baked Potato, Bread, Cole Slaw, Green Tomatoe and Koshel
Pickle.

Chili
Chili ...... Cup $1.00 .... Bowl $1.95
Served with oyster crackers.

Baby Barbecued Back Ribs
Barbecued Back Ribs $4.95
Ribs and Chicken 4.95
Ribs and Beef 4.95
All above items served with Creamed Cole Slaw, Cottage Chips, Kosher
Pickle, Green Tomatoe and Bread.

Specialties

"Walton Salad" $2.25
A Real Special Treat, Bib Lettuce, Hearts of Palm Artichoke, Onions,
Sliced Eggs and Choice of Dressing.
Farber's Salad .... .75
Chilled crisp fresh greens tossed with our own
special blended dressing
With Roquefort Dressing .... 50 Ex
Creamed Cole Slaw
French Fried Onion Rings
Cottage Fries
Hash Brown
French Fries
Baked Potato & Special Bake
Grilled Onions

Beverages

Coffee, Sanka, Tea, Milk
Soft Drinks

Wine

Daily "POT LUCK" Specials
Check our blackboard.

— *Browse Around* —
...all these interesting objects are for sale
"Ask for Bob"

"NO SUBSTITUTIONS PLEASE"

the Other Side

AL FARBER'S

the Other Side

Fast Food that Isn't

The Other Side
Belden Stratford Hotel,
2300 Lincoln Park West,
Chicago, Illinois.

The largely, but not entirely, under-forty group that crowds The Other Side six nights a week (the house is dark on Sunday) may or may not be familiar with New York's Maxwell's Plum, and even though Bob Farber, the proprietor of The Other Side, was partially motivated by the success and decor of the Big Apple's Plum, his establishment is very much his own, and very much north side Chicago.

The Lincoln Park West highrise hotel and residential strip, which runs for four blocks along Lincoln Park's western boundary, is one of Chicago's more interesting lively-but-quietly-active restaurant rows. The northern end has long been the reserve of the Farber family. Al Farber's, a white tablecloth steak house, has been an attraction of the Belden Stratford Hotel since 1956 when it moved there from a downtown location.

Bob Farber grew up in the restaurant business with particular experience in his father's meat-and-potato specialty area, an area which is, after all, a large part of Chicago's dining-out scene.

When Bob Farber, with his partner, Nathan Silver, opened The Other Side in 1972, he wanted to draw on his experience but open a new kind of market place. The location was ideal, the same address, same hotel, and directly across the lobby from the established steak house. His interesting challenge: to operate a restaurant that would complement, not compete with, Al Farber's. Bob also wanted a lower food cost, higher turnover, and as much volume business as a seventy-eight-seat establishment could manage. He decided that the appearance of his new restaurant was the make-or-break factor in drawing the lively crowd who would be his new customers.

183

Bob Farber's very personal bistro, The Other Side, allows customers to fast-fork their food or dawdle in style, as they prefer.

The Other Side is a happy melange. The room is cluttered but not crowded, filled with a few antique pieces, and smaller decorative accessories from Victorian stained glass panels and lampshades to old posters, farmhouse furnishings, and a stop signal that blends its three colors gently in the background. Almost everything is for sale; what goes is replaced by something new/old. Thus, change and variety.

Also in the background: the sound of jukebox records, music from the 40s and 50s. The whole thing works. It creates the atmosphere that Farber had in mind. But this feeling of eclectic clutter is deceptive because, for Farber's business purposes, it does not get in the way of an efficiently planned, quick-food, fast-service operation.

The Other Side does three to four turns during the week and, on Friday and Saturday nights, four to six sittings. Nine people, including the host, can handle the volume; in The Other Side's relaxed-but-hustle atmosphere, people do not mind waiting. Too, there is always the bar, which does a very good business indeed.

Bob Farber's restaurant is a juggle of different foodservice concepts, and his act a balancing one. He has made the most of a new generation's attitude towards "hurried leisure."

"The Other Side satisfies the public's need for change and variety. We offer both a brief encounter and a total experience; we're friendly and the food is awfully good," says Farber.

The food *is* good and Farber's menu is central to his concept. It could best be called an expansive/limited menu. There are six appetizers and a special appetizer tray, onion soup, a deservedly popular cabbage soup, as well as the house chili. Steak, chicken, and barbecued back ribs offer solid entrees, and there are, of course, sandwiches, salads, and hamburgers. "Our hamburgers are different. We call them 'Farberburgers,' seasoned with fresh green peppers and Bermuda onions and broiled with our 'Charcrust.' " (Charcrust is the Farbers' special seasoning used for broiling steaks and other meats in both restaurants.)

The Other Side's daily potluck specials ("check our blackboard") are of particular merchandising note because, at $4.50 and $5.50 they provide a bit of personal down-home cookin'. These items range from chicken roquefort, chicken cacciatore and pan-fried sole or perch, to Russian meatballs and sauteed chicken livers in Burgundy with spaghetti. Because of Farber's promotion imagination, The Other Side also offers a very successful "Thanksgiving Dinner" on the last Thursday of every month. The overall check average is $7.95.

Although the idea behind his establishment may not have originated with Bob Farber, the successful Chicago execution of the idea bears Farber's personal imprint.

"Ours is a changing market with changing customer tastes. The Other Side is never monotonous. We try to give people variety and change. It's a difficult thing, maintaining the interest of a volatile market, but it's our goal to meet that challenge," notes Farber.

A challenging goal. A lively realization.

Images of the original Other Side.

Shortly before the publication of this book, Bob Farber's Other Side closed its doors for the first time since 1972, because of a lease dispute with the property owners. The new location of the Other Side (and Farber's Steak House) has not yet been determined. As of March 1979, Farber was seeking a location where he could recreate his successful menu and service concepts in a setting "as close as possible" to the original Other Side.

ONION SOUP

The Other Side

Ingredients:

Yield: 10 gallons

Onion, chopped	30 pounds
Butter	1 pound
Paprika	2 tablespoons
Hydrolyzed Vegetable Protein	1 cup
Water	10 gallons
Beef Base	1 pound
Pepper, white	2 tablespoons
Worcestershire Sauce	4 ounces
Bread Crusts, toasted, cubed	as needed
Mozzarella Cheese, thin slices	as needed
Paprika	as needed

Procedure:

1. Saute onion with butter, paprika, and hydrolyzed vegetable protein until onion is only slightly firm.
2. Add water, beef base, pepper, and Worcestershire sauce.
3. Simmer 30 minutes. Pour into serving crocks.
4. Sprinkle toasted bread cubes on each crock. Top with slice of cheese. Bake in oven at 400°F. for 4 minutes or until cheese bubbles. Sprinkle with paprika.

CABBAGE SOUP

The Other Side

Ingredients:

Yield: 10 gallons

Beef Chuck, diced	9 pounds
Cabbage, medium, chopped	12
Onions, large, chopped	3
Tomatoes, canned, whole, peeled	1 #10 can
Beef Base	1 pound
Sour Salt	$\frac{3}{4}$ cup
Sugar	7 pounds
Water	$8\frac{3}{4}$ gallons

Procedure:

1. Cover meat with water, bring to a boil, drain, and rinse meat.
2. Put meat into soup kettle and add remaining ingredients.
3. Simmer 45 minutes.

CHOPPED EGG SALAD

The Other Side

Ingredients:

Yield: 1 gallon

Pepper, white	$\frac{1}{4}$ cup
Salt	3 tablespoons
Salad Dressing	3 quarts
Sour Cream	3 pints
Eggs, hard-cooked, coarsely chopped	15 dozen
Onions, Bermuda, medium, chopped	15

Procedure:

1. Blend seasonings with salad dressing and sour cream.
2. Add eggs and onion and toss lightly together.

ROAST SIRLOIN OF BEEF

The Other Side

Ingredients: Yield: 30 to 35 portions

Sirloin of Beef	12 to 15 pounds
Celery, medium bunch, chopped	2
Carrots, bunch, chopped	1
Onions, Bermuda, chopped	3
*Roto-Roast Seasoning	as needed

Procedure:

1. Place roast in pan with vegetables. Cover entire roast with Roto-Roast.
2. Bake, uncovered, in oven at 400°F. for 1 hour and 20 minutes, turning roast every 15 minutes. Meat will be extra rare.

*Note:

"Roto-Roast" is Farber's own blend of spices and herbs for use as coating on items to be cooked in a rotisserie, broiler, or oven.

FARBERBURGER

The Other Side

Ingredients: Yield: 65 portions

Prime Aged Beef, medium ground	30 pounds
Onions, Bermuda, finely chopped	6
Green Peppers, chopped	10
Eggs	18
Garlic Powder	2 tablespoons
*Charcrust Seasoning	as needed

*Note:

"Charcrust" is Farber's own special blend of herbs and spices. It is used over surface of meat to form a crust that seals in all the juices. No other seasoning is needed.

RUSSIAN MEAT BALLS

The Other Side

Ingredients: Yield: 25 portions, 4 balls each

Prime Beef, ground	10 pounds
Onions, large, finely chopped	6
Eggs, beaten	1 dozen
Bread Crumbs, fresh, coarse	2 quarts
Lemon Juice	$1\frac{1}{2}$ pints
Dry Sherry	2 quarts
Sugar, brown	1 pound
Raisins	1 pound
Gingersnaps, finely crushed	1 pound
Beef Stock	2 quarts
Salt	as needed
Pepper	as needed
Noodles, broad, cooked	as needed

Procedure:

1. Mix meat, onions, eggs, bread crumbs, lemon juice, and 1 quart sherry. Refrigerate 24 hours.
2. Roll mixture into half-dollar sized balls.
3. Roll balls in brown sugar, then in raisins.
4. Put in greased pan and add 1 quart sherry, gingersnap crumbs, beef stock and seasoning.
5. Bake in oven at 350°F. until crust forms on top of meat balls, about 20 minutes.
6. Serve over cooked noodles and top with the sauce.

FARBERBURGER *(cont'd.)*

Procedure:

1. Mix all ingredients together thoroughly.
2. Form into patties, 1 to 8 ounces each.
3. Sprinkle each patty liberally with Charcrust on both sides.
4. Grill to desired doneness.

CHICKEN CACCIATORE

The Other Side

Ingredients: Yield: 20 to 22 portions

Chickens, fryers, 3 pounds each, cut up	1 dozen
Salt	as needed
Pepper	as needed
Flour	2 cups
Olive Oil	1 cup
Tomatoes, canned	2 cups
Tomato Paste	$\frac{1}{4}$ cup
Red Wine	12 ounces
Green Peppers, large, 1-inch pieces	4
Garlic Cloves, crushed	3
Onions, medium, quartered	3
Mushrooms, fresh, sliced	3 cups
Noodles, cooked, buttered	as needed

Procedure:

1. Sprinkle chicken with salt and pepper and roll in flour. Brown on both sides in hot olive oil for 10 or 15 minutes.
2. Mix other ingredients except noodles, and add to chicken. Cover tightly and cook slowly about 45 minutes or until chicken is tender.
3. Add mushrooms and cook 10 minutes.
4. Serve with buttered noodles.

CHICKEN ROQUEFORT

The Other Side

Ingredients: Yield: 2 portions

Chicken, fryer, cut up	1
Eggs, beaten	2
Flour	as needed
Bread Crumbs	as needed
Roquefort Cheese, crumbled	as needed
Mayonnaise	1 teaspoon
Sour Cream	1 teaspoon

Procedure:

1. Mix flour, bread crumbs, and crumbled cheese, using enough to coat chicken rather thickly.
2. Dip chicken in egg, then in crumb mixture.
3. Place in oiled pan and bake in oven at 350°F. for 1 hour.
4. Brush with mayonnaise and sour cream, return to oven, and bake 3 minutes more.

SHRIMP DE JONGHE TOPPING

The Other Side

Ingredients: Yield: 100 very thin slices

Bread Crumbs, toasted, fine	10 pounds
Roto-Roast Seasoning	3 pounds
Butter, lightly salted	9 pounds
Parsley, minced	4 bunches
Garlic Bulbs, minced	5
Lemon Juice	3 cups

Procedure:

1. Combine all ingredients and mix very thoroughly.
2. Form into rolls, pressing firmly together.
3. Slice wafer-thin as needed as topping for "Shrimp De Jonghe" or *coquilles St. Jacques.*

SOUR CREAM ROQUEFORT DRESSING

The Other Side

Ingredients: Yield: 5 gallons

Sour Cream	8 quarts
Roquefort Dressing	2 gallons
Dijon Mustard	1 pound
Lemon Juice, fresh	1 cup
Roquefort Cheese, crumbled	5 pounds

Procedure:

1. Combine sour cream, roquefort dressing, mustard, and lemon juice. Mix well.
2. Add Roquefort cheese and mix.

PAN-FRIED PERCH OR SOLE

The Other Side

Ingredients:

Yield: 22 portions

Milk	$1\frac{1}{2}$ quarts
Eggs	8
Perch of Sole Fillets	10 pounds
Flour	1 pound
Roto-Roast Seasoning	$\frac{3}{4}$ cup
Butter	1 pound

Procedure:

1. Beat milk and eggs together.
2. Dip fillets into flour, then into Roto-Roast, then into egg mixture, then again into flour.
3. Pan fry in hot butter, browning on both sides. Sole will require about 3 minutes, each side; perch, about 4 or 5 minutes.

PLENTYWOOD

PLENTYWOOD TODAY

BENSENVILLE, ILLINOIS

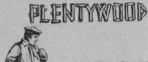

PLENTYWOOD

LUNCHEON

Soup of the Day   Chilled Tomato Juice

Fresh Fruit Cocktail

CHEF'S SPECIAL $3.50

KING CRABMEAT, SHRIMP
Mornay, Gratin Amandine 3.95
FILET OF SOLE
Lemon Butter, Parsley Potato, Vegetable 3.25
SHIRRED EGGS WITH PORK LINK SAUSAGE
Bercy, Apple Sauce, Sweet Potato 2.95
BROCHETTE BEEF TENDERLOIN
Colbert.. 3.45
FARM STYLE CHICKEN POT PIE
Fluffy Crust, Vegetable 3.25
CALVES LIVER SAUTE
Lyonnaise Potatoes, Vegetable.. 3.55
CLUB SALAD BOWL
Greens, Turkey, Ham, Swiss Cheese, Asparagus,
Artichoke, Egg, Tomato, 1000 Island Dressing................. 3.15
MEN'S GRILL SPECIAL SIRLOIN STEAK
Potato and Vegetable 3.85
INTERNATIONAL CHOPPED BEEF STEAK
Topped with Tomato, Mushroom, Vegetable..................... 3.25
TURKEY CLUB STYLE SANDWICH
A Businessman's Delight, Garni... 2.75
CHEF SPECIAL SANDWICH:
Grilled Butt Steak, Onion Ring, on Toast, Garni.............. 3.75
ARISTOCRAT SANDWICH
Turkey, Ham, Bleu Cheese on Toast, Gratin 3.00

DESSERTS

Ice Cream or Sundae   .45   Southern Pecan Pie   .55
Cheese Cake   .55   Aunt Bessie's Pie   .55
Meringue Glace, English Lemon Sauce   .55

BEVERAGE   .25

PLENTYWOOD FARM
SINCE 1932

PLENTYWOOD FARM
A Professional Success Story

Plentywood Farm
130 Church Street,
Bensenville, Illinois.

The menu still features Aunt Bessie's Pie and other early favorites, but Plentywood's original log cabin is now part of a large dining and entertainment empire. This onetime country restaurant, sired by depression necessity in 1932, has long since become big business (1978 volume, approximately $1.6 million) in the city-suburban sprawl.

It is always a new era, and Plentywood moves with the times, while fundamentals remain unchanged. Perhaps "you can take the boy out of the country, but. . . ." Plentywood maintains its own tucked-away country atmosphere despite the bustle, being only ten minutes from O'Hare International Airport, and despite "the madding crowds" that make the restaurant busy and famous.

Plentywood's founding family still thrives. Katherine Howell (who borrowed $200 from her mother to start it all, forty-seven years ago) and her two sons Pete and Sandy are very much in evidence. Even the sons' wives and children help out in this trans-generational foodservice operation. Although the distinguished, white-haired Mrs. Howell isn't as active as she once was, she keeps in regular contact with the business.

Plentywood's beautiful kitchen and bake shop is typical of the Howells' "pride of professionalism." Designed in tile and wood, with decorative lighting, it is as spacious and attractive as any of the restaurant's own dining rooms. "How can cooks be creative and efficient unless their work area is functional, beautiful, and even inspirational?" asks Mrs. Howell.

Plentywood Farm's handsome, rambling, main building, built in 1962—Sandy jokingly calls it "early American Shinto shrine"—seats 260 in four spacious dining rooms. The original structure now seats an additional 150. Beyond the dining facilities, Plentywood's sylvan fourteen and a half

197

The menus of Plentywood Farm . . . from a log cabin to a dining-out empire.

acres includes two shops—a gift emporium and a country store. And on the planning board for 1979: a new banquet hall to seat 500 people.

Plentywood Farm's customers are nearby business people who come during the week, plus many "ladies who lunch" from all over; and, on weekends, families, families, and more families.

The Howells seem to know them all—there can be as many as 700 on a Saturday night in the summer—and they take great pleasure in their familiarity with customers, a good reason why sixty percent of Plentywood's business is repeat.

The Howell family also takes great pleasure in the accomplishments of their employees over the years. (At present the staff numbers 130.) No restaurant in the Chicago area has done more to train young people and encourage their interest in foodservice as a vocation, than Plentywood. Beginning in the 1930s, when Katherine Howell informally

Views of Plentywood Farm. Opposite, the hand-some rambling main building, built in 1962. Right, a section of Plentywood's unusually beau-tiful and efficient kitchen—a mark of the Howell family's "pride of professionalism." Below, one of the spacious, light and woody dining rooms at Plentywood Farm.

taught local farm youngsters to work in her kitchen, down to the present, Plentywood has always been actively involved in foodservice apprentice programs and on-the-job training. Two generations of professionals have learned the practicalities of cooking and restaurant management at Plentywood Farm.

The restaurant's high back-of-the-house morale translates directly into loving customer-care-and-feeding throughout the house. Plentywood's food is wide ranging, from American traditional to familiar continental. It is imaginative and much of it is ambitious, from the Seafood Boat Veloute and Veal en Papillote, to Plentywood's curried shrimp, lobster, and crabmeat Rijstafel.

If these items seem a far cry from Plentywood's original menu of fried chicken and chicken salad, it is because the restaurant's menu has become more sophisticated in keeping with the customers' changing tastes, shaped as they have been by Plentywood's glittering array of executive chefs. At present, Chef Wolfgang Beyer, a German-trained chef, by way of Australia, is very much in charge.

Still it is reassuring to know that Plentywood Farm has a great variety of good old home cooking. "For example," says Mrs. Howell, "chicken pot pie is one of our famous staples. The filling is always all chicken meat; no vegetables, no potatoes, nothing but chicken. The crisp crust is baked separately. It goes in the oven until it is bubbling hot, and is still bubbling when it reaches the patron. For fish, we serve red snapper throats. And we always have a shrimp dish, baked so that it's not greasy. Other things that people like are broiled chicken livers, lamb curry, and our wonderful selection of soups."

Sunday offerings and weekend dinners on the regular menu range from $7 to $9.50; dinners on the "gourmet menu," from $9 to $12.

Plentywood Farm is anything but a stay-put plantation. Rather, it is a launching pad for hundreds of young people whose dedicated service there has made the restaurant "very good indeed," and the foodservice industry even better.

Plentywood Farm's gift shops offer cooking utensils, kitchen items, and various imported foodstuffs.

HAM AND SAUERKRAUT COCKTAIL BALLS

Plentywood Farm

Ingredients: Yield: 6 dozen

Onions, medium, minced	2
Butter	6 tablespoons
Ham, cooked, chopped	4 ounces
Corned Beef, cooked, chopped	12 ounces
Garlic, crushed	1 clove
Sauerkraut, drained, chopped	2 pounds
Beef Bouillon or Consomme	1 cup
Flour	$\frac{3}{4}$ cup
Eggs, beaten	2
Salt	$\frac{1}{4}$ teaspoon
Worcestershire Sauce	1 dash
Parsley, fresh, chopped	2 tablespoons
Eggs, beaten	4
Bread Crumbs, fine	2 cups

Procedure:

1. Saute onion in butter about 5 minutes.
2. Add ham, corned beef, and garlic and saute another 10 minutes, stirring as needed. Add sauerkraut and remove from heat.
3. Beat 2 eggs and bouillon together. Add flour and beat smooth. Mix in salt, Worcestershire sauce, and parsley.
4. Stir into sauerkraut mixture, return to heat, and stir until thickened, about 3 minutes.
5. Cover and chill.
6. Shape mixture into 1-inch balls.
7. Dip in 4 beaten eggs and roll in bread crumbs.
8. Fry in hot fat at 375°F. until lightly browned, about 2 or 3 minutes.
9. Drain well. Serve on picks with bowls of sour cream or mustard sauce for dipping.

Note:

These may be frozen. To serve, reheat in oven at 350°F. for 20 to 25 minutes.

POTATO LEEK SOUP

Plentywood Farm

Ingredients:

Yield: 15 gallons

Butter, melted	1 pound
Leeks, minced	1½ gallons
Onion, minced	½ gallon
Potatoes, peeled, thinly sliced	3 gallons
Celery, minced	1 quart
Chicken Stock	12 gallons
Monosodium Glutamate	½ cup
Pepper, white	1 teaspoon
Salt	as needed
Chicken Base	as needed
Milk	2½ gallons
Cream	1½ gallons
Butter, creamed	2 pounds
Cornstarch	as needed
Cold Water	as needed

Procedure:

1. Saute vegetables, except potatoes, in melted butter until soft and shiny.
2. Add potatoes and stock, bring to a boil, and simmer until smooth, about 2 hours.
3. Force through a sieve, add monosodium glutamate, pepper, salt, chicken stock, milk, cream, and butter. Bring to a boil.
4. Adjust thickness, if necessary, with cornstarch mixed with cold water.
5. Chill and serve.

LENTIL SOUP

Plentywood Farm

Ingredients: Yield: 15 gallons

Bacon, finely diced	1 pound
Bacon Fat or Margarine	1 pound
Celery, finely diced	$\frac{1}{2}$ gallon
Onion, finely diced	$\frac{1}{2}$ gallon
Carrots, finely diced	$\frac{1}{2}$ gallon
Garlic Cloves, finely minced	4
Flour	1 pound
Stock, Ham or Beef	15 gallons
Tomato Puree	$\frac{1}{2}$ gallon
Lentils, soaked overnight	7 pounds
Bay Leaves	6
Vinegar	$1\frac{1}{2}$ cups
Sugar	$\frac{1}{4}$ cup
Nutmeg	1 teaspoon
Pepper, white	1 teaspoon
Salt	as needed
Worcestershire Sauce	$\frac{1}{4}$ cup
Liquid Hot Pepper Seasoning	$\frac{1}{2}$ teaspoon
Cornstarch	as needed
Water, cold	as needed

Procedure:

1. Fry bacon until crisp. Drain and set aside. Add fat, as necessary, to make 1 pound.
2. Add celery, onion, carrots, and garlic to fat and saute until soft.
3. Stir in flour and cook about 8 minutes.
4. Slowly stir in stock and bring to a boil, stirring constantly, until smooth.
5. Add tomato puree, lentils, and bay leaves. Simmer until lentils are soft, about $2\frac{1}{4}$ hours.
6. Add bacon, vinegar, sugar, and seasonings.
7. Adjust thickness with cornstarch mixed with cold water as necessary. Stir and cook until thickened and smooth.

DUTCH PEA SOUP

Plentywood Farm

Ingredients: Yield: 15 gallons

Bacon Fat	8 ounces
Carrots, diced	1 gallon
Celery, diced	1 gallon
Onion, diced	1 gallon
Garlic Cloves, crushed	3
Green Split Peas	10 pounds
Ham Stock	15 gallons
Barley, pearl	1 pound
Pepper	1 teaspoon
Monosodium Glutamate	$\frac{1}{4}$ cup
Nutmeg	1 teaspoon
Worcestershire Sauce	$\frac{1}{4}$ cup
Sugar	$\frac{1}{4}$ cup
Chicken Soup Base	as needed
Salt	as needed
Cornstarch	as needed

Procedure:

1. Saute carrots, celery, onion, and garlic in bacon fat until soft.
2. Add peas and stock and simmer until peas are soft, about $2\frac{1}{2}$ hours.
3. Cook barley separately, drain, and add to soup.
4. Add remaining ingredients except cornstarch. Bring to a boil.
5. Adjust thickness, if necessary, using cornstarch mixed with cold water.

GAZPACHO

Plentywood Farm

Ingredients: Yield: 2 quarts

Garlic, finely minced	1 clove
Tomatoes, medium, fresh, finely chopped	6
Cucumbers, medium, finely chopped	2
Green Pepper, medium, minced	1
Onion, medium, minced	1
Tomato Juice, canned	1 quart
Lemon Juice	3 tablespoons
Parsley, chopped	$\frac{1}{4}$ cup
Salt	as needed
Pepper	as needed
Liquid Hot Pepper Seasoning	dash

Procedure:

1. Mix all ingredients and chill.
2. To serve, put 1 ice cube in each bowl, pour in soup, and garnish with chopped parsley.

CHOPPED GRENADINES OF BEEF
TOPPED WITH BLEU OR ROQUEFORT CHEESE

Plentywood Farm

Ingredients: Yield: 25 to 30 portions

Beef Trimmings, Flank Tenderloin, cubed	10 pounds
Bread, broken into pieces	6 slices
Salt	2 tablespoons
Pepper, black, ground	1 teaspoon
Monosodium Glutamate	2 tablespoons
Catsup or Tomato Juice	2 cups
Water	2 to 3 cups
Eggs	6
Oil	1 cup
Cheese, Bleu or Roquefort, crumbled	1 quart
Colbert Wine Sauce	5 to 6 cups

Procedure:

1. Mix all ingredients except cheese and wine sauce together.
2. Grind mixture through $\frac{1}{2}$-inch blade. Grind again through $\frac{3}{16}$-inch blade. Do not mix after second grind.
3. Shape into 2-ounce sized portions, making a round, thin shape.
4. Cook on griddle to desired doneness.
5. Top each grenadine with cheese. Place under broiler to melt cheese slightly.
6. Allow 3 grenadines per luncheon order, 4 per dinner order. To serve, put $1\frac{1}{2}$ ounces wine sauce on plate, lay grenadines on sauce. Garnish plate with vegetables, potato, and parsley sprigs.

BEEF CASSEROLE PLENTYWOOD

Plentywood Farm

Ingredients: Yield: 40 portions

Top Sirloin of Beef, $\frac{3}{4}$-inch cubes	20 pounds
Butter	$1\frac{1}{4}$ pounds
Wine	$\frac{1}{5}$ gallon
Onion, Bermuda, $\frac{3}{4}$-inch cubes	12 to 15 pounds
Bordelaise Sauce	$1\frac{1}{2}$ gallons
Potato Balls	240
Petite Belgian Carrots, canned	2 #10 cans
Celery, cut $1\frac{1}{2}$-inch lengths	8 to 10 pounds
Salt	as needed
Pepper	as needed
Parsley, minced	1 quart

Procedure:

1. Saute beef in 6 ounces butter for about 5 minutes, or until lightly browned.
2. Add wine and simmer 5 minutes.
3. Saute onion in 6 ounces butter until transparent, then add to meat.
4. Add Bordelaise sauce and simmer over low heat.
5. Deep-fry potato balls at 365°F. for about 8 minutes. Set aside to keep warm.
6. Braise celery in 8 ounces butter until slightly soft. Add carrots, season to taste with salt and pepper, and keep warm.
7. To serve, put 8 to 10 ounces of meat with sauce into heated earthenware casseroles of 10 to 12 ounce capacity. Put seasoned vegetables and potatoes on top of meat. Garnish with chopped parsley.

BAKED STUFFED PORK CHOPS, FARM-STYLE

Plentywood Farm

Ingredients: Yield: 50 portions

Pork Chops, center cut, $1\frac{1}{4}$-inch, thick, $6\frac{1}{2}$ ounces each	50
Salt	1 tablespoon
Pepper, black	$\frac{1}{2}$ teaspoon
Monosodium Glutamate	2 teaspoons
Pork Fat Trimmings, rendered	1 cup

Stuffing	
Bacon, finely chopped	$\frac{1}{2}$ pound
Celery, finely chopped	2 cups
Onion, finely chopped	1 cup
Apples, tart, coarsely chopped	$1\frac{1}{2}$ pounds
Bread Crumbs, dry, finely diced	5 cups
Eggs, slightly beaten	2
Salt	1 tablespoon
Monosodium Glutamate	$\frac{1}{2}$ teaspoon
Thyme, powdered	$\frac{1}{4}$ teaspoon
Stock or Milk	as needed

Procedure:

1. Cut halfway through pork chops from fat to bone, making a pocket for stuffing.
2. Saute bacon until almost crisp. Add celery and onion and saute until softened. Cool.
3. Add apples, bread crumbs, eggs, 1 tablespoon salt, $\frac{1}{2}$ teaspoon monosodium glutamate, and thyme. Mix well. This mixture should be moist enough. If not workable, add a little stock or milk, as needed.
4. Put stuffing into pockets in chops and pin together.
5. Mix 1 tablespoon salt, black pepper, and 2 teaspoons monosodium glutamate. Sprinkle over stuffed chops.
6. Brown on both sides in rendered pork fat.
7. Arrange in roasting pan and bake in oven at 350°F. for about 45 to 60 minutes, or until tender.

VEAL EN PAPILLOTE
(Veal in Parchment)

Plentywood Farm

Ingredients: Yield: 6 portions

Veal, ¼-inch slices, 4 ounces each	12
Mushroom Caps, large, fresh	12
Artichoke Hearts, large, cut in half	6
Parchment Papers, 24- by 16-inch	6 pieces
Oil	as needed
Bordelaise Sauce	1 quart
Chateau Potatoes	as needed
Asparagus Hollandaise	as needed

Procedure:

1. Lay out 6 slices veal. On each slice place 2 mushroom caps and two pieces of artichoke. Top with second veal slice.
2. Cut parchment paper into shape of large heart. Brush with oil. Fold paper in half through center. Starting from heart point, make an overlapping fold around edge about ¾ of the way up.
3. Insert stuffed veal into opening in heart. Add 3 or 4 ounces cold Bordelaise sauce.
4. Finish overlapping and folding the paper so that it becomes an airtight seal.
5. Bake in oven at 350°F. about 20 minutes.
6. To serve, place packages on silver tray. Garnish with potatoes, asparagus, or other vegetable. Maitre d'hotel will lift veal from paper at side table.

BREAST OF TURKEY AND HAM MALTAISE

Plentywood Farm

Ingredients: Yield: 20 portions

Turkey Breast, boneless, cooked	5 pounds
Baked Ham, thin slices	20
Oranges, fresh, peeled and sectioned	6
Hollandaise Sauce	1 quart

SEAFOOD WALDORF

Plentywood Farm

Ingredients:

Yield: $2\frac{1}{2}$ gallons

Mushrooms, fresh, sliced	3 pounds
Butter	$\frac{2}{3}$ cup
Onion, minced	$\frac{1}{2}$ cup
Scallops, quartered	4 pounds
Lobster Meat, cooked, diced	4 pounds
Crabmeat, cooked, flaked	4 pounds
Dry Vermouth	3 cups
Monosodium Glutamate	2 tablespoons
Fish Veloute, medium	3 quarts
Heavy Cream	3 cups
Rice, cooked	as needed

Procedure:

1. Saute mushrooms in butter about 5 minutes.
2. Add onion and scallops. Cook 5 minutes.
3. Add lobster and crabmeat. Cover and heat through.
4. Add vermouth, monosodium glutamate, and fish veloute. Place over hot water and cook about 5 minutes.
5. Stir in cream and heat through.
6. Serve on hot fluffy rice.

BREAST OF TURKEY AND HAM MALTAISE *(cont'd.)*
Procedure:

1. Cut turkey into 4-ounce slices and place on buttered baking sheet.
2. Top with a slice of ham and 2 or 3 orange sections.
3. Bake in oven at 350°F. for 10 or 15 minutes.
4. Before serving, cover with hollandaise sauce and place under broiler until brown.

SEAFOOD BOAT VELOUTE

Plentywood Farm

Ingredients: Yield: 40 portions

Pineapples, whole with tops	20
Butter or Shortening	as needed
Onions, large, finely chopped	5
Mushrooms, fresh, sliced	4 pounds
Fish Veloute Sauce	1 gallon
Shrimp, raw, shelled, deveined	5 pounds
Scallops	5 pounds
King Crab Meat	5 pounds
Parmesan Cheese, grated	5 cups

Procedure:

1. Cut pineapples in half, cutting through green tops. Hollow out center, saving fruit for later use.
2. Saute onions and mushrooms in butter or shortening until onions are transparent. Add veloute sauce.
3. Saute shrimp and scallops about 5 minutes. Add to mushroom mixture.
4. Fold crab meat into the mixture very gently. Simmer about 5 minutes.
5. Place seafood mixture into pineapple shells. Sprinkle lightly with cheese.
6. Place under broiler until lightly browned.

RIJSTAFEL

Plentywood Farm

Ingredients: Yield: 1 portion

Shrimp, cooked, peeled, deveined
Lobster Meat
Curry Sauce (see recipe)
Crab Meat
Rice, cooked, buttered
Kumquats
Raisins
Coconut, grated

EASTERN SEABOARD CRAB CAKES

Plentywood Farm

Ingredients: Yield: 100 crab cakes, 2 ounces each

Mayonnaise	$\frac{3}{4}$ cup
Egg Yolks, beaten	1 dozen
Salt	1 ounce
Monosodium Glutamate	2 teaspoons
Pepper, white	2 to 3 teaspoons
English Mustard, dry	2 to 3 teaspoons
Liquid Hot Pepper Seasoning	dash
Parsley, minced	$1\frac{1}{2}$ ounces
Crab Meat, flaked	12 pounds
Flour	as needed
Dipping Batter	as needed
Bread Crumbs	as needed

Procedure:

1. Mix mayonnaise, egg yolks, and seasonings and blend thoroughly.
2. Add crabmeat and mix lightly but well.
3. Portion cakes with a #16 scoop.
4. Dip in flour, then in batter, then in crumbs.
5. Pan fry quickly in lightly greased skillet until delicately browned on both sides.
6. Allow 2 cakes per serving for luncheon.

RIJSTAFEL *(cont'd.)*

Procedure:

1. Use equal portions of shrimp, lobster, and crabmeat.
2. Saute shrimp and lobster in butter.
3. Add enough curry sauce to achieve a good proportion between sauce and seafood. Add crab meat last to prevent shredding.
4. Serve *en casserole* with hot buttered rice. Garnish with kumquats, raisins, and grated coconut.

CURRY SAUCE

Plentywood Farm

Ingredients: Yield: 3 gallons

Shortening or Vegetable Oil	5 cups
Onion, chopped	1 quart
Celery, chopped	1 pint
Parsley, chopped	few sprigs
Apples, cooking, chopped	6 medium
Garlic, crushed	2 cloves
Flour	6 cups
Curry Powder	$\frac{3}{4}$ to 1 cup
Chicken Stock	3 gallons
Bay Leaves	3
Sugar	$\frac{1}{2}$ cup
Lemon Juice	$\frac{1}{2}$ cup
Monosodium Glutamate	$\frac{1}{4}$ cup
Ginger Ale	1 pint
Salt or Chicken Base	as needed
Bananas, mashed	2 medium
White Wine	$\frac{1}{2}$ cup
Sherry Wine	$\frac{1}{2}$ cup
Worcestershire Sauce	$\frac{1}{4}$ cup
Butter, softened	$\frac{3}{4}$ pound

Procedure:

1. Saute onion, celery, parsley, apples, and garlic in hot shortening (margarine, chicken fat, butter) or vegetable oil until soft.
2. Add flour. Stir and cook slowly about 8 minutes.
3. Add curry powder and cook together for 3 minutes.
4. Slowly add stock, stirring constantly until thick and smooth.
5. Add remaining ingredients except wine, Worcestershire sauce and butter. Simmer 25 minutes, stirring often to prevent scorching.
6. Strain. Add wine and Worcestershire sauce. Cream in the butter. Heat through.

BANANA CAKE

Plentywood Farm

Ingredients: Yield: 18 to 20 pans

Butter	$3\frac{1}{2}$ pounds
Sugar, granulated	$3\frac{1}{2}$ pounds
Sugar, brown	$3\frac{1}{2}$ pounds
Salt	$1\frac{1}{4}$ ounces
Vanilla	3 tablespoons
Egg Yolks	1 quart
Flour, cake	6 pounds
Baking Power	2 ounces
Buttermilk	1 quart
Baking Soda	1 ounce
Banana Pulp	6 pounds

Procedure:

1. Cream butter, add sugar, salt, and vanilla in 5 stages. Cream thoroughly.
2. Add egg yolks 3 or 4 at a time and blend well.
3. Sift flour and baking powder together.
4. Combine buttermilk and baking soda.
5. Alternately add flour, buttermilk, and banana pulp. Blend until smooth.
6. Scale batter into greased loaf pans, about 1 pound per pan.
7. Bake in oven at 375°F. until done, (about 50 minutes). Remove from pans and allow to cool.
8. Do not frost.

ENGLISH LEMON SAUCE
(for use over meringue glace)

Plentywood Farm

Ingredients: Yield: 2 gallons

Eggs, whole	2 quarts
Sugar	1 gallon
Egg Yolks	2 quarts
Lemons, fresh, juice and grated rind	8
Butter	2 pounds

Procedure:

1. Mix whole eggs, sugar, and egg yolks thoroughly.
2. Whip in lemon juice and rind.
3. Cook slowly until thick, stirring occasionally.
4. Cut butter into chunks and stir in. Mix well.
5. Cool. Store in 1 gallon containers and use as needed.

Note:

Two 30-ounce cans of frozen lemon juice may be substituted for fresh lemons.

ZUIDER ZEE
(a custard pie)

Plentywood Farm

Ingredients: Yield: 40 portions

Sugar	1 pound
Cornstarch	5 ounces
Milk	2 quarts
Eggs	10
Vanilla	2 tablespoons
Salt	as needed
Graham Cracker Crust Mix	as needed
Whipping Cream	1 pint

SOUTHERN PECAN PIE

Plentywood Farm

Ingredients: Yield: 8 9-inch pies

Sugar, brown	3 pounds
Eggs	3 pints
Honey	1 quart
Corn Syrup, light	$1\frac{1}{2}$ pints
Corn Syrup, dark	1 pint
Vanilla	1 tablespoon
Salt	1 ounce
Pecans	3 pounds
Pie Shells, unbaked, 9-inch	8

Procedure:

1. Put all ingredients except pecans in mixer and mix on #1 speed for 5 to 10 minutes. Add pecans.
2. Pour into pie shells. Bake in oven at 350°F. for 40 to 45 minutes.

ZUIDER ZEE *(cont'd.)*

Procedure:

1. Mix sugar and cornstarch together. Blend with 1 pint cold milk to dissolve. Add eggs and mix well.
2. Heat remaining milk. Just before boiling add above mixture very slowly. Cook for about 5 minutes, stirring constantly. Add salt to taste. Add vanilla.
3. Line a 14- by 16- by 2-inch pan with crumb mix.
4. Pour filling into pan. Chill.
5. Whip cream and spread in a thin layer over pudding just before serving.

APPLE CRISP

Plentywood Farm

Ingredients: Yield: 75 portions

Filling
Apple Slices, frozen	$7\frac{1}{2}$ pounds
Apple Juice, drained from apple slices	$\frac{1}{2}$ gallon
Cornstarch	4 ounces
Sugar	1 pound
Salt	$\frac{1}{2}$ ounce
Nutmeg	$\frac{1}{4}$ teaspoon
Cinnamon	$\frac{1}{2}$ teaspoon
Lemon Juice	1 tablespoon

Topping
Eggs	10
Sugar	1 quart
Flour, pastry	1 quart
Baking Powder	2 teaspoons

Procedure:

1. Drain apples. Juice should be about 2 quarts. Use 1 pint of juice to dissolve cornstarch. Bring remaining $1\frac{1}{2}$ quarts of juice to a boil. Slowly stir in cornstarch and cook, stirring constantly, until clear.
2. Mix 1 pound sugar, salt, nutmeg, and cinnamon together. Add to thickened juice.
3. Add lemon juice and apples.
4. Fill individual ramekins $\frac{2}{3}$ full.
5. Warm eggs and 2 cups sugar together as for sponge cake. Whip until light and fluffy.
6. Mix 2 cups sugar with flour and baking powder. Fold into egg mixture lightly.
7. Place mixture on top of each filled ramekin.
8. Bake in oven at 325°F. for 45 minutes.

appetizers
enjoy with a cocktail...

GUACAMOLE DIP (FOR TWO) 3.35
CHILE CON QUESO DIP (FOR TWO) 3.00

MINIATURE SOPES (6) 4.25
Soft Tortilla topped with beans,
Mexican sausage, lettuce and cheese

CEVICHE ACAPULCO 3.00
Marinated White Fish with
Chef's own blend of spices

BOTANA
Mexican Hors D'Oeuvres
Small 3.00   Large 5.00

OUR FAMOUS TEXAS
chili con carne
DISHES

ENCHILADAS (TWO) FILLED WITH CHEESE
AND ONIONS TOPPED WITH
CHILI CON CARNE 3.50

SAN ANTONIO SPECIAL 5.00
Tamales Covered with
Our Famous Texas Chili
(Served with Rice and Beans)

BOWL CHILI CON CARNE 1.75
Quart Chili To Go 3.50
(With or Without Beans)

antojitos
BEEF, CHICKEN OR CHEESE
TACOS (TWO) 3.35

ENCHILADAS (TWO) 3.35
Beef, Chicken or Cheese and Onions
Served with your choice of sauce
Red, Green or Mole

CHALUPA COMPUESTA 3.50
Crisp Tostada with Chicken or Beef,
Lettuce and Avocado

GUACAMOLE 1.75   TAMALES (THREE) 2.75
RICE .60   REFRIED BEANS .60

hacienda dinners
(SERVED WITH COFFEE OR TEA)

SU CASA SPECIAL #1
CHICKEN AND BEEF TACO
TAMALE WITH CHILI
Rice   Guacamole Salad   Refried Beans
Sherbet or Fruit Plate (In Season)
6.00

SU CASA SPECIAL #2
THREE CHICKEN ENCHILADAS
(With Green Sauce and Sour Cream)
Rice   Guacamole Salad   Refried Beans
Sherbet or Fruit Plate (In Season)
6.00

SU CASA SPECIAL #3
PELO ROJO
Your Choice of Two Beef or Chicken Enchiladas
with Cheese and Onion Casseroled in Tomato Sauce
Topped with Melted Cheddar Cheese
Rice   Guacamole Salad   Refried Beans
Sherbet or Fruit Plate (In Season)
6.00

CHILE RELLENO
Bell Pepper Stuffed with Cheese or Lean Ground Beef
Souffléed in Egg Batter Covered in Tomato Sauce
Rice   Guacamole Salad   Refried Beans

su casa specialties
(SERVED WITH COFFEE OR TEA)

SU CASA DE-LUXE COMBINATION — 8.50
A Strip of Carne Asada   ½ Chile Relleno
Cheese Taco   Chicken Enchilada
Rice   Guacamole Salad   Refried Beans
Sherbet or Fruit Plate (In Season)

CARNE ASADA
Butterfly Cut of Prime
Guacamole Sal
Rice
Sherbet or Fruit Pl

CAMARONES A LA
Large Shrimp in the
Served with Guac

Sherbet o

COMBINA
A Strip
and F
Rice
Sher

(Brock
with gar
and cu

Pollo

chef carlos' suggestions
APPETIZER
"QUEZADILLAS" — 2.75
TOSTADA — 1.25
Beef, Chicken or Cheese

DINNERS
PESCADO — 5.25
TAMPICO STYLE
White Fish Baked in a Mild Sauce
of Tomato, Wine, Capers and Olives
with Mexican Rice and Sliced Tomato
Fruit Plate or Sherbet

SU CASA — 5.75

BIENVENIDO • MI CASA ES SU CASA
ENTERTAINMENT
DOORMAN PARKING

LUNCH - DINNER - SUPPER
11:30 A.M. to 1:00 A.M.
MONDAY THRU FRIDAY
SATURDAY 5:00 P.M. to 2:00
CLOSED SUNDAY

WE ARE PLEASED TO ENCLOSE
YOUR SU CASA CREDIT CARD AND
HOPE YOU WILL FIND OCCASION
TO USE IT REGULARLY.

Su Casa
MI CASA ES SU CASA
Su Casa
49 EAST ONTARIO ST., CHICAGO PHONE 943-4041

WE WELCOME YOU IN SPIRIT OF HOSPITALITY
EXCELLENT MEXICAN FOODS AND COCKTAILS
TELEPHONE FOR RESERVATIONS
4041

Su Casa

PIZZERIA

PIZZERIA DUE

CHICAGO'S FINEST MARTINI
made with
FLEISCHMANN'S DISTILLED
DRY GIN

"HAPPY MANHATTAN"
dry or sweet made with
FLEISCHMANN'S PREFERRED
WHISKEY

SELECT YOUR PIZZA

both
WINES
selection
BEER, and
Anheuser-Busch Michelob
ON DRAUGHT

SOFT DRINKS
Coca Cola - Pepsi Cola - 7 Up
We also carry a
COMPLETE LINE OF WHISKEYS,
CORDIALS AND LIQUEURS

MENU
MIDGET CHEESE PIZZA . . . 2.90
MIDGET CHEESE AND
SAUSAGE PIZZA 3.70
MEDIUM CHEESE PIZZA . . . 4.20
MEDIUM CHEESE AND
SAUSAGE PIZZA 5.20
LARGE CHEESE PIZZA . . . 5.20
LARGE CHEESE AND
SAUSAGE PIZZA 6.20
Anchovies, Onions, Green Pepper or
Mushrooms Additional Charge

Our Famous Italian
SALAD BOWL 1.25
Deliciously dressed with
Wine Vinegar and pure Olive Oil
Topped with Onion Rings
SPECIAL SALAD 2.25
DESSERT .60
Spumoni Ice Cream
Bisque Tortoni
Choice of
BEVERAGE
Our Special Blend Coffee .30
or Grade A Milk .40
Per Serving
SOFT DRINKS .15

BACCHUS

At the entrance to Pizzeria Due, Bacchus, the God
of Wine bids you welcome. This bust was the landmark and tribute to the wines of the Piedmont
Provinces during the 18th century. It stood at the
entrance to the vineyards of the Barolo villa, Asti
District. We are proud and happy to possess and
display him.

PIZZERIA SPECIALS
Your Choice of Delicious
SANDWICHES
ITALIAN SAUSAGE $2.25
with Special Homemade Sauce
IMPORTED SALAMI $2.25
with imported Swiss Cheese
POORBOY (Ragazzo-Povero) $2.25
a combination of Italian Sausage
and Imported Salami with Swiss Cheese

OVER 10,000,000 PIZZAS HAVE BEEN PREPARED BY OUR EXPERTS
15% GRATUITY FOR 10 PERSONS OR MORE

SU CASA PIZZERIAS 1&2
As "Chicago" as Pizza Pie and Guacamole

Su Casa, 49 E. Ontario Street,
Pizzeria Uno, 29 E. Ohio Street,
Pizzeria Due, 619 N. Wabash Avenue,
Chicago, Illinois.

There is a lot of "Chicago" in these three restaurants; two of them represent the city's premiere pizza palaces and the other, the city's first and reigning-class Mexican restaurant. As "inborn" as anything is the fact that all three restaurants are owned by Ike Sewell, a well-known Chicago business-man and sportsman. Sewell had wanted to open a Mexican restaurant in the city as far back as the late 1930s, when he first came to Chicago from Texas to head up the midwest division of Fleischman's Distillers. Sewell was deflected from his goal by his good friend, the late Ric Riccardo, the most colorful restaurateur in the annals of the city.

Early in World War II, Riccardo went behind enemy lines to visit his family in northern Italy. He came back with the idea of serving pizza as a one dish meal and opening a genuine Italian pizzeria in Chicago. The idea of Sewell's Mexican restaurant was shelved for almost twenty years as the partners united to push pizza, then generally unknown in the United States except in Italian neighborhoods where it was regarded as a snack or an hors d'oeuvre. In June 1943, Ike and Ric opened Pizzeria Uno. It took several months for Uno to catch on, but once the word started to spread about this new restaurant serving cheese-tomato-meat-et cetera pie, it was SRO.

By the time Uno was joined by its sister pizzeria, Due (located a block north), it had become a Chicago favorite. By now, it is estimated that the 125-seat Uno and the 140-seat Due have served over twelve million pizzas between them. Uno opened with a staff of six. Today there are 100 employees at both pizzerias.

Since 1943, more than 2500 pizza places have sprung up in

Ike Sewell's pioneering trio—Pizzerias Uno & Due and the high-style Su Casa Mexican restaurant.

the Chicago area alone, but Uno was unquestionably the first to serve pizza as a main course in the United States.

Though many have tried, no one has been able to duplicate Uno's original pizza. Part of the secret is the high-temperature (600°F.) gas ovens that the pizzas are put into for 15 minutes, followed by 5 minutes more at 450°F. Also part of the secret is the large, deep pans in which they are cooked, not to mention the proportions of Mozzarella cheese, pear tomatoes, Italian sausage, olive oil, and pinches of various herbs and spices that go into the pizza.

Now, for the first time since it opened thirty-six years ago, changes have been made at Uno. After a generation of use, the kitchen has been replaced with the finest equipment available. A new entrance has been built, and the exterior of the building painted Roman pink-orange.

Two things have not changed: the quality of the pizza, and the graffiti on the walls. Thousands of signatures are there in all their carved up, cartooned, and handwritten glory.

The Uno and Due are frequented by much the same crowd, although there is an older group of "pizzaficionados" that remains faithful to Uno, regarding Due as an upstart. Both restaurants have a check average of about $6.25, and do three-plus turns during the week, with five to six sittings on weekends. In addition to their celebrated pizza, both Uno

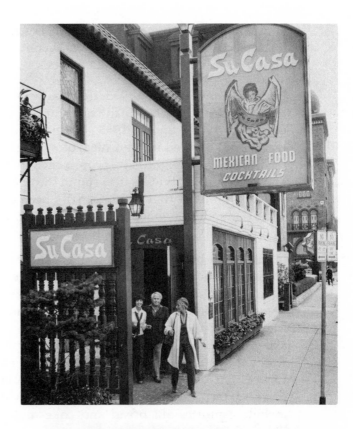

Two of the three Ike Sewell restaurants, Su Casa and Pizzeria Due, are within the same block on Chicago's Near North Side. The other one—the original Pizzeria Uno—is two streets away. All occupy vintage Chicago buildings, and all are Chicago originals.

and Due serve Italian sandwiches, a green salad, spumone for dessert, and between them have become one of the largest outlets for Chianti in the United States.

It was not until January 1963, that Ike Sewell realized his ambition of opening a Mexican restaurant. If pizza was largely unknown in Chicago in 1943, the great cookery of Mexico was all but ignored in the Chicago of the early 1960s. It was Su Casa that brought it to prominence in a setting of style and authenticity. Su Casa is around the corner from Pizzeria Due in a building that had originally been the stables for the Victorian mansion which Sewell splendidly restored to serve as office-headquarters for the three restaurants.

Su Casa is a beauty! Its interiors are those of an eighteenth-century Mexican hacienda. On one wall are giant doors with pediments from a house in Taxco; bronze Cathedral bells hang from the ceiling nearby. Jose Clemente Orozco, one of Mexico's greatest painters, painted two large panels of Veracruz Indian dancers that are on display. On another wall are two large wood sculptures of St. Peter and St. Paul, carved in 1670 for the altar of a Mexican cathedral. Other pieces of art, strikingly set off against white brick walls, include centuries-old bread and cake molds, large candle-

sticks, handcarved grilles, balconies, and draperies made from hand-loomed rebozos.

Su Casa does a handy business among local professionals and out-of-towners who recognize it as one of the city's top places to go. With 152 seats, Su Casa will serve an average of 300 dinners during the week and up to 400 on weekends.

The food at Su Casa is quite good, if less adventuresome than its outstanding ambience would indicate. In addition to traditional offerings of tacos, enchiladas, guacamole, and Chili Rellenos, the restaurant features a really excellent broiled shrimp Veracruz style, Arroz con Pollo, Crepes de Pollo (Mexican chicken crepes), Estofado (Mexcian beef stew), and Trucha al Cilantro (brook trout with fresh coriander). If not indigenous to Mexico, the house Chili con Carne is one of the best in town. Su Casa's dinner check average is $10.50, including liquor. (At lunch, $7.50.)

Between them—Su Casa and the Pizzerias—the three Sewell restaurants to approximately 3\frac{1}{2}$ million volume annually.

Two views of Su Casa, one of the city's best-designed restaurants. Comfortable, warm and inviting, it's totally "artless" in its overall effect.

CHILI CON CARNE

Su Casa

Ingredients: Yield: 8 gallons

Lean Ground Beef, coarsely ground	50 pounds
Onions, large, chopped	6
Garlic Cloves, chopped	10
Bay Leaves	6
Thyme, leaf	$\frac{1}{4}$ cup
Pepper, black, ground	$\frac{1}{2}$ cup
Cumin	3 cups
Chili Powder	1 quart
Salt	$1\frac{1}{2}$ cups
Water	6 gallons
Flour	$2\frac{1}{2}$ quarts

Procedure:

1. Cook beef with garlic and onion until done.
2. Add spices and salt. Cook 20 minutes. Pour off fat and save for the roux.
3. Add water to beef and bring to boiling. Lower heat and simmer for 30 minutes.
4. Make roux from reserved fat and flour. Slowly stir in roux. Simmer 45 minutes with occasional stirring.

CHILI CON QUESO DIP

Su Casa

Ingredients: Yield: 6 portions

Processed Cheese Spread, diced	1 pound
Cheddar Cheese, diced	$\frac{1}{2}$ pound
Tomatoes, fresh, diced	$\frac{1}{2}$ cup
Onion, minced	$\frac{1}{2}$ cup
Parsley, chopped	2 tablespoons
Green (Hot) Chilies, chopped	2 or more

ESTOFADO
(Mexican Beef Stew)

Su Casa

Ingredients:

Yield: 25 portions

Beef Shank, lean, cubed	10 pounds
Garlic Cloves, minced	2
Onion, large, chopped	1
Salt	as needed
Pepper	dash
Flour	$\frac{3}{4}$ cup
Tomato Puree	$\frac{1}{2}$ cup
Thyme	1 teaspoon
Bay Leaves	2
Pepper, Cayenne	dash
Pepper, black	dash
Beef Base	1 tablespoon
Beef Stock	$2\frac{1}{2}$ quarts
Carrots, large, cut up	8
Celery Ribs, cut up	2
Potatoes, Idaho, large, cut up	5
Green Peas, frozen, cooked	1 cup

Procedure:

1. Saute beef with garlic and onion. Sprinkle with flour. Stir and cook 6 or 7 minutes over low heat. Add puree, spices, salt, pepper, beef base, and stock.
2. Cook in oven at 350°F. for 90 minutes.
3. Add vegetables except peas and cook 60 minutes.
4. Use green peas as garnish over stew.

CHILI CON QUESO DIP *(cont'd.)*
Procedure:

1. Put cheese in double boiler and add remaining ingredients.
2. Heat until cheese is melted and onion is soft.

ITALIAN SAUSAGE SANDWICH

Pizzerias Uno & Due

Ingredients: Yield: About 1 gallon of sauce

Veal Bones, cut up	3 pounds
Fat	as needed
Onion, sliced	4 pounds
Celery, chopped	2 pounds
Green Pepper, chopped	2 pounds
Pear Tomatoes, peeled	1 #10 can
Italian Sausage, mild, 5 ounce pieces	as needed
Italian Bread Small Loaf Buns	as needed
Italian Vegetable Garnish, (a prepared sweet-sour garnish)	as needed

Procedure:

1. Saute veal bones until brown. Cover with onion, celery, and green pepper. Simmer until vegetables are soft.
2. Remove bones. Add tomatoes and mix well. Refrigerate overnight to develop flavor.
3. Bake sausage until brown. Refrigerate until needed.
4. To serve, place browned Italian sausage in sauce and heat.
5. Split sausage lengthwise and place in bun. Pour sauce over sausage.
6. Garnish with Italian vegetable garnish.

CHILI RELLENO

Su Casa

Ingredients: Yield: 6 portions, 3 crepes each

Bell Peppers, medium, parboiled	6
Oil	as needed
Vinegar	as needed
Cheese, Monterey Jack, grated	1 pound
Eggs	3
Onion, medium, thinly sliced	1
Garlic Clove	1
Olive Oil	3 tablespoons
Chicken Stock	$3\frac{1}{2}$ cups
White Wine	$\frac{1}{2}$ cup
Tomatoes, canned, solid pack	3 #303 cans
Oregano	1 teaspoon
Bay Leaf	1
Salt	1 tablespoon
Pepper	1 teaspoon

Procedure:

1. Broil peppers evenly. Place in paper bag, close tightly. Allow them to steam in closed bag for approximately 20 minutes. Remove from bag, peel off outer skin.
2. Cut $\frac{1}{2}$ inch from stem end of pepper, remove seeds with spoon. Marinate overnight in equal parts of oil and vinegar.
3. Drain peppers and fill with cheese.
4. Separate eggs. Beat whites until stiff, fold in slightly beaten yolks.
5. Roll peppers in flour, dip in egg mixture one at a time. Drop into deep fat at 360°F. Cook until evenly browned, 2 or 3 minutes. Drain well.
6. Saute onion and garlic in olive oil until onion is clear. Strain tomatoes through sieve and combine with onion and garlic. Add chicken stock, wine, spices, and seasoning.
7. Simmer for 8 to 10 minutes.
8. Twenty minutes before serving, place peppers in sauce and simmer until heated through.

CREPAS DE POLLO
(Chicken Crepes)

Su Casa

Ingredients: Yield: 6 portions, 3 crepes each

Chicken, cut-up, 3 pounds	1
Tomatoes, canned	12 ounces
Onion, small, chopped	$\frac{1}{2}$
Garlic Cloves, chopped	2
Salt	as needed
Pepper	pinch
Cumin	pinch
Cloves	pinch
Oregano	pinch
Chicken Base	1 teaspoon
Raisins	$\frac{1}{2}$ cup
Crepes	
Eggs	2
Milk	1 cup
Flour	$\frac{1}{2}$ cup
Baking Powder	$\frac{1}{4}$ teaspoon
Sugar	1 teaspoon
Salt	$\frac{1}{2}$ teaspoon
Vanilla	3 drops
Butter, melted	5 ounces
Sour Cream	1 cup

Procedure:

1. Cook chicken in water until done. Remove meat from bones. Reserve broth.
2. Blend tomatoes, onion, garlic, spices, chicken base, raisins, salt, and 2 cups broth. Simmer for 15 minutes. Add chicken meat and cook another 5 minutes.
3. Mix eggs and milk. Mix baking powder with flour, then slowly beat into liquid. Stir in sugar, salt, vanilla, and butter. Beat well to avoid lumps.
4. Using a 2-ounce measure, drop batter on hot griddle. Bake until lightly browned on bottom and cooked on top. Baking time will be about 4 minutes for each crepe.
5. Baked crepes may be stacked on the side until all are done.
6. To serve, place some of the chicken mixture on each crepe, top with a spoonful of sour cream, and roll up. Place three crepes, seam side down, in small casserole. Pour more of chicken mixture over them and bake in oven at 350°F. for 10 minutes.

ARROZ CON POLLO

Su Casa

Ingredients: Yield: 4 portions

Frying Chickens, 2½ pound each, cut-up	2
Onion, medium, chopped	½
Parsley, chopped	¼ bunch
Oregano, leaf	1 teaspoon
Garlic, granulated	¼ teaspoon
Salt	as needed
Chicken Stock	1 cup
Butter, melted	½ pound
Tomato, fresh, diced	1 medium
Green Peas, cooked	1 cup
Rice, cooked (see recipe)	6 cups

Procedure:

1. Place chicken on a baking pan. Sprinkle with oregano, parsley, garlic, onion, and salt. Pour stock and melted butter over chicken.
2. Bake in oven at 375°F. for 1 hour, 15 minutes.
3. Mix green peas and tomato with rice. Place chicken on top of rice and bake in oven at 350°F. for 10 minutes.

CAMARONES A LA VERACRUZANA
(Shrimp Veracruz-Style)

Su Casa

Ingredients: Yield: 2 portions

Garlic Cloves	2
Oil	$\frac{1}{2}$ cup
Shrimp, in shell	12 large
White Wine	3 ounces
Parsley, chopped	2 teaspoons
Salt	as needed

Procedure:

1. Chop garlic and place in oil. Let stand for at least 1 hour.
2. To clean shrimp, remove legs and cut lengthwise from bottom, being careful not to cut shell. With fingers force shrimp halves open to expose intestine and hold under running cold water.
3. Remove garlic from oil. Pour oil into frying pan and heat. Place shrimp one at a time, shell side up, in hot oil. Place a smaller pan on top of shrimp to weight them down and fry for approximately 13 minutes.
4. Remove from heat. Pour off oil. Return to heat and sprinkle with wine and parsley. Serve at once.

COOKED RICE

Su Casa

Ingredients: Yield: 75 portions

Oil	2 cups
Garlic Cloves	7
Converted Rice	8 pounds
Salt	$\frac{1}{4}$ cup
Onions, medium, finely chopped	2
Tomatoes, canned, whole	1 #10 can
Chicken Base	5 ounces
Chicken Stock, hot	4 gallons

TRUCHA AL CILANTRO
(Brook Trout with Fresh Coriander)

Su Casa

Ingredients: Yield: 6 portions

Brook Trout, boneless, 4 to 6 ounces each	6
Lime Juice	3 ounces
Salt	as needed
Pepper	as needed
Flour	6 ounces
Butter, clarified	6 ounces
Oil	4 ounces
Cucumbers, medium, cut lengthwise, seeded, sliced	2
Coriander, Fresh, chopped	3 teaspoons

Procedure:

1. Sprinkle trout with 2 ounces lime juice, salt, and pepper. Flour on both sides.
2. Saute fish in oil and 3 ounces butter, three at a time, until brown on both sides. Place on heated, greased baking sheet. Bake in oven at 350°F. for 11 minutes.
3. Saute cucumbers in 3 ounces butter until clear and soft. Sprinkle with 1 ounce lime juice and chopped coriander.
4. Place fish on hot platter and arrange cucumbers over and around it.

COOKED RICE *(cont'd.)*

Procedure:

1. Heat oil with 3 cloves garlic. Wash rice and drain well. Saute in hot oil until golden brown. Mince 4 cloves garlic. Add salt, onions, minced garlic, tomatoes, chicken base, and chicken stock.
2. Mix well. Cook until almost dry.
3. Remove quantity of rice needed, place in covered pan and bake in oven at 350°F. for 10 or 12 minutes.

REFRIED BEANS

Su Casa

Ingredients: Yield: 50 portions

    Pinto Beans   10 pounds
    Water   as needed
    Salt $1\frac{1}{2}$ cups
    Lard   3 pounds

Procedure:

1. Cook beans with enough water to cover until very soft. Drain and whip in mixer.
2. Heat lard in large frying pan. Add beans and fry over low heat. Stir to prevent sticking.

SPECIAL SALAD

Su Casa

Ingredients:

    Iceberg Lettuce Head, pulled apart   1
    Tomato Wedges, fresh   as needed
    Swiss Cheese, cut in strips   as needed
    Italian Sausage, cut in strips   as needed
    Italian Vegetable Garnish, (a prepared
      sweet-sour garnish)   as needed
    Red Wine and Olive Oil Dressing
      with Garlic   as needed
    Parmesan Cheese, grated   as needed

Procedure:

1. Toss vegetables, Swiss cheese, and sausage lightly with dressing.
2. Sprinkle with Parmesan cheese.

TANGO

WINE LIST

---

brewery

superburgers

(12 ounces of chopped steak served open face plain or with choice of toppings)

super burger	$2.95
super cheese	$3.50
super super burger	$4.00

any or all toppings

hamburgers

(1/2 pound hamburger)

hamburger	$2.10
cheeseburger	$2.25
swissburger	$2.25
cheddarburger	$2.25
bleu cheeseburger	$2.40
mushroom-bacon cheeseburger	$2.75

fresh mushrooms only

pizzaburger	$2.50
crabmeat burger	$3.50

fresh crabmeat mounded on our hamburger topped with baked cheese

kiddie burgers $1.65 ✳

weight watchers hamburger $1.65 ✳

weight watchers steak—new york strip $2.50

appetizers and side orders

fried mushrooms (fresh)	$1.50
giant steak onion rings	$1.00
cottage fries	$1.00
zucchini fingers	$1.25
home made chili (seasonal)	$1.50
brunswick stew	$1.50

robert woods style

onion soup	$1.50

(home made)

none better in chicago

in order to maintain the high quality of our fruit and salad buffet, please no sharing ; no waste. cheaters will be dealt with handily.

salad

our new concept salad and fruit bar

with meals	$.99

without a meal

lunch	$1.95
dinner	$3.25

and weekend

other brewery specialties

filet mignon (8 oz.)	$6.50
frog legs	$4.75

sautéed in garlic butter

chicken itza	$3.50

breast of chicken, mushrooms and rice covered with a chile chili flavored sauce and served in parchment

the deli

POULTRY

Roast Duckling Montmorency	10.25
dark bing cherry sauce	
Savory Broiled Chicken	8.50
half a chicken, disjointed	

SALADS

Caesar Salad	2.00
Sliced Tomato Salad	2.00

ENTREE SALADS

served with warm bread and herbed butter

Watercress Salad	4.50
with onions, shallots, water chestnuts, bacon and mushrooms with herb dressing	
Seafood Salad à La Russe	6.75
poached fresh salmon resting on a bed of vegetables with mustard sauce	

A LA CARTE VEGETABLES

Fried Eggplant Fingers with Sour Cream	2.25
Fried Carrot Fingers with Sour Cream	2.00
Potato Skins	2.25
served with either sour cream or applesauce	

bit 'o' italy

veal parmesan	$3.95

eggplant parmesan brewery

slices of baked eggplant covered with our tomato sauce covered with delicious baked cheese	$3.25
vegetables monreale	$2.75

fresh vegetables lightly sautéed with tomato sauce covered with baked cheese

italian steak sandwich	$3.50

sirloin breaded & broiled, and covered with melted italian cheeses.

HOT APPETIZERS

Escargots

Escargots

Baked Mussels Tango	3.50
herb garlic topping baked on the half-shell	
Steamed Mussels Tango	3.25
cloves of fresh garlic, wedges of orange and onion	
Mussels Marseillaise	3.75
steamed in a seafood broth touched with saffron	
Baked Shrimp Dijonnaise	3.75
baked shrimp in garlic, butter and mustard	
Coquille of Crab Meat	3.25
crab meat baked in white wine sauce gratiné	
Oysters St. George	3.00
fresh oysters, topped with spinach, crab meat and cheese and baked on the half-shell	
Fried Oysters	3.00
crisp with a savory butter sauce	
Ratatouille	1.75
the classic mediterranean vegetable stew baked au gratin	2.25
Fresh Mushroom Caps	2.50
sautéed in butter and garlic	

COLD APPETIZERS

Smoked Salmon Paté	3.00
with shrimp, served with fresh dill sauce	
King Crab Legs	4.25
served with mustard sauce	
Shrimp Cocktail	3.75
Bluepoint Oysters on the Half Shell	3.25
Chilled Poached Salmon à La Russe	3.50
poached fresh salmon resting on a bed of vegetables with mustard sauce	
White Asparagus	2.50
dressed with mustard sauce	
Ratatouille	1.75

ENTREE SOUP

served with warm bread, herbed butter and salad

Bouillabaisse de Marseilles	13.75
the classic seafood dish of the Mediterranean	

*price subject to change with season, inquire for correct price.

FISH

tureen of soup, salad, rice tango and bread	
superior Whitefish	
broiled	8.50
almondine sautéed	9.50
Trout, broiled or sautéed	10.00
Fresh Brook Trout, sautéed almondine	11.00
Fresh Brook Trout, stuffed with crab meat and sautéed	11.25
Fresh Broiled Walleye Pike—when available	9.50

OCEAN FISH

served with tureen of soup, salad, rice tango and bread

Fresh Boston Scrod, sautéed	8.50
French Turbot	
sautéed	12.50
almondine	13.50
Dover Sole	12.50
sautéed and served with sauce albert	

SHELL FISH

served with tureen of soup, salad, rice tango and bread

King Crab Legs	13.00
cold with mustard sauce	

DINNER

Prime Aged Filet Mignon	13.75
Prime Aged New York Cut Sirloin	14.00
Grilled Spring Lamb Chops	11.75
Ice Tea	.75

TANGO
The Contemporary Chicago Classic

Tango
3172 N. Sheridan Road,
Chicago, Illinois.

Classics! The double-breasted polo coat, a '41 Lincoln Continental, Gucci loafers, Mies's Barcelona chair, Walter Huston's "September Song."

And a restaurant called Tango.

Classics, all of them. Each is one-of-a-kind, beyond trendiness and the vagaries of taste, and occupies its own space/time niche. And each has a tremendous influence on anything that follows.

While the climb to "classicality" usually takes a while, Tango merely catapulted there. In the short time since August 1973, when George Badonsky opened the glass doors of his establishment, Tango has become a classic, as both a restaurant design and a foodservice concept.

The experience of Tango is more than visual. It is also a mood of excitement and anticipation. As a sculptured space, the restaurant is deceptively simple, four rooms on two levels, flowing into each other but apart so there is a sense of sharing, yet privacy. For every yin, Tango offers a yang: Some floors are marble, some deeply carpeted. There are open spaces and closed, sharp edges and curves. And at first, one sees only color: Apollonian white and Dionysian brown. Then one notices the delight of detail: beautiful glasses, a fine piece of Senefu sculpture, a Cuevas painting, precise theatre lighting; but nothing intrudes. Chicago has not seen a restaurant like this before—totally sophisticated yet utterly simple.

As an *oeuvre*, Tango is restaurant-designer Tony Barone's finest hour.

As a restaurant, Tango is the joyous summation of George Badonsky's foodservice knowledge. "Dining out should be

237

George Badonsky's restaurants include The Brewery, the new Bastille, and Tango—which has become a classic in six years.

an act of participation, a sharing. I want to turn people on to things, to introduce them to a wine or maybe a new dish that I'm enthusiastic about," says Badonsky.

The food at Tango is exceptional. All domestic fish is purchased port fresh daily by Badonsky. The Tango menu is large, more than thirty entrees, including three shrimp dishes, three trout preparations, bouillabaisse, walleyed pike, French turbot, and two kinds of mackerel. It is, however, the nonmenu daily specialties which account for sixty-five percent of Tango's business and give the place its unusual distinction. How many fish restaurants serve sea bass, gray sole, fresh tuna, shark, fresh sturgeon, hake (French colin), fresh water white bass, and fresh herring? The food is creatively prepared by Chef John Stolzman, formerly of Maxim's in Chicago, and attractively presented by Tango's crew of alert waiters and waitresses.

Opposite, the sleek bar area at Tango offers uncluttered seating "coves." Below, Tango's main dining room: a simple sculptured space with delightful details.

Indeed, Tango is a superb fish house, but many people think of it for its "other" offerings: Tournedos Helder, Rack of Spring Lamb en Croute, or Roast Duckling Montmorency. And then there are Tango's inimitable vegetables—fried carrot and eggplant fingers with sour cream, potato skins with apple sauce or sour cream, and eggplant Provencal.

Food always comes first at Tango, then show-biz. Badonsky re-introduced the intimate supper club to Chicago when he hired the legendary Bricktop to sing in the ninety-seat main dining room for ten weeks, then later for six weeks more. It was a sell out with two shows a night as were the performances of harmonica virtuoso Larry Adler.

Because of his passionate involvement in the restaurant business and his great originality, George Badonsky is singular in the Chicago foodservice world. Perhaps he is making up for lost time. Ten years ago at the age of thirty-three, he left "the music business" where he was an independent record producer and publisher. Badonsky got involved in The Brewery, a typical Chicago-style hamburger pub, and the foodservice business hooked him. Being a quick learner, Badonsky absorbed all of the information and knowledge that he could. For example, "Ten years ago I knew nothing about fine wine, now I'm a fanatic. I learned everything from a friend, Dave Schnell, the greatest wine man alive, and now I want to share my pleasure with others. That's why Tango has the lowest priced wines in the city . . . a 1974 classified Bordeaux for $9, can you imagine that? And a '59 Chateau Meyney for $19. For $19! That's why Tango sells thirty-five to fifty-five cases of wine a week."

Badonsky's foodservice education continued when he opened Tango, and then in 1975 when a new Brewery replaced the old, physically and in market approach. The second Brewery seeks a broader base as an upper-middle-class neighborhood establishment. "It's a really good contemporary saloon with a variety of food from burgers and sauteed king crab legs to veal Parmesan and large baked cornish hens," says Badonsky. The new Brewery, also designed by Barone, has a different look. There are several levels, natural oak walls, copper-topped, kidney-shaped tables, a garden room area whith a twelve-foot square skylight, and ceilings that were cunningly devised "to roll" or seemingly undulate.

Interesting comparisons: at the Brewery there are 150 seats and a check average of $6.50, including liquor; at Tango, 175 seats and a check average of $22, with liquor. The Brewery serves 700 to 900 meals on a Saturday, perhaps 400 on Wednesday; at Tango, which is predominantly a dinner business, 400 on a Saturday, 225 on Wednesday. Together, the two restaurants gross about $2.5 million a year, a figure that should go higher now that Badonsky's third restaurant, the renovated Bastille, has opened on the near north side.

Within his organization, Badonsky's relationship with his employees is special: demanding, but based on give-and-take. "I don't want sycophants. I want lively, dedicated people with a point of view, whether it agrees with mine or not." The Badonsky operations are staffed with unusually talented younger people who are anxious to learn about wine, food, and the celebration of life that restaurants provide. They are learning fast, not unlike their employer, except that he has learned faster.

ESCARGOTS TANGO

Tango

Ingredients: Yield: 4 portions

Mushroom Caps, fresh, large, blanched	16
Bacon, chopped, cooked	$\frac{1}{4}$ cup
Escargots	16
Garlic Butter (see recipe)	as needed

Procedure:

1.   Arrange mushroom caps in small casseroles.
2.   Put bacon into each cavity.
3.   Place an escargot on top of each mushroom.
4.   Heat garlic butter until consistency of thick paste and pour over escargots.
5.   Bake in oven at 350°F. for 5 to 10 minutes, or until butter is boiling.

KING CRAB LEGS SAUTEED IN GARLIC BUTTER

Tango

Procedure:

Split shell along one side of each leg. Cut crab legs in 2-inch pieces and saute in garlic butter (see recipe).

GARLIC BUTTER

Tango

Ingredients:

Yield: 1 pound

Butter	1 pound
Parsley, minced	1 bunch
Garlic, cloves, minced	5
Shallots, minced	5
Pernod or Richard (Anisette) Liqueur	$\frac{1}{2}$ ounce
Salt	as needed
Pepper	as needed

Procedure:

1. Soften butter and mix in all ingredients.
2. Mixture may be frozen until needed.

POTATO SKINS

Tango

Ingredients:

Yield: 1 portion

Baking Potato, large	1

Procedure:

1. Bake potato. When cool cut in half, then in quarters.
2. Scoop potato out of skins and save for other uses.
3. Just before serving, fry skins in deep fat at 380°F. until crisp.
4. Serve with sour cream.

BOUILLABAISSE DE MARSEILLES

Tango

Ingredients: Yield: 1 portion

Mussels	5
Clam	1
Oyster	1
Crab Claw	1
Lobster Tail, 3 ounces	1
Scampi	2
Fillet of Red Snapper, 6 ounces	1
Scallions, chopped	2 ounces
Base Stock (see recipe)	3 cups

Procedure:

1. Cut all fish in uniform sized pieces. Place in a pot and add base stock.
2. Simmer 20 minutes.
3. Serve in large bowl; garnish with parsley.

BASE STOCK
(for Bouillabaisse de Marseilles)

Tango

Ingredients: Yield: 30 portions

Leeks, thinly sliced	10 pounds
Onion, chopped	5 pounds
Tomatoes, fresh, diced	4 gallons
Garlic, minced	$\frac{1}{3}$ cup
Olive Oil	$1\frac{1}{2}$ quarts
Saffron	1 tablespoon
White Wine	3 gallons
Fish Stock	6 gallons
Salt	as needed
Pepper	as needed

Procedure:

1. Saute leeks, onion, garlic, and tomatoes in olive oil.
2. Add saffron and wine and simmer for 30 minutes.
3. Add fish stock and simmer for 1 hour. Add salt and pepper to taste. Refrigerate until used.

CREAM OF CAULIFLOWER SOUP

Tango

Ingredients:

Yield: 35 gallons

Cauliflower, fresh	15 pounds
Onions, large	10
Celery Stalk	1
Chicken Stock	30 gallons
Garlic Cloves, crushed	4
Cream	1 gallon
Butter	3 pounds
Cornstarch	$2\frac{3}{4}$ pounds
Salt	as needed
Pepper, white	as needed
Monosodium Glutamate	as needed
Parsley, chopped	1 quart

Procedure:

1. Grind cauliflower, onions, and celery very fine.
2. Add chicken stock and simmer gently for 45 minutes.
3. Add cream and butter.
4. Blend cornstarch with enough cold water to make a paste. Stir into hot soup. Cook, stirring constantly, until thickened. Add salt, pepper, and monosodium glutamate.
5. Garnish each serving with a sprinkle of chopped parsely.

CASSOULET

Ingredients: Yield: 25 portions

White Beans	2 quarts
Cold Water	as needed
Boiling Water	as needed
Salt Pork	$1\frac{1}{3}$ pounds
Bouquet Garni	
Carrots, medium, fresh	2
Celery Rib	1
Parsley	as needed
Bay Leaves	as needed
Thyme	as needed
Onion, small	1
Cloves	as needed
Goose Fat	$\frac{1}{2}$ cup
Pork Loin, cubed	3 pounds
Breast of Lamb, cubed	2 pounds
Onions, large, chopped	4
Garlic Cloves, chopped	6
Veal Stock	3 cups
Pork Sausage, Stuffed, 1-inch pieces	4 pounds
Roast Goose Meat, cubed	4 pounds
Bacon, diced	4 pounds
Potato, diced	1 large
Salt	as needed
Pepper	as needed
Monosodium Glutamate	as needed
Bread Crumbs, coarse	1 quart
Butter or Goose Fat	$\frac{1}{2}$ to $\frac{3}{4}$ cup

CASSOULET *(cont'd.)*
Procedure:

1. Soak beans in cold water overnight.
2. Drain beans and cover with boiling water. Add bouquet garni composed of carrot, celery, parsley, bay leaves, thyme, and 1 small onion stuck with cloves.
3. Simmer for about 1 hour.
4. Saute pork, lamb, onion, and garlic in goose fat.
5. When meat is brown, add veal stock and simmer about 1 hour or until meat is tender.
6. Saute sausage and cook bacon. Discard fat.
7. Combine cooked beans, meats, sausage, and bacon in one pot. Add potato, salt, pepper, and monosodium glutamate. Simmer about $\frac{1}{2}$ hour.
8. Place about 8 ounces in individual casseroles. Top with bread crumbs, dot with butter or goose fat, and bake in oven at 350°F. for 30 minutes.

BREWERY CHILI

The Brewery and Tango

Ingredients: Yield: 10 gallons

Ground Beef	30 pounds
Onion, chopped	3 pounds
Garlic, minced	$\frac{1}{4}$ cup
Tomatoes, canned, diced	4 #10 cans
Salt	$\frac{1}{2}$ cup
Chili Powder	1 pound
Cumin	1 cup
Red Chili	as needed
Monosodium Glutamate	$\frac{1}{4}$ cup
Water	1 gallon
Beans, red, canned	6 #10 cans

Procedure:

1. Combine beef, onion, and garlic and saute until onions are transparent.
2. Add seasonings, tomatoes, and water. Bring to rapid boil and simmer for 1 hour.
3. Add beans and simmer 30 minutes, stirring occasionally.

BROILED ROCK CORNISH GAME HEN DIJON

Tango

Ingredients: Yield: 1 portion

Cornish Hen, quartered	1
Butter, melted	2 tablespoons
Salt	as needed
Pepper	as needed
Dijon Mustard	$\frac{1}{4}$ cup
White Wine	$\frac{1}{4}$ cup

CHICKEN ITZA

Tango

Ingredients: Yield: 24 portions

Chicken Breasts, boneless, 5 ounces each	24
Salt	$1\frac{1}{2}$ tablespoons
Pepper	$1\frac{1}{2}$ teaspoons
Flour	2 pounds
Oil	1 quart
Butter	1 pound
Onion, chopped	1 pound
Garlic Cloves, chopped	10
Tomatoes	2 #10 cans
Oregano, leaf	$\frac{1}{4}$ cup
Cumin	$\frac{1}{4}$ cup
Mushrooms, fresh, sliced	2 pounds
Parchment Papers, 12- by 12-inch pieces	24
Rice, cooked	4 pounds

Procedure:

1. Dredge chicken in flour mixed with salt and pepper.
2. Saute in hot oil until golden brown.
3. Combine $\frac{1}{4}$ pound butter, onion, and garlic and saute until onion is soft.
4. Add tomatoes and cook for 30 minutes.
5. Add oregano and cumin and cook 20 minutes more.
6. Grind sauce through fine blade, add remaining butter, and blend well.
7. Place a spoonful of rice on each piece of parchment paper, top with a chicken breast, then with some mushrooms. Cover with sauce.
8. Fold paper to form a seal. Place on sheet pan and bake in oven at 350°F. for 25 minutes.

BROILED ROCK CORNISH GAME HEN DIJON *(cont'd.)*
Procedure:

1. Brush hen with butter; sprinkle with salt and pepper.
2. Broil about 25 minutes, basting with a mixture of mustard and wine about 4 times during cooking.

PRESIDENT'S TUNA

Tango

Ingredients: Yield: 16 portions

Butter	18 ounces
Flour	10 ounces
Fish Stock	1 gallon
Heavy Cream	1 pint
Salt	as needed
Pepper	as needed
Noodles, cooked (6 pounds AP)	1 gallon
Tuna, canned, drained, flaked	3 pounds
Mushrooms, fresh, sliced	2 pounds
Mozzarella Cheese, sliced	3 pounds

Procedure:

1. Heat 10 ounces butter, blend in flour, and cook slowly for 10 minutes. Do not brown.
2. Whip in fish stock and cook until thickened and smooth, stirring constantly.
3. Add salt and pepper and simmer 30 minutes.
4. Strain. Add cream, then fold in 8 ounces butter.
5. In each casserole put: 3 ounces cream sauce, 3 ounces noodles, 3 ounces tuna, 2 ounces mushrooms, 2 ounces cream sauce, and 2 slices cheese in that order. Use 14-ounce casseroles.
6. Bake in oven at 350°F. for 25 minutes.

DOVER SOLE EN CROUTE

Tango

Ingredients: Yield: 4 portions

Dover Sole Fillets	2 pounds
White Wine	$\frac{1}{5}$ gallon
Salt	as needed
Pepper	as needed
Monosodium Glutamate	as needed
Thyme	pinch
Spinach, fresh, cooked	2 pounds
Onion, medium, chopped	1
Butter	$\frac{1}{2}$ pound
Nutmeg	pinch
Puff Pastry	2 pounds
Egg Yolk, beaten	1

Procedure:

1. Poach sole in wine seasoned with salt, pepper, monosodium glutamate, and thyme. Drain, cool, and flake apart with fork.
2. Chop spinach and saute with onion in butter. Season with nutmeg, salt, and pepper. Cool.
3. Roll out puff pastry (see recipe) to $\frac{1}{8}$-inch thickness. Cut 8 5-inch squares.
4. Place about 3 ounces of spinach on each of 4 squares. Top with 5 ounces sole.
5. Brush egg yolk around edges of pastry squares and top with a second pastry square. Press together to seal edges. Refrigerate until ready to use.
6. Bake in oven at 350°F. for 10 to 15 minutes.
7. Serve with lemon butter sauce.

FEUILLETAGE
(Puff Pastry)

Tango

Ingredients: Yield: 4 pounds

Flour, sifted	$3\frac{3}{4}$ cups
Salt	$1\frac{1}{2}$ teaspoon
Water	$1\frac{1}{4}$ to $1\frac{1}{2}$ cups
Butter, kneaded	1 pound

Procedure:

1. Mix flour and salt. Put on a board in a circle, making a well in the middle. Add water in well as needed, working in until smooth and elastic. Roll into a ball and let stand for 25 minutes.
2. Roll out into a sheet 8 inches square and of an even thickness. Put the kneaded butter in the middle and fold the paste over it to enclose it completely. Let stand for 10 minutes in cold place.
3. Give two turns to this paste. This operation, called *tourage* in French, is done in two parts:
    a. Roll out on a lightly floured board to a rectangle 24 inches long, 8 inches wide and $\frac{1}{2}$ inch thick.
    b. Re-fold this strip in thirds. You have now completed one turn. The second turn is done by rolling out the folded paste in the opposite direction and folding again.
4. Give 4 more turns to the paste, leaving it to stand for 10 minutes between each turn. It is now ready to use.

Note:

The purpose of turning and rolling is to spread the butter evenly in the paste. During preparation the pastry should be kept in a cold place but never put directly on ice.

OYSTERS ST. GEORGE

Tango

Ingredients: Yield: 60 portions

Spinach, fresh, cooked, chopped	10 pounds
Onions, large, chopped	3
Butter	4 ounces
Cream	1 quart
Salt	1 teaspoon
Pepper	$\frac{1}{2}$ teaspoon
Nutmeg	$\frac{1}{8}$ teaspoon
King Crab Meat, chopped	10 pounds
Light Cream Sauce	2 quarts
Swiss Cheese, grated	3 pounds
Parmesan Cheese, grated	3 pounds
Oysters on half shell	120

Procedure:

1. Saute chopped spinach and onions until onions are clear. Add cream, salt, pepper, and nutmeg. Cool.
2. Mix crabmeat with light cream sauce.
3. Mix Swiss cheese with Parmesan cheese.
4. Place oysters on baking sheets. Put small amount of spinach on each oyster, then some of the crabmeat mixture. Top with grated cheese.
5. Bake in oven at 350°F. for 10 to 15 minutes.

CEVICHE
(Marinated Fish)

Tango

Ingredients: Yield: 150 portions, 2 ounces each

Fish Fillets, cubed	20 pounds
Lemon Juice	2 quarts
Olive Oil	2 quarts
Onion, chopped	4 pounds
Tomatoes, fresh, diced	6 pounds
Green Peppers, diced	6 pounds
Ripe Olives, sliced	1 quart
Tomato Puree	1 #10 can
Oregano, leaf	$\frac{1}{4}$ cup
Salt	$\frac{1}{3}$ cup
Worcestershire Sauce	$\frac{1}{2}$ cup
Liquid Hot Pepper Seasoning	as needed
Parsley, fresh, chopped	$\frac{1}{2}$ cup

Procedure:

1. Marinate fish in lemon juice overnight.
2. Mix remaining ingredients.
3. Drain half the lemon juice off fish. Add remaining juice and fish to the other ingredients and toss lightly together.
4. Chill overnight and serve.

POACHED POMPANO WITH SHALLOT SAUCE

Tango

Ingredients: Yield: 60 portions

Butter	1 pound
Shallots, sliced	4 cups
Mushrooms, fresh, thinly sliced	4 cups
Brandy	1 cup
White Wine	1 quart
Veal Stock	1 quart
Whipping Cream	2 quarts
Cornstarch	4 to 5 table-spoons
Cold Water	as needed
Salt	1 teaspoon
Pepper	1 teaspoon
Thyme, leaf	$\frac{3}{4}$ teaspoon
Pompano Fillets, 8 ounces each	60
White Wine and Water, equal parts	as needed
Salt	as needed
Pepper	as needed
Thyme, leaf	pinch
Bay Leaf	1

Procedure:

1. Saute shallots and mushrooms in butter.
2. Add brandy and white wine. Reduce by one half.
3. Add veal stock and reduce by one third.
4. Add whipping cream. Mix cornstarch with enough cold water to make a thin paste. Slowly stir into creamed mixture as needed to thicken to desired consistency.
5. Cook until smooth and thickened, stirring constantly.
6. Stir in 1 pound butter. Season with salt, pepper, and thyme.
7. Poach pompano in equal parts of wine and water seasoned with bay leaf, salt, pepper, and thyme, until tender.
8. Top with shallot sauce and serve.

CHEESECAKE

Tango

Ingredients: Yield: 8 9-inch cakes

Graham Cracker Crusts, 9-inch	8
Sour Cream	2 quarts
Cream Cheese	6 pounds
Eggs	20
Vanilla	$\frac{1}{4}$ cup
Sugar	7 cups

Procedure:

1. Blend all ingredients at medium speed until smooth. Pour into graham cracker crusts.
2. Bake in oven at 275°F. for 40 minutes.
3. Cool and serve same day.

STRAWBERRIES TANGO

Tango

Ingredients: Yield: 20 portions

Sour Cream	$1\frac{1}{2}$ quarts
Brown Sugar	$\frac{1}{2}$ pound
Amaretto Liqueur	1 cup
Strawberries, fresh	5 pints

Procedure:

1. Combine sour cream, brown sugar, and Amaretto.
2. Fold in strawberries.
3. Serve in glass topped with sprinkling of brown sugar.

U of C HOSPITALS & CLINICS

A Special Kind of Restaurant

The Dietary Services Department
The University of Chicago Hospitals and Clinics,
950 East 59th Street, Chicago, Illinois.

It is interesting to consider that the word "restaurant," coined in late eighteenth-century France, originally meant a place where "restoratives" were served. That original meaning has particular relevance for the huge "restaurant" (more than 4000 meals a day) run by The University of Chicago Hospitals and Clinics, an amalgam of seven distinct healthcare institutions.

A hospital's dining-in restaurant differs from other forms of dining-out foodservices in that guests don't want to come to dinner. It is the unique challenge of hospital foodservice to please these reluctant guests.

For the hospital patient, food and the so-called hotel services (the room, a clean bed, bathing facilities) are the only two comforting "familiars" in an otherwise unfamiliar and dehumanizing situation. Because of this, the level of "familiar" expectation is very high. Thus, ironically, the unwilling guest is also a very demanding one. Patients expect their food hot, on time, and they want it to taste "as if mother had made it." Patients don't care—and shouldn't have to care—about the logistics of serving a large number of meals in rooms, managing transportation from a central kitchen to distant areas of the building, and preparing a variety of special diet foods. What patients *do* care about is the end product: is the food cold and unappealing?

At the University of Chicago Hospitals and Clinics the food *is* served hot and it *is* appealing; perhaps a homelike veal Parmesan, or sweet and sour pork, or a chicken cacciatore—not unlike mother used to make. To be sure the food is served hot, the Dietary Services Department uses a food distribution system, specifically designed for the health-care industry, that utilizes a heating element in transit, one which is preheated to 225°F. in the kitchen. Meals remain hot and

259

When patrons are patients, the University of Chicago Hospitals and Clinics may be *the* place to eat.

appetizing 45 minutes after they have been placed on the tray and in the transit cart.

The Department is also concerned about the presentation of food—how it looks when the patient receives it. All food items are carefully arranged on compact trays, with bright, cheerful placemats and napkins that resemble what one might see (and eat from) in a Boeing 747.

The key to an efficient hospital foodservice operation is menu planning. At the University of Chicago Hospitals, menu planning is not only a matter of cost efficiency with nutritional needs paramount but it is an ultimate aid to patient morale. All menus are prepared on a two-week cycle for variety.

The Dietary Services Department offers a selective menu to all patients, regardless of diet type. This has particular meaning at the University Hospitals because sixty-five percent of the patients are on a special diet by physician's prescription. But, whether on a general or special diet, patients are offered a choice of three entrees: two hot and one cold. If patients are on a liquid diet, they still receive a menu which allows them to select the kind of beverage they want and make a choice between gelatin, custard, or ice cream (they can even choose the flavor of gelatin they want). Small things, but vastly important to an uneasy or uncomfortable hospital patient who looks upon mealtime as *the* event of the day.

All menus are prepared by a registered dietician who takes many considerations into account: the nutritional value of the food; the ethnic background of the patient; the Department's ability to individualize the menu for patients' nutritional and medical needs; the availability of the food product; the capabilities of the production equipment and personnel; and, of course, economics.

Menu making that offers a patient a choice of food is a relatively recent development. Two decades ago, little attention was paid to patient preference in menu planning. Very few hospitals offered any type of selectivity on their menus. The menu was written to satisfy daily dietary requirements, and every patient received the same food, "diet allowing."

The U of C Hospitals' Dietary Services Department regards the patient's right to select his own food as very important. Not only is it psychologically valuable, but a selective food menu is the beginning of a learning process. The patient gets used to seeing all the foods he is allowed to have on his particular diet, thus reinforcing the diet instruction he receives at the time of his dismissal from the hospital.

The University of Chicago Hospitals and Clinics offer the traditional three meals a day plus a night snack—a "pleasant familiar" of high nutritional value.

In back of the "pleasant familiar" foodservice that the patient experiences, the large Dietary Services Department operates on detailed specificity and clockwork efficiency. To protect against waste and labor, all food is prepared in multiples of fifty because studies indicate that University of Chicago Hospitals' patients order meals in quantities of fifty, by type. All recipes are detailed and implemented exactly. Even the recipe for roast beef is carefully spelled out and followed to the letter.

If the U of C's hospital foodservice operation were in the public sector, it would be big business indeed. To serve 4000 meals a day, there are over 200 employees and a department that is divided into these major areas: patient services—offering dietary care to patients; food systems, including food procurement and preparation; special pediatric nutrition services; non-patient food services (for employees and patient families).

The annual budget of the Dietary Services Department for 1978–79 was almost $4,700,000, with 45% of that amount to cover food and supplies, and 55% for labor (which is unionized).

From 1974 to late 1977, a period of major reorganization and innovation, the Director of Food Services for the University of Chicago's Hospitals and Clinics was Gareth R. Campbell, whose background covered industrial catering, inflight feeding, and experience in hospital foodservice including administration, research, and development. In early 1978 Campbell became Director of Plant and Facilities Management for the University of Chicago's Hospitals and Clinics. His successor is Helen Simons, who bears the changed title Director of Dietary Services Department. Simons has been with the U of C since 1973 as Director of Dietetics, responsible for clinical services. She has had notable experience in management and administration developing the dietary department in the Winfield State Mental Hospital in Kansas, where she served for 17 years. Then she taught food management and nutrition at Oklahoma State (where she received her masters degree in nutrition) before coming to Szabo Food Services in Chicago in 1971 as corporate staff dietician, and then to The University of Chicago two years later.

Under Campbell and Simons, the goal at The University of Chicago's Hospitals and Clinics remains the same: "customer satisfaction"—a goal that recognizes the patient as the most *important* kind of patron.

CANADIAN CHEESE SOUP

U of C Hospitals and Clinics

Ingredients: Yield: 50 portions, 6 ounces each

Margarine	8 ounces
Onion, chopped	8 ounces
Flour	1 cup
Cornstarch	$\frac{1}{3}$ cup plus 2 tablespoons
Paprika	1 teaspoon
Salt	1 tablespoon
Pepper, white	1 teaspoon
Milk, skimmed	1 gallon
Chicken Stock	$1\frac{1}{2}$ gallons
Carrots, diced, cooked	1 pound
Celery, diced, cooked	1 pound
Cheddar Cheese, sharp, diced	1 pound
Parsley, chopped	$\frac{1}{2}$ cup

Procedure:

1. Saute onion in margarine until lightly browned.
2. Mix flour and cornstarch. Blend into onion and cook 3 or 4 minutes.
3. Blend in paprika, salt, and pepper.
4. Add milk and stock slowly. Cook and stir until thickened.
5. Add carrots and celery.
6. Just before serving, add cheese and bring to serving temperature.
7. Garnish each serving with chopped parsley.

CREAM OF POTATO SOUP

U of C Hospitals and Clinics

Ingredients: Yield: 50 portions, 6 ounces each

Potatoes, fresh, peeled, ½-inch dice	3 pounds
	6 ounces
Celery, diced	9½ ounces
Onion, diced	1¾ pounds
Bacon, diced	10¾ ounces plus
White Sauce	6 pounds
	12 ounces
Milk, whole	1 pound plus
	8 ounces
Salt	as needed

Procedure:

1. Cook potatoes until half done. Add celery and onion. Cook until tender.
2. Cook bacon and drain well.
3. Heat white sauce to simmer point. Add cooked vegetables and bacon. Stir.
4. Add milk. Salt to taste.
5. Heat through and serve.

MINESTRONE

U of C Hospitals and Clinics

Ingredients: Yield: 50 portions, 6 ounces each

Beef Bones	15 pounds
Water, cold	4 gallons
Bay Leaves	2
Salt	3 tablespoons
Kidney Beans, canned	2 #10 cans
Onion, chopped	1 pound
Potatoes, fresh, diced	1 pound
Carrots, thinly sliced	$1\frac{1}{2}$ pounds
Parsley, chopped	$\frac{1}{2}$ cup
Spaghetti, cooked	12 ounces

Procedure:

1. Combine bones, water, bay leaves, and salt. Bring to boiling and simmer 3 to 4 hours.
2. Remove bones and chop meat.
3. Add meat to stock along with vegetables. Cover and simmer 1 hour. Replace water as necessary.
4. Add spaghetti. Season to taste.
5. Heat and serve.

NAVY BEAN SOUP

U of C Hospitals and Clinics

Ingredients: Yield: 50 portions, 6 ounces each

Water	1 gallon plus 1 cup
Navy Beans	1 pound $\frac{3}{4}$ cup
Onions, yellow, diced	$4\frac{1}{4}$ ounces
Bacon, raw, diced	$4\frac{1}{4}$ ounces plus 1 pound
Potatoes, peeled, diced	6 ounces
Salt	dash
Pepper, black	dash
Ham Shanks	$10\frac{3}{4}$ ounces
Water	as needed

Procedure:

1. Put cold water and washed beans into stock pot. Bring to a boil and cook 1 hour.
2. Add remaining ingredients and enough water to make 4 gallons. Continue cooking until beans are tender.

BAKED STUFFED PORK CHOPS

U of C Hospitals and Clinics

Ingredients:　　　　　　　　　　Yield: 50 portions, 6.5 ounces each

Pork Chops	17 pounds plus 8 ounces
Salt	1½ ounces
Pepper, black	1½ teaspoons
Bread Crumbs, dry	2 pounds plus 6 ounces
Onion, chopped	12 ounces
Pepper, black	½ teaspoon
Poultry Seasoning	1 tablespoon
Salt	9 grams
Oil	2¼ ounces
Eggs, whole, frozen, beaten	4 ounces
Water	1½ quarts
Green Pepper Rings, fresh	1 pound plus 8 ounces
Water	as needed

Procedure:

1. Brown chops on both sides on lightly greased griddle. Sprinkle with 1½ ounces of salt and 1½ teaspoons pepper.
2. Place chops on 18- by 26-inch sheet pans.
3. Combine bread crumbs, onion, ½ teaspoon pepper, poultry seasoning, 9 grams salt, oil, eggs, and 1½ quarts water. Mix lightly but thoroughly.
4. Place 1 pepper ring on each chop.
5. Top each with ¼ cup bread mixture.
6. Pour enough water in each pan to cover bottom.
7. Bake in oven at 350°F. for 1 to 1½ hours or until done.

FRIED GIBLETS WITH BACON

U of C Hospitals and Clinics

Ingredients:

Yield: 50 servings, 4 ounces each

Chicken Gizzards	8 pounds plus 13 ounces
Flour	4 pounds plus 12 ounces
Salt	2 ounces
Eggs	6
Milk	2¼ cups
Crumbs, cornflake	2 pounds plus 6 ounces
Bacon, cooked, crumbled	3¼ cups

Procedure:

1. Wash and drain gizzards. Place in 2-inch full-sized steamtable pan and steam cook 30 minutes. Drain.
2. Mix 2 pounds 6 ounces flour with salt.
3. Mix eggs and milk.
4. Mix remaining flour with cornflake crumbs.
5. Dip giblets into ingredients listed in 2), 3), and 4) above in order.
6. Fry in deep fat at 350°F. not more than 5 minutes.
7. Serve 5 giblets per order. Top each serving with 1 tablespoon bacon bits.

SWEET SOUR PORK

U of C Hospitals and Clinics

Ingredients: Yield: 50 portions, 8 ounces each

Eggs, whole, frozen, slightly beaten	1 cup
Soy Sauce	1 cup
Cornstarch	1¾ cups
Salt	3 tablespoons
Pork Cubes, ½-inch	15 pounds
Garlic Cloves, minced	2
Oil	6 ounces
Bean Sprouts, canned	6 pounds
Pineapple Chunks, canned	3 pounds
Juices plus Water	3½ quarts
Vinegar	2½ cups
Soy Sauce	½ cup
Salt	1½ tablespoons
Sugar	4 cups
Cornstarch	1 cup
Green Pepper, fresh, sliced	1 pound

Procedure:

1. Combine eggs, 1 cup soy sauce, 1¾ cups cornstarch, and 3 tablespoons salt. Pour over meat, stir, and let stand 10 minutes.
2. Add garlic to oil and heat. Brown pork.
3. Drain bean sprouts and pineapple chunks. Combine juices with vinegar, ½ cup soy sauce, and enough water to make 3½ quarts. Add 1½ tablespoons salt and bring to a boil.
4. Combine sugar and 1 cup cornstarch. Slowly stir into hot liquid and cook 10 minutes or until thick and clear, stirring constantly.
5. Add browned meat, bean sprouts, pineapple, and green pepper to sauce. Simmer 5 minutes.
6. Serve over cooked rice.

SPAGHETTI WITH MEAT SAUCE

U of C Hospitals and Clinics

Ingredients: Yield: 50 portions, 11.7 ounces each

Ground Beef	12 pounds
Garlic Powder	½ teaspoon
Salt	1¼ ounces
Oregano, ground	1 tablespoon
Pepper, cayenne	1 teaspoon
Tomatoes, canned, crushed	2 #10 cans
Tomato Paste	5 pounds plus 12 ounces
Water	1 gallon
Water (for spaghetti)	1½ gallons
Salt	2½ ounces
Spaghetti	3 pounds

Procedure:

1. Braise beef in its own fat. Drain off excess fat.
2. Add garlic powder, salt, oregano, thyme, and cayenne pepper. Cook 5 minutes.
3. Add tomatoes, tomato paste, and 1 gallon water.
4. Cook over low heat about 3 hours, stirring frequently to prevent sticking. Add more water if sauce becomes too thick. Skim off fat before serving.
5. Bring 1½ gallons water to boiling, add 2½ ounces salt, and spaghetti.
6. Cook about 15 minutes, stirring occasionally. Drain.
7. Serve sauce over spaghetti.

CHICKEN CACCIATORE

U of C Hospitals and Clinics

Ingredients: Yield: 50 portions

Chicken, fryers, quartered, 2½ pounds each	12½ pounds
Flour	12 ounces
Salt	2 ounces
Oil	14 ounces
Tomatoes, whole, canned	1 #10 can
Green Peppers, EP	2 pounds plus 4 ounces
Garlic, minced	¼ clove
Pepper, black, ground	1½ teaspoon
Oregano, ground	1½ teaspoon

Procedure:

1. Wash and drain chicken.
2. Mix flour and salt and dredge chicken.
3. Place chicken quarters on well-greased, 18- by 26- by 1-inch sheet pans, 25 pieces per pan.
4. Brush generously with oil. Place in oven at 425°F. until brown, 30 to 40 minutes.
5. Crush tomatoes in steam-jacketed kettle. Add green pepper cut into lengthwise strips ¼ to ½ inches wide.
6. Add remaining ingredients and heat to boiling.
7. Place browned chicken in serving pans. Do not overlap or crowd.
8. Distribute hot sauce uniformly over chicken. Bake, uncovered, in oven at 325°F. for 30 to 40 minutes.

CHICKEN TETRAZZINI

U of C Hospitals and Clinics

Ingredients: Yield: 50 portions, 6.1 ounces each

Chicken Cubes, frozen	7 pounds plus 15 ounces
Spaghetti	1 pound plus 5 ounces
Water, boiling	$3\frac{1}{4}$ quarts
Salt	1 ounce
Onion, chopped	2 ounces
Green Pepper, chopped	2 ounces
Mushroom Pieces, canned	1 #10 can
Margarine	$8\frac{1}{2}$ ounces
Flour	$4\frac{3}{4}$ ounces
Chicken Soup Base	$3\frac{3}{4}$ ounces
Water, boiling	3 pints, $1\frac{1}{2}$ cups
Milk, non-fat, dry	$3\frac{1}{2}$ ounces
Water, warm	1 quart
Pimiento, canned, chopped	$5\frac{1}{2}$ ounces
Pepper, black, ground	$\frac{1}{4}$ teaspoon
Cheddar Cheese, grated	as needed

Procedure:

1. Cook chicken cubes in steamer 20 minutes or until tender.
2. Cook spaghetti in boiling salted water about 15 minutes. Drain.
3. Saute onion, pepper, and mushrooms in margarine until tender.
4. Combine flour, chicken soup base, and $1\frac{1}{2}$ cups water. Stir until smooth. Add to sauteed vegetables.
5. Gradually add 3 pints boiling water. Stir and cook until smooth and thickened.
6. Reconstitute dry milk in warm water and add to above mixture. Simmer 10 minutes.
7. Add pimientos, pepper, chicken, and spaghetti.
8. Pour mixture into steamtable pans.
9. Sprinkle grated cheese over each.
10. Bake in oven at 425°F. about 20 minutes or until cheese is browned.

TUNA SUPREME ON NOODLES

U of C Hospitals and Clinics

Ingredients: Yield: 50 portions, 6.1 ounces each

White Sauce, medium	2 pounds
	4 ounces
Peas, frozen	10 ounces
Carrots, diced, frozen	8 ounces
Celery, diced, frozen	12 ounces
Onion, dehydrated	14 grams
Pimiento, canned	4 ounces
Mushroom Stems and Pieces, canned	4 ounces
Pepper, white	dash
Tuna, light, canned	3 pounds
Noodles	1 pound plus 4 ounces
Water, boiling	1 gallon

Procedure:

1. Heat white sauce.
2. Steam-cook peas, carrots, and celery. Combine with white sauce, onion, pimientos, mushrooms, and pepper.
3. Drain tuna and break into small pieces. Add to creamed mixture.
4. Place in serving pans and keep hot.
5. Cook noodles in boiling water and drain.
6. Serve sauce over noodles.

ROAST BEEF

U of C Hospitals and Clinics

Ingredients: Yield: 50 portions, 3.1 ounces each, cooked weight

Beef Roast, boneless sirloin butt	15 pounds plus 1 ounce
Salt	1½ ounce
Pepper, black, ground	2¼ teaspoons

Procedure:

1. Rub each roast with salt and pepper.
2. Place with fat side up without crowding in pans.
3. Insert meat thermometer into thickest part on main muscle.
4. Roast, uncovered, in oven at 325°F. for 2 to 4 hours until thermometer registers 160°F.
5. Let stand 20 minutes before slicing.

ASPARAGUS AU GRATIN

U of C Hospitals and Clinics

Ingredients: Yield: 50 portions, 4.4 ounces each

Asparagus Spears, frozen	10 pounds
Salt	2 teaspoons
White Sauce, medium	5 pounds
Cheddar Cheese, shredded	12 ounces

Procedure:

1. Arrange single layer of asparagus in steam cooker pans.
2. Sprinkle with salt.
3. Cook at 5 pounds pressure for 5 to 8 minutes or until tender.
4. Combine white sauce and cheese. Heat and stir until cheese melts.
5. Pour sauce over asparagus and serve.

BROCCOLI POLONNAISE

U of C Hospitals and Clinics

Ingredients: Yield: 50 portions, 3 ounces each

Broccoli Spears, frozen	10 pounds
Salt	2 teaspoons
Bread Crumbs	$\frac{3}{4}$ cup
Margarine, melted	1 pound plus 4 ounces
Eggs, hard-cooked, chopped	7
Parsley, chopped	$\frac{1}{4}$ cup

Procedure:

1. Arrange single layer of broccoli spears in 2 full-size steam cooker pans.
2. Cook at 5 pounds pressure for 5 to 8 minutes or until tender.
3. Brown crumbs in margarine. Spread over broccoli in each pan.
4. Garnish each with chopped eggs and parsley.

BROILED FRESH TOMATOES

U of C Hospitals and Clinics

Ingredients: Yield: 50 portions, 4 ounces each

Tomatoes, fresh, 5 ounces each	14 pounds plus 3 ounces
Margarine, pre-portioned pats, 1 gram each	50
Bread Crumbs	$6\frac{3}{4}$ pounds

Procedure:

1. Core tomatoes neatly. Arrange in pans core side up.
2. Place 1 margarine pat and 2 ounces crumbs on each tomato.
3. Place in oven at 300°F. for 10 to 12 minutes.
4. Place in broiler until toasted on top, 1 to 2 minutes.

HOT SPICED BEETS

U of C Hospitals and Clinics

Ingredients:

Yield: 50 portions, 2.8 ounces each

Beets, sliced, canned	2 #10 cans
Beet Liquid and Water	$3\frac{3}{4}$ cups
Vinegar	1 cup plus 3 tablespoons
Cinnamon, ground	$\frac{7}{8}$ teaspoon
Cloves, ground	$1\frac{7}{8}$ teaspoons
Salt	$1\frac{1}{2}$ teaspoons
Pepper, black, ground	$\frac{1}{8}$ teaspoon
Sugar, granulated	$\frac{1}{2}$ cup
Sugar, brown	$1\frac{2}{3}$ cups
Margarine, melted	$\frac{1}{2}$ cup

Procedure:

1. Drain beets. Combine liquid with enough water to meet required volume.
2. Add remaining ingredients except margarine and beets. Bring to a boil, reduce heat, and simmer 10 minutes.
3. Add beets and margarine. Heat to serving temperature.

BAKED HUBBARD SQUASH

U of C Hospitals and Clinics

Ingredients:

Yield: 50 portions, 2.9 ounces each

Hubbard Squash, fresh	14 pounds plus 8 ounces
Oil	8 ounces
Salt	2 tablespoons
Pepper, black	$\frac{1}{2}$ teaspoon
Brown Sugar	$\frac{3}{4}$ cup

Procedure:

1. Cut squash in half. Remove seeds. Cut into $4\frac{1}{2}$ ounce pieces.
2. Place in 18- by 24-inch roasting pans. Brush with oil.
3. Mix salt, pepper, and brown sugar, and sprinkle over squash. Cover pans.
4. Bake in oven at 350°F. for 45 minutes. Remove covers and bake 15 minutes more or until tender and lightly browned.

WALDORF SALAD

U of C Hospitals and Clinics

Ingredients: Yield: 50 portions, 3.5 ounces each

Apples, cored	5 pounds plus 10 ounces
Lemon Juice	3 tablespoons plus $\frac{1}{2}$ tea-spoon
Celery, $\frac{1}{4}$-inch dice	2 pounds
Walnuts, chopped	$6\frac{1}{2}$ ounces
Salad Dressing	1 pound plus 3 ounces
Lettuce	1 pound 10 ounces

Procedure:

1. Quarter apples. Do not peel. Cut into $\frac{1}{2}$-inch cubes. Place in salted water until ready to use.
2. Drain apples well. Mix with juice, celery, walnuts, and dressing. Mix lightly. Chill.
3. Portion 3 ounces with a #12 scoop.

SOFT FRUIT WITH SOUR CREAM DRESSING

U of C Hospitals and Clinics

Ingredients: Yield: 50 portions, 3.9 ounces each

Peaches, canned, sliced, drained	4 pounds plus 9 ounces
Pears, canned, sliced, drained	4 pounds plus 9 ounces
Apricots, canned, sliced, drained	4 pounds plus 9 ounces
Sour Cream Dressing	3 pounds plus 7 ounces
Lettuce Leaf	4 ounces

ORANGE AMBROSIA

U of C Hospitals and Clinics

Ingredients: Yield: 50 portions, 2.7 ounces each

Oranges, fresh, AP	11 pounds plus 9 ounces
Lettuce Leaf	12 ounces
Coconut, toasted	$3\frac{1}{4}$ ounces

Procedure:

1. Place oranges in full steamtable pans and steam for 4 minutes. Remove peel while hot.
2. Slice oranges on meat slicer into approximately 25-gram slices on number 30 setting. This makes about 4 center slices per orange.
3. Place lettuce leaf on salad plate and arrange 3 slices of orange on each plate.
4. Garnish with 1 teaspoon coconut.

SOFT FRUIT WITH SOUR CREAM DRESSING *(cont'd.)*
Procedure:

1. Mix fruit together gently.
2. Add sour cream dressing.
3. Serve in a lettuce-lined bowl.

PERFECTION SALAD

U of C Hospitals and Clinics

Ingredients: Yield: 32 servings, 4.6 ounces each

Water, hot	3 pints, $\frac{1}{4}$ cup
Gelatin, lemon-flavored	17 ounces
Salt	$1\frac{1}{2}$ teaspoons
Water, cold	plus 4 pounds 3 ounces
Vinegar	$\frac{1}{2}$ cup plus 1 teaspoon
Cabbage, finely shredded	1 pound plus 1 ounce
Carrots, finely chopped	$4\frac{1}{4}$ ounces
Celery, finely diced	1 pound plus 9 ounces
Green Pepper, chopped	$4\frac{1}{4}$ ounces
Pimiento, canned, chopped	$7\frac{1}{4}$ ounces
Lettuce	1 pound plus 9 ounces

Procedure:

1. Dissolve gelatin and salt in hot water.
2. Add cold water and vinegar. Chill until slightly thickened.
3. Add vegetables to gelatin. Mix thoroughly.
4. Pour the mixture into a counter pan. Chill until set.
5. Cut pan 4 servings by 8 servings. Serve on lettuce cup.

Poissons

Sole Louis XIV
Poached Filet of Sole with Shrimp and Julienne Vegetables

Homard Sauce Champagne
Lobster Tails in Champagne Sauce

Casserole D'Ecrevisses
Crayfish in Casserole

Coquille St. Jacques Provençale
Sautéed Bay Scallops Provençale

Dover Sole Grillée

Médaillon De Saumon Au Beurre Blanc
Medallion of Salmon Meunière in Wine and Butter Sauce

Viandes

Ris De Veau Aux Morilles
Sweetbreads with Morels

Filet De Boeuf Au Poivre Vert
Filet with Green Peppercorn

Côte De Veau Prince Orloff
Veal Chop Cream Mushroom Sauce

Médaillon De Veau Oscar
Veal Medallion with Crabmeat Asparagus and Sauce Béarnaise

Canard Roti À L'Orange
Roast Duckling Served with Orange Sauce

Tournedos Forestière
Beef Filet with Sauce of Morels, Chanterelles and tomato

The Whitehall Club

Desserts

Crème Glacés, Sorbets
Raspberry or Lemon Sherbet 1.25   Strawberry Parfait 1.75
Vanilla, Coffee or Whitehall Special Chocolate Ice Cream 1.50

Coupes Glacés
1.75   Coupe Angele 1.75   Pear Belle Helene 2.00   Snowball 1.50

Dessert Flambés
3.00   Crepes Suzette (for two) 3.75 per person
Baked Alaska (for two) 3.50 per person

Fruits
omanoff 3.50   Fruit Frais au Porto 2.50
Melon in Season (Cantaloupe, Cranshaw) 1.50

Special
hall S   undae 1.75

Fresh Berries 1.50

Sliced Bananas with
Pineapple, Prune, Tom

Whitehall S
Choice of
Corned Beef Hash wi
Pastry Bas
Jams, Preserves,
Choice of Be
4.95

Choice of Juice,

One Egg,

The Whitehall Club

Sunday Brunch

12 Noon to 3:00 p.m.

Appetizers

Smoked Scottish Salmon 5.25   Escargots 4.00   Iced Fruit Juices 1.00
Mackerel in White Wine 2.50   Prosciutto with Melon 3.25
Cut Fresh Fruit in Season 1.50   Grapefruit, Apricot Dressing
Hearts of Palm, Vinaigrette 2.25   Avocado Stuffed with C
Blue Point Oysters on the Half Shell 3.75   Cherrystone Cl

Champagne

Imported:

1. Bollinger Brut 1970
2. Dom Pérignon 1969-71
3. Taittinger Blanc de Blancs 1969-71
4. Taittinger Brut "La Francaise" N.V.
5. Veuve Clicquot Extra Dry N.V.   23.
6. Laurent Perrier Blanc de Blancs 1966-70   24.0
7. Mumm's Cordon Rouge Brut 1971   22.00

American:

8. Korbel Natural N.V.   12.00
9. Almaden Blanc de Blancs N.V.   13.00
10. Great Western Extra Dry N.V.   12.00

The Whitehall Club

The Whitehall Club
A Public View of a Private Club

The Whitehall Club
105 E. Delaware Place,
Chicago, Illinois.

Members have known it for 22 years as the place that served the "biggest drink in town," for its outstanding wine library, and for its fine food specialties: Steak au Poivre, the legendary Corned Beef Hash Whitehall; Canneloni Quo Vadis; Broiled Langoustines with Sauce Choron, or Veal Pescadore. And the desserts . . .

Almost 4000 members of this dining club have become addicted to The Whitehall's standards of excellence in both food and service. They know they will always receive cordial attention from the friendly, but never familiar staff of sixty, many of whom were with the Club when it opened in 1956. When the original maitre d' Toni Tontini left in February 1977, to open his own restaurant, there was fear that a strong link of continuity would be missing. After all, Toni had been with The Whitehall since the beginning when there were only 55 members. And Toni *is* missed. Nevertheless, his successor as maitre d', Swiss-born-and-raised Josef Reif is also one of those all too rare people who take great pleasure in serving. And service is, after all, the hallmark of The Whitehall.

As a matter of professional pride, Reif, who worked the Maisonette Restaurant and the Gourmet Room in Cincinnati, is rapidly becoming familiar with the personal preferences of Club members, even those who are infrequent guests. Private clubs, much more than public places, need this unbroken bridge of personal recognition, even though the person giving attention to members may change.

Two other notable figures on the strong management team tunning The Whitehall's foodservice operation: Lee Grossbard, the food and beverage chief who came aboard in 1977, and chef Jean Pierre Henry who joined The Whitehall Club in March 1978. French-trained, Henry cooked at the

283

Since 1956, the Whitehall has maintained its reputation as the
top private club for fine dining in Chicago.

Cafe Chauveron in Miami before coming to Maxim's in Chicago as souschef, where he worked with the near-lengendary Jean Banchet. (See Le Francais Restaurant, in these pages.) Henry is responsible for maintaining the high standards of The Whitehall's French, Italian, and American cookery, and has introduced a great amount of decorative *garde manger* presentations. In 1977 The Whitehall Club opened a new section, enlarging the area, but rather than crowding in more tables and chairs, actually reduced the total seating capacity to 120, down from 160. Again, members of private clubs expect space as well as service.

The interior of The Whitehall is warm and gracious with its crystal chandeliers, dark-tan suede cloth on walls, and overall color scheme of muted browns and reds. There are red leather chairs, a mirrored bar, an antique marble fireplace and, everywhere, fresh flowers—usually roses. Silver service plates and fine English bone china are beautiful embellishments.

The Whitehall has often been the site of annual meetings for various wine and food societies, and the Club is one of the few US establishments that has been mentioned in the distinguished publication *Tradition et Qualite.* The Whitehall Club has also received four-star Mobile Guide mention; and was given the *Institutions/Volume Feeding* Ivy Award in 1976.

Opposite, the posh Whitehall Hotel on Chicago's Near North Side is home to the Whitehall Club. Below, the hotel's luxurious little lobby serves as entry way to the Club. The feeling of the entire establishment: restrained richness.

It was only five years ago that The Whitehall Hotel, then semi-residential, was crisply turned into an active guest hotel by Lex, Inc., of London. Thus began the complete renovation and reorganization of public and private spaces, which continues. As part of the hotel's hospitality, all guests now receive temporary Club membership privileges for dining, while they are staying at The Whitehall.

As of 1978, The Whitehall Club's check average was $11.50 for lunch and $19.50 for dinner. These two figures exclude liquor, although the Club's $1.8 million a year volume includes both food and liquor. The initiation fee for members is $150, with annual dues of $75.

Opposite, dining *a deux* before the Whitehall's antique fireplace. Tables are set with fresh flowers, silver service plates, fine bone china. This page, "Members Only" (plus Whitehall Hotel guests) enjoy the pleasures of Chef Jean Pierre Henry's decorative *garde manger* treats.

STEAK TARTARE

The Whitehall

Ingredients: Yield: 1 portion

Onion, chopped	2 tablespoons
Parsley, chopped	1 teaspoon
Capers	1 teaspoon (about 12)
Anchovy Fillets, chopped	3
Egg Yolk	1
Mayonnaise	1 tablespoon
Salt	as needed
Pepper	as needed
Beef Tenderloin, 8 ounces	1
Cognac	1 tablespoon

Procedure:

1.   Thoroughly mix all ingredients except meat and cognac.
2.   Chop the tenderloin with a knife and add. Sprinkle with cognac. Form into a patty.
3.   Sprinkle with a pinch of chopped parsley and serve with rye bread.

ESCARGOT (BOURGUIGNONNE) BUTTER

The Whitehall

Ingredients: Yield: 32 pounds

Butter, sweet, softened	25 pounds
Garlic, minced	2 pounds
Shallots, minced	$2\frac{1}{2}$ pounds
Parsley, minced	2 pounds
Salt	1 ounce
White Pepper	$\frac{1}{2}$ ounce
Lemon Juice	1 cup
Snails, boiled	as needed

PETITE MARMITE HENRY IV

The Whitehall

Ingredients: Yield: 8 portions

Shin of Beef	2 pounds
Frying Chicken with Giblets	1
Water	3 quarts
Salt	3 teaspoons
Pepper	$\frac{3}{4}$ teaspoon
Celery Rib, julienne	1
Carrots, medium, julienne	4
Leeks, julienne	2
Onion, medium, thinly sliced	1
Turnip, medium, julienne	1
Salt	as needed
Pepper	as needed

Procedure:

1. Cut chicken into parts and put in a large kettle with giblets and beef shin.
2. Add water, salt, and pepper. Bring to a boil, reduce heat, and simmer for 3 hours, skimming as necessary.
3. Take out meat and chicken. Cut shin meat and breast of chicken into fine julienne strips. (Save remaining chicken for other use.)
4. Strain broth into a clean kettle through a sieve lined with cheesecloth.
5. Add remaining ingredients, correct seasoning, and simmer for 15 minutes.
6. Add chicken and meat strips and simmer 2 minutes.
7. Serve in large bowls with some of each kind of meat and vegetables. Accompany with hot french bread.

ESCARGOT (BOURGUIGNONE) BUTTER *(cont'd.)*

Procedure:

1. Put all ingredients except snails in mixer. Blend thoroughly.
2. Put cooked snails in pots or shells, and stuff with butter. Cook for about 10 minutes in oven at 425°F.

STEAK AU POIVRE

The Whitehall

Ingredients: Yield: 4 servings

Sirloin Steak, 3 pounds, 1¼ inch thick	1
Peppercorns, whole	2 tablespoons
Butter	3 tablespoons
Oil	1 teaspoon
White Wine, dry	⅔ cup
Brandy	1 tablespoon

Procedure:

1. Coarsely crush peppercorns. Pound into both sides of steak, covering thickly. Let stand 2 hours.
2. Heat 1 tablespoon butter with oil in a heavy skillet. Sear steak quickly over high heat on both sides. Cook 5 minutes each side. Remove to hot platter.
3. Stir wine and brandy into the pan. Boil rapidly for 2 minutes, scraping up brown meat drippings.
4. Remove from heat and swirl in 2 tablespoons butter.
5. Strain sauce over the steak and serve. (If loose bits of pepper are desired, do not strain.) Garnish with watercress.

CORNED BEEF HASH WHITEHALL

The Whitehall

Ingredients: Yield: 12 portions

Brisket of Corned Beef, 5-pound, cooked	1
Potatoes, Idaho, large, cooked in peel	4
Half and Half	1 cup
Poached Eggs	12
Chili Sauce	as needed

VEAL PESCADORE

The Whitehall

Ingredients: Yield: 12 portions

Veal Scallopini	24 slices (approximately 6 pounds)
Olive Oil	as needed
Shallots, chopped	1 tablespoon
Mushrooms, fresh, chopped	1 cup
King Crab Meat, chopped	1 pound
Cream Sauce	3 cups
Egg Yolks, beaten	2
Parmesan Cheese, grated	1 cup
Whipped Cream	1 cup
Spinach, fresh	$1\frac{1}{2}$ pounds
Butter	as needed
Espagnole Sauce	as needed

Procedure:

1. Saute scallopini in olive oil until tender.
2. Combine and saute the shallots and mushrooms. Add crab meat.
3. Stir in cream sauce, bring to a boil, and remove from heat.
4. Stir in egg yolks, $\frac{1}{4}$ cup Parmesan cheese, and whipped cream.
5. Cook spinach, drain, and saute in butter. Place 2 ounces of cooked spinach on each service plate.
6. Top with 2 slices of scallopini and cover with crabmeat sauce.
7. Sprinkle with remaining Parmesan cheese and place in hot salamander.
8. Serve with cordon of Espagnole sauce (i.e., brown sauce).

CORNED BEEF HASH WHITEHALL *(cont'd.)*

Procedure:

1. Trim fat off beef and chop coarsely.
2. Peel and dice potatoes. Put into bowl and add half and half. Mix in corned beef and toss lightly.
3. Using 10 to 12 ounces per portion, brown on each side in a small pan.
4. Serve with poached egg and chili sauce.

BREAST OF CHICKEN AU CHAMPAGNE

The Whitehall

Ingredients: Yield: 4 portions

Double Breasts of Chicken, boned	
or Single Breasts of Capon, boned	4
Flour	$\frac{1}{4}$ cup
Salt	1 teaspoon
Pepper	$\frac{1}{2}$ teaspoon
Butter or Oil	$\frac{1}{2}$ cup
Mushrooms, fresh, sliced	$\frac{1}{2}$ pound
Cream	1 cup
French Champagne	$\frac{1}{4}$ cup
Mushroom Caps, sauteed	4

Procedure:

1. Place boned breasts between 2 pieces of waxed paper and pound until slightly flattened.
2. Mix flour, salt, and pepper together. Roll chicken breasts in this mixture and shake off excess.
3. Melt butter in heavy skillet and cook chicken breasts until lightly browned on both sides.
4. Add sliced mushrooms, cover, and cook for 10 minutes. Drain off any excess fat.
5. Add cream and simmer over low heat for 10 minutes.
6. Transfer breasts to warm platter. Add champagne to the liquid in skillet. Bring to a rapid boil and cook until sauce is reduced to a creamy consistency.
7. Spoon sauce over breasts. Garnish with mushroom caps.

BROILED LANGOUSTINES, SAUCE CHORON

The Whitehall

Ingredients: Yield: 12 servings

Tarragon Vinegar	$\frac{1}{2}$ cup
Pepper, black	1 teaspoon
Tarragon, fresh, chopped	1 tablespoon
Tomato Puree	$\frac{1}{4}$ cup
Lemon Juice	1 teaspoon
Egg Yolks	4
Water	1 tablespoon
Butter, clarified	$1\frac{1}{2}$ pounds
Langoustines, 9 to 12 count	48 pieces
Butter	as needed
Paprika	as needed

Procedure:

1. Combine and reduce to one-fourth: tarragon vinegar, pepper, tarragon, tomato puree, and lemon juice.
2. In a *bain marie,* mix egg yolks and water, then whip until thick and smooth.
3. Stir butter into yolks, then add reduced mixture. Keep in a warm place.
4. Split langoustines lengthwise and loosen meat from shell.
5. Put on sheet pan, top with butter and paprika, and cook in oven at 450°F. for about 5 minutes.
6. Serve directly from oven to table with sauce on side. (Do not permit langoustines to sit before serving because they lose flavor and become hard.)

CHEESE BLINTZES

The Whitehall

Ingredients: Yield: 4 portions

Eggs	3
Milk	$1\frac{1}{2}$ cups
Sifted Flour	1 cup
Salt	$\frac{1}{4}$ teaspoon
Sugar	2 teaspoons
Butter, melted	1 teaspoon
Cottage Cheese	2 cups
Egg Yolks	2
Sugar	2 tablespoons
Vanilla	$\frac{1}{4}$ teaspoon
Nutmeg	$\frac{1}{4}$ teaspoon
Salt	$\frac{1}{2}$ teaspoon
Butter	as needed
Sour Cream	as needed

Procedure:

1. Beat eggs and milk together.
2. Combine flour, salt, and 2 teaspoons sugar. Add milk-egg mixture and beat until smooth. Add 1 teaspoon melted butter and mix. Refrigerate for 30 minutes.
3. Heat a 7-inch skillet and grease with a little butter.
4. Pour in batter to cover the bottom thinly, about 1 ounce, tilting pan to spread the batter evenly.
5. Bake until underside is browned. Turn out, browned side up, on clean towel. Stack pancakes until all are made, about 16.
6. Drain cottage cheese by putting it into a large sieve and pressing out liquid with back of spoon.
7. Mix drained cottage cheese with egg yolks, 2 tablespoons sugar, vanilla, nutmeg, and salt.
8. Place 1 tablespoon of the cheese filling in the center of the browned side of each pancake. Fold ends in, then roll up.
9. Heat 2 tablespoons butter in a skillet. Brown the pancakes (blintzes) in it on all sides.
10. Serve hot and crisp with sour cream spooned on top.

COTTAGE FRIED POTATOES

The Whitehall

Ingredients: Yield: 4 portions

Idaho Potatoes	3 medium
Butter, clarified	$\frac{3}{4}$ cup
Oil	$\frac{1}{4}$ cup
Salt	as needed
Pepper	as needed

Procedure:

1. Peel potatoes. Cut into slices $\frac{1}{8}$ inch thick. *Do not wash them.*
2. Lay the slices, one by one, on the bottom of a cold, heavy skillet, starting from the center. Place them in circles with each slice overlapping the other.
3. Combine butter and oil in saucepan and heat. Pour the hot fat over potatoes and cook over medium heat for 10 minutes.
4. The slices should stick to each other and be brown on the bottom. Turn them over with a spatula, being careful not to break the circle.
5. Cook another 10 minutes. When each side is crisp and golden brown, drain fat from the pan.
6. Turn out on a hot round platter. Sprinkle with salt and pepper and serve.

CANNELONI, QUO VADIS

The Whitehall

Ingredients: Yield: 12 portions

Spinach, creamed	1 pound
Parmesan Cheese, grated	1 pound
Sweetbreads, calf, cooked	1 pound
Hydrolyzed Vegetable Protein	1 tablespoon
Worcestershire Sauce	1 teaspoon
Pepper	as needed
Salt	as needed
Bread Crumbs	$\frac{1}{2}$ cup
Cream Sauce, medium	2 cups
Egg Yolks, beaten	2
Parmesan Cheese, grated	$\frac{1}{2}$ cup
Whipped Cream	1 cup
French Pancakes (without sugar)	12

Procedure:

1. Mix spinach, 1 pound Parmesan cheese, and sweetbreads. Put through fine-hole grinder.
2. Add seasonings and bread crumbs and mix well. Refrigerate for 1 hour.
3. Fill pancakes with sweetbread mixture. Roll up and heat in oven at 325°F. about 20 minutes.
4. Mix cream sauce, egg yolks, and $\frac{1}{2}$ cup Parmesan cheese. Fold in whipped cream.
5. Pour over canneloni. Heat under broiler until golden in color.

EGG CUSTARD

The Whitehall

Ingredients: Yield: 12 portions

Milk	1 quart
Eggs	12 ounces
Sugar	6 ounces
Coffee Cream	10 ounces
Salt	pinch
Vanilla	1 teaspoon
Yellow Food Coloring	as needed

Procedure:

1. Mix all ingredients thoroughly.
2. Pour through strainer into buttered custard cups.
3. Set cups in water bath.
4. Bake in oven at 350°F. until set, about 35 to 40 minutes.

WHITEHALL CHOCOLATE ROLL

The Whitehall

Ingredients: Yield: 8 portions

Egg Yolks	5
Sugar	$\frac{1}{2}$ cup
Vanilla	$\frac{1}{2}$ teaspoon
Cocoa	3 tablespoons
Flour	$\frac{3}{4}$ cup
Egg Whites	5
Butter	$\frac{1}{4}$ cup
Cream	$\frac{2}{3}$ cup
Chocolate, dark, sweet	13 ounces
Coffee Liqueur	3 ounces
Cream, heavy	1 cup
Chocolate, semi-sweet, shaved	as needed

Procedure:

1. Combine egg yolks, sugar, and vanilla and beat with electric mixer for 5 to 10 minutes until eggs are thick and pale.
2. Combine cocoa with flour and sift together. Beat egg whites until stiff. Fold gently into the cocoa/flour mixture along with 2 tablespoons melted butter.
3. Butter a 10- by 14-inch baking sheet, line with waxed paper, and butter the waxed paper.
4. Spread batter on baking sheet $\frac{1}{2}$ inch deep. Bake in oven at 350°F. for 8 to 10 minutes.
5. Remove from oven and roll cake immediately, lengthwise, leaving cake on waxed paper.
6. Combine cream with 2 tablespoons butter and bring to a rapid boil. Remove from heat and add 10 ounces chocolate, cut into pieces. Stir until chocolate melts and mixture is smooth. Refrigerate until proper consistency for spreading.
7. Unroll cake and remove waxed paper. Spread with filling and roll again.
8. Melt 3 ounces chocolate with 1 ounce of coffee liqueur. Whip heavy cream and fold into chocolate, thoroughly but gently.
9. Swirl the whipped cream topping over top and sides of roll. Sprinkle generously with shaved chocolate.
10. Refrigerate until served.

Whether you dine at The Whitehall Club (below) or any other excellent restaurant discussed in *Restaurants Chicago–Style,* the author wants to take this final opportunity to say, "Bon Appetit!"

RECIPE INDEX

CONVERSION SCALES

Volume

1 teaspoon	=	5	milliliters
1 cup	=	250	milliliters
¾ cup	=	185	milliliters
½ cup	=	125	milliliters
⅓ cup	=	83	milliliters
1 tablespoon	=	15	milliliters
1 fluid ounce	=	29.57	milliliters
1 milliliter	=	.03	fluid ounce
1 pint	=	437.18	milliliters
1 quart	=	.95	liter
1 gallon	=	3.79	liters

Weight

1 gram	=	.035	ounce
1 ounce	=	28.35	grams
1 pound	=	453.6	grams
1 kilogram	=	2.20	pounds
1 pound	=	.45	kilograms

Temperature

To convert degrees Fahrenheit to degrees Celsius:
1) Subtract 32 from Fahrenheit reading.
2) Multiply step #1 result by $5/9$.

To convert degrees Celsius to degrees Fahrenheit:
1) Multiply Celsius reading by $9/5$.
2) Add 32 to step #1 result.